Studies in the Political Economy of Public Policy

Studies in the Political Economy of Public Policy presents cutting edge, innovative research on the origins and impacts of public policy. Going beyond mainstream public policy debates, the series encourages heterodox and heterogeneous studies of sites of contestation, conflict and cooperation that explore policy processes and their consequences at the local, national, regional or global levels. Fundamentally pluralist in nature, the series is designed to provide high quality original research of both a theoretical and empirical nature that supports a global network of scholars exploring the implications of policy on society. The series welcomes manuscript submissions from scholars in the global South and North that pioneer new understandings of public policy.

More information about this series at
http://www.palgrave.com/gp/series/14465

Steven Rolf

China's Uneven and Combined Development

palgrave
macmillan

Steven Rolf
Digit Centre
University of Sussex
Brighton, UK

ISSN 2524-7441 ISSN 2524-745X (electronic)
Studies in the Political Economy of Public Policy
ISBN 978-3-030-55558-0 ISBN 978-3-030-55559-7 (eBook)
https://doi.org/10.1007/978-3-030-55559-7

This Palgrave Macmillan imprint is published by the registered company Springer Nature Switzerland AG
The registered company address is: Gewerbestrasse 11, 6330 Cham, Switzerland

To my mother, Sharon.

Acknowledgements

This work grew out of my PhD thesis which I researched at the University of Bristol's School of Sociology, Politics and International Studies (SPAIS) between 2012 and 2017. There, my supervisors Jeff Henderson and Adam Dixon provided invaluable guidance and support. Jeff also worked hard to secure me funding for language training and fieldwork trips, and kindly provided countless meals and drinks.

My thanks to all those who helped out during my fieldwork in China, and those who kept me company while working on the thesis and eventually the book. To Soraya and Robin for hosting me for a significant period of the writing. And to my family: Jeff, Dai, Jo, Dave, Mike, Sophia, Joseph and Jacob.

Most of all, my gratitude and love are extended to Rosa.

Praise for *China's Uneven and Combined Development*

"China's geopolitical and economic 'catch up' is usually discussed in terms of a new global 'power' challenging an established world order or of types of capitalism—Anglo-American vs. state-capitalist, and so on—rather than in terms of the intersection between global and national capitalisms, on the one hand, and different types of polity, on the other. In a powerful synthesis of original theoretical discussion and up-to-date detailed empirical analysis, Steve Rolf shows how much can be gained from reframing China's startling economic trajectory of the past thirty years by highlighting dynamic processes of uneven and combined development, rather than those of static comparative models that ignore necessary within-country as well as country-by-country differences in how economic growth takes place."

—John Agnew, *Distinguished Professor of Geography, UCLA, USA*

"Through the lens of the Marxian theory of uneven and combined development, Rolf meticulously weaves together a coherent account of China's rise from the initiation of market reform to the Belt and Road Initiative and the trade war with the US. It sheds new lights on the many contradictions within China and in the global geopolitical economy that the China boom brings."

—Ho-fung Hung, *Henry M. & Elizabeth P. Wisenfeld Professor in Political Economy, The John Hopkins University, USA*

Contents

List of Figures

List of Tables

CHAPTER 1

Introduction: China Shakes the World System

1.1 Overview

Since 1978, the People's Republic of China (PRC) has pulled off a developmental miracle. China leapt from its position as one of the lowest income economies in the world into the bracket of upper middle-income countries—a truly rare feat for a large, poor state in the history of the capitalist world economy. During this period, its achievements in poverty reduction, industrialisation, urbanisation and improvements in agricultural productivity and the bureaucratic capacity of the state were, taken collectively, of a world historic scale. Explosive economic development, moreover, has catapulted the PRC into the role of the world's second superpower; encouraging the view—now increasingly mainstream—that China may be likely to play a hegemonic role in (an Asian-centric) world politics during the twenty-first century, reprising that of the United States in the latter part of the twentieth (though whether this is to be welcomed or not remains an open question: cf. Jacques 2009; Mearsheimer 2006; Rachman 2016). Nor have some major negative upshots of this transformative project gone unnoticed: the high degree of labour exploitation and the creation of a labouring migrant underclass, environmental degradation, rampant corruption and increasing political authoritarianism. Outgrowing its national or even regional impact, China's growth miracle,

S. Rolf, *China's Uneven and Combined Development*,
Studies in the Political Economy of Public Policy,
https://doi.org/10.1007/978-3-030-55559-7_1

alongside the boom in financialisation, the shrinking of welfare states, and the rise of income inequality, ranks as—perhaps *the*—striking fact of the contemporary global political economy. The foundational proposition of this book, then, is that China's 'rise' is real, and that it represents a major restructuring of the capitalist world system.

This monograph is motivated by the urgent need to better understand—both historically and theoretically—the factors and social processes which have enabled and structured China's period of rapid economic growth since the late 1970s. To do so, and from a perspective of critical political economy often lacking in approaches to understanding the 'rise of China', this book first revises and develops, and subsequently mobilises, Leon Trotsky's theory of the uneven and combined development (UCD) of the global capitalist economy.

At the core of my argument is the contention that China's growth spurt has been characterised by the activation of UCD—understood as a distinct set of political-economic processes and possibilities immanent in the capitalist world economy. UCD suggests that—and while the possibility remains an outlier rather than the norm—developing economies suffering poverty and geopolitical subjugation (in a world order bifurcated between national states of global north and south) may, seeking rupture with this inequality, mobilise the 'privilege of historical backwardness' by importing advanced technologies, thus leaping ahead and driving *towards* economic convergence with advanced capitalist economies through an intensive bout of industrialisation and urbanisation. But, a second implication is that true convergence is in fact only rarely facilitated by UCD, precisely because these developmental 'leaps' take place by grafting advanced forms of production and social relations onto antiquated ones; producing sociospatial hybridities which are, more often than not, chronically unstable and unlikely to directly replicate their source material. Instead, these hybridities have developmental trajectories entirely of their own which must be analysed in their specificity and (strictly) cannot be expected to simply repeat established patterns of development. Thus from the outset, UCD injects into Marxism an orientation which some may associate more closely with postcolonial theory. One objective of this book is to firmly root such concepts in a materialist understanding of political economy.

This conception of UCD forms only a subsection of a more general theory of capitalist development and so, unlike the comparative capitalisms perspectives discussed here shortly (and in greater depth in Chapter 2), is itself expressly not applicable in every time and place—but specifically in the case of developing states experiencing 'leaps' towards the level of the leading economies (van der Linden 2007).[1] This more specific application of UCD I develop here seeks to theorise why more abstract propositions regarding capital accumulation as a general process become modified in this context (for example, while technological innovation is generally cumulative and reliant upon deep R&D investments and basic research in the advanced economies, UCD might allow developing economies to appropriate these technological advances while investing far less capital). A core (latent) assumption of UCD in this regard is both of a fundamental geographical distinction in the world economy between developed and developing states (measured by relative income and labour productivity) which is predicated upon differential levels of industrialisation and urbanisation (Dunford and Liu 2017)—*and*, simultaneously, the complex and sporadic diffusion of portions of the most advanced capitalist practices to those states whose *general* level remains at that of a 'developing' economy. It is the emphasis on capitalist temporality and dynamism which distinguishes UCD from (what I regard as) the misleading inertia posited by the major proponents of world systems theory.

Uncovering both why this process of UCD should have been kick-started in the particular case of contemporary China, as well as its implications and outcomes there, requires an extensive historical and empirical exegesis (as is developed from Chapter 4 onwards). But I also contend that UCD, while it takes on novel forms across periods and spaces of capitalist development, also represents a more fundamental condition of the capitalist mode of production as it expands on a global scale. Capital—despite its intrinsically globalising thrust (as Marx [1991, 359] writes, 'the capitalist mode of production is therefore a historical means for developing the material powers of production and for creating a

[1] UCD is conceived here as only being operative under conditions of capitalism, rather than a transhistorical phenomenon (Ashman 2009). Davidson (2010) suggests even stricter criteria—UCD is only operative in states that *are* experiencing rapid development, but are unable to reach the developmental level of the advanced capitalist economies. It seems extremely premature to make a firm judgement on this question in China's case, but it seems self-evident that China *is* experiencing such a process, regardless of whether it makes it to the other side of advanced capitalism or not.

corresponding world market')—also and inevitably relies upon a relatively fixed system of national states to achieve this mobility. The parcellisation of political territory, and the competitive interaction between this multiplicity of sovereign units which capital thus creates, has distinctive and observable effects on the way particular political economies develop. The world economy is thus *uneven* insofar as the gains from economic development are never evenly distributed across space; and yet, the global and expansionary drive of capital to foster market interactions everywhere renders this unevenness *combined* into a world system. The competitive drive for survival by national states entangles them within this combinatory logic, and, moreover, contributes to its enforcement as states become promoters and defenders of the capitals with which they are interwoven. This looser and (under capitalism) general condition of UCD is, rather confusingly, to what recent scholarly debates of the concept have mostly referred (see Chapter 2).

Capitalist development is both uneven and combined in *two* senses then: first, in the nationally bounded sense referred to in the case of China (a *specific* form of UCD comprising of accelerated, but uneven, development in a national economy). Second, on a global scale—a *general* form of UCD in which states competitively coexist as part of a single world economy. The two different senses of UCD are intrinsically linked, because it is the pressure exerted by competitive political multiplicity (referred to simply as 'geopolitics' by the ascetic international relations literature, though more often in this book in an expansive sense as 'geopolitical economy')—or UCD in the second sense—that drives developing states to attempt to initiate the first form of UCD: to combine their development with advanced capitalist economies rather than face the often dire consequences of underdevelopment (what Trotsky termed the 'whip of external necessity') and 'leap' developmental stages towards the technological frontier. As I show in Chapter 3, China experienced most acutely the 'whip of external necessity' in the late 1970s, which motivated it to pursue economic development through reform and opening as the only plausible means of maintaining regime stability during the late Cold War.

While these observations are neither wholly original nor especially illuminating in and of themselves, they do, in my view, present a powerful toolkit for approaching an extended, detailed, and creative exploration of a highly atypical period of rapid growth as China has recently experienced. Disentangling these two different forms of UCD requires a work of fairly lengthy conceptual revision, which is presented across this Introduction and the subsequent two chapters. This book consequently has three objectives:

1. The further development of UCD as a research programme capable of being deployed to analyse aspects of the contemporary global political economy—particularly China's catch-up development under conditions of an increasingly globalised manufacturing system (Chapters 2 and 3).
2. A re-reading of China's reform and opening period through the conceptual 'lens' of UCD which demonstrates how geopolitical-economic determinants shaped China's political economy with effects that persist to date, shaping the ongoing evolution of its distinct system of capital accumulation (Chapters 4–7).
3. An elaboration on how the consequences of China's UCD are increasingly being felt in the contemporary global political economy (Chapter 8).

Before proceeding with my own conceptual elaboration of UCD, this introductory chapter begins by succinctly elaborating some of the conceptual difficulties I understand as inhibiting an adequate theoretical and historical understanding of China's economic rise in order to justify my chosen approach. In particular, I want to identify how important aspects of this process are too often misrepresented by either globalisation theory (which denies many of the critical functions played by states) or, conversely, methodologically nationalist political economy (which frequently conceptualises China in isolation from the global political economy of which it forms a part).

In response to some of the exaggerations and difficulties I identify, Chapter 2 proceeds to lay out the theory of UCD: briefly stating the theory as it was initially deployed, before highlighting some shortcomings of its more general application in the contemporary global political economy (GPE) and international relations (IR) literatures. To make the case for UCD's ability to transcend globalising and methodologically nationalist political economies in a way which is potentially useful to understanding the Chinese case, I develop it in counterposition with a conceptual critique of two of the major schools of thought which inspire the work I pursue during the remainder of the book (but that often fall prey to these difficulties): critical geography, underpinned as it is by the theory of 'uneven development', and Marxist state theory. I contend that both capture important aspects of the dynamics of UCD, but only by integrating their propositions with the effects of political multiplicity as described above can we adequately bring their modes of analysis to bear on the case of China.

Chapter 3 puts this theoretical development to work, considering how contemporary institutionalist and comparative political economy have approached the question of the specific character of state-economy relations in contemporary China. I develop a critique of comparative approaches to political economy that have begun to broach the 'China question' in its institutional specificity: the Varieties of Capitalism (VoC) and its more recent (critical) extension in the Variegated Capitalism approach. The VoC perspective has become the most sustained justification of *dirigisme* and institutional heterogeneity, eclipsing to some extent the earlier 'developmental state' literature. Variegated Capitalism has sought to dig below the national and put scalar theory to work in exploring uneven development between China's urban regions. Neither approach has, however, attempted to locate China in the global division of labour, nor to attend to the ways that geopolitical economy has been constitutive of its economic development. Addressing these lacunae, and to give Chinese institutions the scalar contextualisation lacking from contemporary approaches to comparative statist political economy, I restate the case for drawing upon uneven and combined development (UCD)—but this time at a lower level of abstraction suited towards the kinds of theoretically informed empirical analysis characteristic of the comparative capitalisms literature, which I pursue from Chapter 4 onwards

In Chapter 4, I argue that a prime contributor to China's unusual form of capitalism has been the idiosyncratic character of the global political economy into which China has emerged. Broadly following Robert Brenner's (2006) account, I sketch how the latter stages of postwar globalisation came to be driven by profitability pressures in the advanced capitalist economies, intensified by the emergence of new manufacturing competitors to Europe and the United States (especially Japan and West Germany, followed by the East Asian 'Tiger' economies). China, a Cold War antagonist of the United States, nonetheless took advantage of geopolitical opportunities for *detente* during the 1970s, subsequently facilitating its integration into increasingly modularised manufacturing chains. But emerging at the tail end of this longer historical process and under a new global phase of capitalist development (neoliberalism), it has struggled to repeat the earlier East Asian experience. Instead, China's distinct and geopolitically mediated form of industrialisation had profound ramifications for the country's class structure and state form—not least its distinctive fusion of transnational investors and local governments and the fact that SMEs have formed the vanguard of its economic development—which persist to date. While prior postwar late developers could quite straightforwardly pursue state-led combined development by developing vertically integrated national industries, doing so has since become exceptionally challenging in a neoliberalising global political economy.

Chapters 5 and 6 together sketch the contours of the form of capitalism this geopolitical economy produced, the first prior to and the second in the aftermath of the crisis of 2008. This year is understood as a pivotal moment due to the collapse of China's export sector, despite the appearance of relative continuity achieved by state stimulus programs. Chapter 5 accounts for the scale of the boom—which, as we shall see, principally ensued from 2001–2008—by labelling it as a 'leap' in the sense of UCD, contributing towards China's 'variety of capitalism' substantially different from, but profoundly intertwined with, those of the advanced capitalist world. China's 'exportist system of accumulation' combined elements of East Asian developmental statism ('Keynesianism') with the cell form of flexible and modularised production system ('neoliberalism') to which global production networks have given rise. This interdependence (combination) of forms of capitalist production, I argue, lies behind China's huge sectoral variety and divergent trajectories of state and private control in different industries. Chapter 6 then considers the aftermath of the crisis and the question of economic 'rebalancing'—that is, whether the state has the capacity to re-engineer the structures of the Chinese economy in favour of a model based on domestic consumption, rather than export dependency. I provide a critique of this literature and question whether such attempt at rebalancing is possible or desirable. The substantive conclusion of the empirical study running across these chapters is that China is confronting a severe profitability crisis in its surplus-generating export manufacturing sector, which has been temporarily papered over by loading the economy with debt. One consequence of this is a flight of investment capital into the real estate sector, and away from manufacturing, discussed in Chapter 7. An extended concluding Chapter (8) ties these observations together and examines the 'externalisation' of China's developmental process, as it develops into an increasingly significant economic, diplomatic and military power on the world stage.

I restrict myself primarily to (geo-)*political economy*. UCD has applications far beyond political economy, as a rich and expansive literature is beginning to demonstrate. Many socio-cultural forces shaped by UCD structure social life in contemporary China and deserve scholarly attention. Take the increasing adoption of environmental consciousness by many middle-class Chinese, for instance, which is not a process 'internal' to China alone, but also a product of Chinese adopting and mutating ideas imported by green NGOs—formed in Europe and the United States in the 1960s when those societies were forced to confront the impact of industrial pollution. One could construct an extensive thesis around the idiosyncratic effects of social movements applying such 'externally' generated knowledge to the internal, national environmental politics of China, but I do not attempt to incorporate these areas of social life as determinations here. Finally, while I claim UCD represents a comparative historical-sociological method, I unfortunately am not able to introduce more than cursory comparisons with prior cases of UCD. Stubbs (2017) and Gray (2015) have presented excellent comparative and sequenced primers on East Asian industrialisation. Attempting such analyses from a UCD perspective is a project for the future.

1.2 Theorising China's Rise

The sources of the Chinese boom are vigorously contested: identifying them has become a major task spilling across the disciplinary boundaries of the contemporary social sciences. And while both multidisciplinary and voluminous, the literature has tended to coalesce around two broad explanatory perspectives (for major overviews, see Brandt and Rawski 2008; Fan et al. 2014). On the one hand, proponents of market-led development understand the China boom as an (ongoing) successful example of post-communist market transition. In this account, a progressive dismantling of the state economy led almost inexorably towards perpetual improvements in total factor productivity commensurate with China's size, labour force, and rich natural endowments—improvements which the communist state planning system had hitherto inhibited (Lin et al. 1996). Proponents of statist political economy, by contrast, tend to emphasise the ways in which China borrowed heavily (with its own particularities) from the East Asian model of the developmental state, pioneered earlier by Japan, South Korea and Taiwan—in which the state pursues an interventionist industrial policy based upon 'getting prices wrong', state-led investment, and heavy market regulation to secure a nationally based Listian competitive (rather than a Ricardian comparative) advantage (Stiglitz 2014).[2]

While some convergence of perspectives is evident over historical particularities (cf. Lin 2013; So 2013), both market-led and statist political economies have held firm their core—and opposed—contentions regarding the drivers of Chinese growth (Lee 2014). China, it is claimed, grew either *because* of economic liberalisation, or because of its *resistance* to significant liberalisation vis-à-vis other large economies in structurally similar positions (India, Russia and Brazil). But even while delivering conflicting judgements on the merits of marketisation versus *dirigiste* statism, underpinning both sides of this debate is a faithfulness to methodologically nationalist conceptions of economic development: in which the state is conflated with the national economic territory, and understood as somehow apart from its context in the world economy and states system (Agnew 1994). This double movement proves particularly obscuring in the Chinese case—not least because China's boom has dovetailed with its unprecedented integration into the global political economy. It consequently seems remarkable that both dominant approaches should chiefly explore factors *internal* to China to explain its period of *export* led industrialisation (Moore 2002).[3]

[2] I take the term 'statist political economy' from the work of Ben Selwyn (2014). It aims to capture the broad set of approaches which crystallised in opposition to the Washington consensus on global development, celebrating the Japanese, South Korean and Taiwanese developmental states; this through an intellectual lineage originating with the work of Friedrich List and Alexander Gerschenkron, among others (Chang 2002; Amsden 2001; Wade 1990; Johnson 1982).

[3] Two prominent exceptions stand out here. The first is Arrighi's (2007) *Adam Smith in Beijing*, which (ambitiously) attempts to characterise China's rise as a response to the decline of US imperialism. Despite its promising title, however, the work only considers in a curtailed form those contemporary developments internal to China—and its analysis here is fatally hampered, I suggest, by Arrighi's reluctance to understand development in China as capitalist (preferring the epithet non-capitalist market economy). This allows for creative theorization, but delimits the possibility for understanding China as part of the capitalist global political economy. The second, Hung (cf. 2009, 2015) is in my view the most incisive political economist working on contemporary China. His conclusions regarding the incorporation of China into the US-dominated global political economy suggest, however, that he cleaves somewhat too strongly to the 'state internationalisation' theses of Panitch and Gindin (2012) and Poulantzas (2014). I prefer to show how

This reductionism is evident of a broader trend in the social sciences. As Charnock and Starosta (2016, 11) note, market-led vs. statist debates of the 1990s entailed a 'discernible move away from the consideration of any question of the structural unity of the global accumulation of capital by IPE and cognate literatures, and instead turned towards a widespread focus on national state institutions as autonomous drivers of economic development'. Hamilton and Gereffi (2009, 143) task such theory with using a 'sociological imperialism… to counterbalance the imperialist attitude that they attribute to economists', ignoring in the process 'a world of economic activities in which profits, prices, and efficiencies do matter'. And while neoclassical economics could not reasonably be subjected to this latter charge, nationally grounded conceptions of capitalism do operate just as much in the scalar optics of data collection and policy prescriptions of 'neoliberal' international organisations, as in more manifestly nation state-centric lenses of developmental statists (see Glassman 2004, for an example of this duality at work in the Thai context; and Gray 2011, for the Korean case). It is, after all, the marketisation of *a* state's (in the singular) factors of production that is the neoliberal imperative.

This duality continues to structure discussions of China to date. Take, for example, *the* China economy debate of recent years: between Justin Yifu Lin (former senior vice president of the World Bank, and once proponent of a 'neoliberal' reading of China cited above) and Weiying Zhang (a prominent Chinese 'New Right' economist), both now at Peking University (Lin 2017; Zhang 2017). Lin has spent some years developing his 'new structural economics', a modification of Washington consensus proposals that aims to sanction limited space for industrial policy—always, of course, within the broader bounds of market rationality (for a critique, see Fine and van Waeyenberge 2013). While such statements might not appear especially radical outside the corridors of the World Bank, applying this thesis to China (as a justification of its past growth and as a policy model for only gradual economic liberalisation moving into the future) drew the criticism of Zhang. Zhang had previously argued that the 'reason China made such big achievements is that state intervention was less and less and the scale of SOEs was smaller and smaller. And the reason there are still so many problems is that there are still many SOEs in existence and their scale is still very large!' (cited in Eaton 2015, 115–116). He

capitalist production has a territoriality of its own which tends to produce geopolitical conflagration.

accordingly deemed Lin's 'new structural economics' of Chinese development a 'new look of Soviet-style planning economy' (quoted in Tang 2016). The argument caught the attention of the global business press, perhaps largely due to the spectacle of a leading World Bank economist lecturing a former Chinese official on the virtues of planning—but it simply repeated in a new context the stale state vs. market debates of the 1990s.

Predating and paralleling such approaches, much critical scholarship of the global political economy has attempted to overcome the national optic of classical and neoclassical political economies. World systems theorists have long maintained that social formations do not exist in isolation, but instead form parts of a hierarchical global system made up of core and peripheral areas: in which politics and economics combine to hold some down and allow others to maintain their dominance (Wallerstein 2011; Amin 2010). While the phenomenon of East Asian industrialisation and the development of other 'emerging market' economies in Brazil, Russia, India and further afield, has since shattered the assumption of any static inequity in the global division of labour, the core claim of world systems theory regarding the existence of a 'supranational social space' in the global economy—from which supposedly 'sovereign' states self-evidently cannot be understood in abstraction—retains its validity (Pendenza 2014, 5). Theorists of the 'new international division of labour', similarly, emerged from the world systems tradition, while aiming to take seriously the phenomenon of peripheral industrialisation (Fröbel et al. 1981; Harris 1986; Henderson 1989). And the contemporary rise of scholarship on transborder production networks renders a national perspective on 'development' redundant if it does not explicitly tackle the terms of sectoral particularities of industries, still defined largely by Western lead firms (Henderson et al. 2002; Gereffi et al. 2005). Given the breadth of and empirical research generated by this diverse scholarship, then, it seems clear that methodologically nationalist political economy, by comparison, quite unreasonably disregards factors emanating from structures and conjunctures of the global political economy, beyond the individual state.

Such efforts to overcome methodological nationalism—from a broad range of critical perspectives—have, conversely, often carried with them an unfortunate tendency to reject wholesale the significance of nation states, their forms, and their distinctly geo/political (or 'relatively autonomous') practices for the concrete and varied forms that capitalist development takes. Globalisation—defined simply as the geographical expansion of capitalist production relations—is often now dissociated from the reproduction of state power, as though the two were antithetical (for a critique, see Rosenberg 2005). Cammack (2015, 25), for instance, argues that the deepening global division of labour expressed in the rise of production networks subjugates states ever more intensely to the law of value, concluding that this heralds the birth of a 'genuinely global capitalism... [which] makes international relations as a discipline both obsolete and redundant'. In this understanding, states' (geo)political autonomy is progressively and inexorably subordinated to the functionalist task of lubricating the process of accumulating capital. Inside social formations, in parallel, the state's role is reduced to that of a partner to international organisations, passively enforcing a homogenous logic of 'competitiveness' (2015, 17).[4] Carroll and Jarvis (2015, 295) similarly portray a new politics of global development characterised by 'deep marketisation': 'an extreme pro-private sector agenda designed to transform the state from being an economic actor (typified in the era of state-led development) into a regulatory state providing the institutional resources necessary for market operation'. And, from a networked perspective, Dicken (2014, 236) argues 'transnational production networks slice through national boundaries (although not necessarily as smoothly as some would claim)', implying a (newly operative) power imbalance between firms and states brought about by the 'territorial asymmetry' between geographically fixed states and mobile capital.

Without doubting the reality of these tendencies, or of a tangible deepening of economic globalisation during recent decades, the risk implicit in the directionality of this scholarship is to gravely neglect the persisting significance of states and their politics for the concrete dynamics taken by capitalist social relations (O'Kane 2014). While the GPN literature now abounds with rich case studies of particular networks, the other major assertion of the original research programme—that 'the precise nature and articulation of firm-centred production networks are deeply influenced by the concrete socio-political contexts within which they are embedded', has remained strikingly unexplored by way of comparison (Henderson et al. 2002, 446; cf. Glassman 2011). And this may not just represent an empirical problem. As Adrian Smith (2015, 291) puts it in a recent

[4] This most recent formulation runs against the grain of some of Cammack's (2012) previous work, however, which does recognise the significance of exploring emerging 'varieties of capitalism' and explores the significance of heavy state regulation in Asia.

discussion of production network approaches, this literature has not yet 'provided a framework for understanding the articulation between state regulation, production networks and the wider accumulation strategies of which they are a part'. Very little work has considered exactly how to integrate the fact of qualitatively deepener transborder production relations with the persistence and reconstitution of national politics, broadly conceived.

To illustrate the difficulties this poses with reference to the Chinese case, take Hart-Landsberg and Burkett's (2006, 13) important and influential argument: that the view of China 'as a national success story based on its increasing export prowess, and as an anchor for regional and global growth, is seriously misleading… [because] China and East Asia are being jointly reshaped by a larger transnational corporate restructuring dynamic that also encompasses the more developed capitalist countries in as well as outside the region'. Again—without contesting the rise of transborder production systems—this 'methodological globalism' leaves us without any analytical framework to understand the particularities of capitalist restructuring taking place *in* China. Because East Asia as a discrete economic region is being 'knitted together in a production process that crosses many borders and, in so doing, restructures national activity and resources away from meeting domestic needs', it follows, for these authors, that China's 'autonomous development potential is being eroded as the state loses its planning and directing capability, and resources are taken over and restructured in and by foreign networks largely for the purpose of satisfying external market demands' (Hart-Landsberg and Burkett 2006, 40; 22). Economic integration is consequently understood as synonymous with the rendering of policy and regulatory initiatives subservient to the demands of mobile capital flows. Their account, while marking an advance on purely state-centric perspectives of China, has nothing to say about what remains of national politics after economic integration, beyond the presumed erosion of national differences.

This perceived 'depoliticisation' of state functions and the ensuing rise of docile regulatory (or 'competition') states first ignores the extent to which the abrogation of state functions is itself often a political choice (Burnham 1999). And—in my view more significantly—it also fails to grapple with the extent to which neoliberal policies are rarely strategically beneficial for capitalists, insofar as the logic of short term profitability represents a poor method of governing any economic region over the medium to long term (resulting more often in the deferral of state interventions aimed at rescuing the economy, rather than their abandonment) (Chang 2011). Wang's (2003, 13) recent application of this thesis of depoliticised 'corporate governance' (in the sense of government-by-capital) to China's experience with cross-border economic integration is a case in point, since it posits the fallacious assumption that until very recently China and the CCP were somehow free from the pressures of global capital to pursue genuinely 'political' policy, but that this is no longer the case (he thus writes: 'the boundary between the political elite and the owners of capital grows gradually more indistinct.... the economic functions of the nation-state are ceded to supranational market organizations ... divisions over questions of development become technical disputes about market-adjustment mechanisms. Political divisions between labor and capital, left and right, are made to disappear'.) In fact, as this book demonstrates, politics and the state—and the national state, at that—form a permanent presence in the Chinese political economy simply because of the intrinsically conflictual nature of capitalist accumulation: and typically, not in forms which might be simply judged either rational or irrational. In a compelling critique of the purported convergence of states towards rational, economising forms during the neoliberal period, Streeck (2009, ch. 13) demonstrates how capital—riven by competitive interests—is by definition always unable to collaborate in the design of such ideal type, rational, 'depoliticised' institutions. Capitalists cannot behave as a 'collective societal agent with sufficient intention, control and foresight to design and build social institutions so that they maximise, or continuously increase, the return to economic resources' (Streeck 2009, 173)—rendering the idealised 'competition state' more a will-o'-the-wisp than a reality.

More broadly, the significance of territorial rivalries between regionally grounded groups of capitals—with highly distinctive policy mixtures and considerable 'non-neoliberal' aspects which could not be seen to conform to any globalising logic—persists, and is quite readily observable in the slew of journalistic material heralding the 'end of globalisation' which have appeared more recently. Decades of global neoliberal policy-making have continually reproduced highly heterogenous state forms and differentiated geographies of development (Peck 2011). Hardy (2013), for instance, characterises the multiplicity of means by which contemporary capitalist states continue to engineer their economies in ways designed to favour particular capitals over others. Cognisant of these issues, a critical strand of historical materialist institutionalist analysis has now emerged which aims, within the context of a tendentially global capital system, to articulate the ways in which political institutions themselves both encounter and reproduce geographical differences (Ebenau et al. 2015; Germann 2018). And a burgeoning parallel literature has begun to draw upon such geographical political economy as an explanation for the empirical phenomenon of the persistence of a nation states system under conditions of deep economic integration (cf. Anievas 2010; Sheppard 2016).

Many issues of substance in this literature remain unresolved, and most importantly for this book is the question of the remaining significance of state territoriality for capitalist development. Panitch and Gindin's (2012) contemporary classic *The Making of Global Capitalism* exemplifies this problem. On the one hand, they convincingly argue that US hegemony has been sustained through the exploitation, rather than a transcendence, of multiple, nominally sovereign, national states which have served to integrate most of the world into US-led global production networks. On the other, their conception of 'super-imperialism' and the internationalisation of states risks eroding the content of the concept of sovereignty to such a degree that all other states become essentially vassals of US power, and the system as a whole consequently unlikely to experience serious inter-imperial conflict or tension (though they do grant—in something of an understatement—that China's integration into this system has been among the world's most 'uneven'). Since this question regarding the shifting geography of production and the evolving nature of political autonomy is best answered in the concrete rather than in the abstract, I devote the bulk of this work to empirical questions that collectively explore various aspects of the territoriality of capitalist production in China today. But I begin with an introduction to the theoretical vantage point best suited to undertaking such a study and one which I think is also suited to answering the question regarding the 'why' of multiple national capitalisms: uneven and combined development.

References

Agnew, John. 1994. The Territorial Trap: The Geographical Assumptions of International Relations Theory. *Review of International Political Economy* 1 (1): 53–80.

Amin, Samir. 2010. *The Law of Worldwide Value*. NYU Press.

Amsden, Alice. 2001. *The Rise of "The Rest": Challenges to the West from Late-Industrializing Economies*. Oxford: Oxford University Press.

Anievas, Alexander (ed.). 2010. *Marxism and World Politics: Contesting Global Capitalism*. London: Routledge.

Arrighi, Giovanni. 2007. *Adam Smith in Beijing*. London: Verso.

Ashman, Sam. 2009. Capitalism, Uneven and Combined Development and the Transhistoric. *Cambridge Review of International Affairs* 22 (1): 29–46.

Brandt, Loren, and Thomas G. Rawski (eds.). 2008. *China's Great Economic Transformation*. Cambridge: Cambridge University Press.

Brenner, Robert. 2006. *The Economics of Global Turbulence: The Advanced Capitalist Economies from Long Boom to Long Downturn, 1945–2005*. London: Verso.

Burnham, Peter. 1999. The Politics of Economic Management in the 1990s. *New Political Economy* 4 (1): 37–54.

Cammack, Paul. 2012. Varieties of Private Sector Governance in Asia. Lee Kuan Yew School of Public Policy Working Paper No. 24. Available online at: https://papers.ssrn.com/sol3/papers.cfm?abstract_id=1991772.

Cammack, Paul. 2015. Production and Social Reproduction in the Contemporary World Market: The Social Reproduction Complex. Paper presented at the 9th Pan-European Conference on International Relations, September 23–26, Giardini Naxos, Sicily. Available online at: https://www.academia.edu/15926705/Production_and_social_reproduction_in_the_contemporary_world_market_the_social_production_complex. Accessed 10 November 2016.

Carroll, Toby, and Darryl Jarvis. 2015. The New Politics of Development: Citizens, Civil Society, and the Evolution of Neoliberal Development Policy. *Globalizations* 12 (3): 281–304.

Chang, Ha-Joon. 2002. *Kicking Away the Ladder: Development Strategy in Historical Perspective*. London: Anthem Press.

Chang, Ha-Joon. 2011. *23 Things They Don't Tell You About Capitalism*. London: Penguin.

Charnock, Greig, and Guido Starosta. 2016. Introduction: The New International Division of Labour and the Critique of Political Economy Today. In *The New International Division of Labour*, ed. Greig Charnock and Guido Starosta, 1–22. Basingstoke: Palgrave.

Davidson, Neil. 2010. From Deflected Permanent Revolution to Uneven and Combined Development. *International Socialism* 2: 128.

Dicken, Peter. 2014. *Global Shift: Mapping the Changing Contours of the World Economy*. London: Sage.

Dunford, Michael, and Weidong Liu. 2017. Uneven and Combined Development. *Regional Studies* 51 (1): 69–85.

Eaton, Sarah. 2015. *The Advance of the State in Contemporary China: State-Market Relations in the Reform Era*. Cambridge: Cambridge University Press.

Ebenau, Matthias, Ian Bruff, and Christian May (eds.). 2015. *New Directions in Comparative Capitalisms Research: Critical and Global Perspectives*. Palgrave: Basingstoke.

Fan, Shenggen, Ravi Kanbur, Shang-Jin Wei, and Xiaobo Zhang (eds.). 2014. *The Oxford Companion to the Economics of China*. Oxford: Oxford University Press.

Fine, Ben, and Elisa van Waeyenberge. 2013. A Paradigm Shift That Never Was: Justin Lin's New Structural Economics. *Competition & Change* 17 (4): 355–371.

Fröbel, Folker, Jürgen Heinrichs, and Otto Kreye. 1981. *The New International Division of Labour*. Cambridge: Cambridge University Press.

Gereffi, Gary, John Humphrey, and Timothy Sturgeon. 2005. The Governance of Global Value Chains. *Review of International Political Economy* 12 (1): 78–104.

Germann, Julian. 2018. Beyond 'Geo-Economics': Advanced Unevenness and the Anatomy of German Austerity. *European Journal of International Relations* 24 (3): 590–613.

Glassman, Jim. 2004. *Thailand at the Margins: Internationalization of the State and the Transformation of Labour*. Oxford: Oxford University Press.

Glassman, Jim. 2011. The Geo-political Economy of Global Production Networks. *Geography Compass* 5 (4): 154–164.

Gray, Kevin. 2011. The Social and Geopolitical Origins of State Transformation: The Case of South Korea. *New Political Economy* 16 (3): 303–322.

Gray, Kevin. 2015. *Labour and Development in East Asia: Social Forces and Passive Revolution*. London: Routledge.

Hamilton, Gary, and Gary Gereffi. 2009. Global Commodity Chains, Market Makers, and the Rise of Demand-responsive Economies. In *Frontiers of Commodity Chain Research*, ed. Jennifer Bair, 136–161. Stanford: Stanford University Press.

Hardy, Jane. 2013. New Divisions of Labour in the Global Economy. *International Socialism Journal* 2 (137): 101–125.

Harris, Nigel. 1986. *The End of the Third World: Newly Industrialising Countries and the Decline of an Ideology*. London: I.B. Tauris.

Hart-Landsberg, Martin, and Paul Burkett. 2006. China and the Dynamics of Transnational Accumulation: Causes and Consequences of Global Restructuring. *Historical Materialism* 14 (3): 3–43.

Henderson, Jeffrey. 1989. *The Globalisation of High Technology Production: Society, Space, and Semiconductors in the Restructuring of the Modern World*. London: Routledge.

Henderson, Jeffrey, Peter Dicken, Martin Hess, Neil Coe, and Henry Wai-Chung Yeung. 2002. Global Production Networks and the Analysis of Economic Development. *Review of International Political Economy* 9 (3): 436–464.

Hung, Ho-Fung. 2009. America's Head Servant? *New Left Review* 60: 5–25.

Hung, Ho-fung. 2015. *The China Boom: Why China Will Not Rule the World*. Chichester: Columbia University Press.

Jacques, Martin. 2009. *When China Rules the World*. Harmondsworth: Penguin.

Johnson, Chalmers. 1982. *MITI and the Japanese Miracle: The Growth of Japanese Industrial Policy, 1925–1975*. Stanford: Stanford University Press.

Lee, Ching Kwan. 2014. A Chinese Developmental State: Miracle or Mirage? In *The End of the Developmental State?* ed. Michelle Williams, 128–151. London: Routledge.

Lin, Justin Yifu. 2013. Demystifying the Chinese Economy. *Australian Economic Review* 46 (3): 259–268.

Lin, Justin Yifu. 2017. Industrial Policies for Avoiding the Middle-income Trap: A New Structural Economics Perspective. *Journal of Chinese Economic and Business Studies* 15 (1): 5–18.

Lin, Justin Yifu, Fang Cai, and Zhou Li. 1996. *The China Miracle: Development Strategy and Economic Reform*. Hong Kong: Chinese University Press.

Marx, Karl. 1991. *Capital Volume III*. London: Penguin.

Mearsheimer, John. 2006. China's Unpeaceful Rise. *Current History* 105 (690): 160–162.

Moore, Thomas G. 2002. *China in the World Market: Chinese Industry and International Sources of Reform in the Post-Mao Era*. Cambridge: Cambridge University Press.

O'Kane, Chris. 2014. State Violence, State Control: Marxist State Theory and the Critique of Political Economy. *Viewpoint*, October 29. Available online at: https://www.viewpointmag.com/2014/10/29/state-violence-state-control-marxist-state-theory-and-the-critique-of-political-economy/. Accessed 25 October 2016.

Panitch, Leo, and Sam Gindin. 2012. *The Making of Global Capitalism*. London: Verso.

Peck, Jamie. 2011. Geographies of Policy: From Transfer-diffusion to Mobility-mutation. *Progress in Human Geography* 35 (6): 773–797.

Pendenza, Massimo. 2014. Introduction. In *Classical Sociology Beyond Methodological Nationalism*, ed. Massimo Pendenza, 1–26. Leiden: Brill.

Poulantzas, Nicos. 2014. *State, Power, Socialism*. London: Verso.

Rachman, Gideon. 2016. *Easternisation: War and Peace in the Asian Century*. London: Bodley House.

Rosenberg, Justin. 2005. Globalization Theory: A Post Mortem. *International Politics* 42 (1): 2–74.

Selwyn, Benjamin. 2014. *The Global Development Crisis*. John Wiley & Sons.

Sheppard, Eric. 2016. *Limits to Globalization: Disruptive Geographies of Capitalist Development*. Oxford: Oxford University Press.

Smith, Adrian. 2015. The State, Institutional Frameworks and the Dynamics of Capital in Global Production Networks. *Progress in Human Geography* 39 (3): 290–315.

So, Alvin Y. 2013. *Class and Class Conflict in Post-Socialist China*. Singapore: World Scientific Publishing.

Stiglitz, Joseph. 2014. Transition to a Market Economy. In *The Oxford Companion to the Economics of China*, ed. Shenggen Fan, Ravi Kanbur, Shang-Jin Wei, and Xiaobo Zhang. Oxford: Oxford University Press.

Streeck, Wolfgang. 2009. *Re-forming Capitalism: Institutional Change in the German Political Economy*. Oxford: Oxford University Press.

Stubbs, Richard. 2017. *Rethinking Asia's Economic Miracle: The Political Economy of War, Prosperity and Crisis*. Basingstoke: Palgrave.

Tang, Frank. 2016. To Embrace Market or State: Chinese Economists Debate the Country's Future. *South China Morning Post*, November 12. Available online at: http://www.scmp.com/news/china/economy/article/2021088/leading-economists-debate-alue-state-intervention-chinas. Accessed 13 November 2016.

van der Linden, Marcel. 2007. The "Law" of Uneven and Combined Development: Some Underdeveloped Thoughts. *Historical Materialism* 15 (1): 145–165.

Wade, Robert. 1990. *Governing the Market*. Princeton: Princeton University Press.

Wallerstein, Immanuel Maurice. 2011. *Historical Capitalism: With Capitalist Civilization*. London: Verso.

Wang, Hui. 2003. *China's New Order: Society, Politics, and Economy in Transition*, trans. Theodore Huters. Cambridge: Harvard University Press.

Zhang, Weiying. 2017. China's Future Growth Depends on Innovation Entrepreneurs. *Journal of Chinese Economic and Business Studies* 15 (1): 19–40.

CHAPTER 2

Uneven and Combined Development and the Capitalist States System

2.1 Introduction

The global financial crisis of 2008 and its aftermath have put states back at the centre of attention. State-led economic stimulus; the rise of increasingly interventionist forms of capitalism in the form of the BRICS; and the return of significant geopolitical tensions and conflagrations from the Caucasus, Ukraine, Syria and the broader MENA region, to the South and East China Seas; have decisively challenged the notion that states and geopolitics have been undermined by the pressures of global economic integration (Callinicos 2010; Klassen 2014; Nowak and Ekrem 2018). The levelling of global geoeconomic space conjectured by both neoliberals (cf. Wolf 2005; Bhagwati 2004) and some Marxists (cf. Hardt and Negri 2000; Robinson 2005) alike, has not materialised. The 'globalisation' of the 1990s and early 2000s instead revealed itself as a new phase in the world expansion and deepening of geographically differentiated and antagonistic capitalist social relations (Barrow 2005; Rosenberg 2005).

As globalist ontologies have come under challenge, critical voices have again proposed (and celebrated already existing) state developmentalist alternatives to globalisation as more equitable and sustainable models of growth, especially for late developers (cf. Evans 2014). The implication is that the 'ideology' of neoliberalism, the 'vested interests' of (usually financial) capitalists, or a 'lack of institutional capacity' are to blame for

S. Rolf, *China's Uneven and Combined Development*,
Studies in the Political Economy of Public Policy,
https://doi.org/10.1007/978-3-030-55559-7_2

the cases where these policies are not enacted and development stalls as a result (Selwyn 2014). While this shift plainly represents an improvement on the Washington consensus prescriptions of the first stage of rollout neoliberalism, such statist perspectives are plainly vulnerable to the charge of 'methodological nationalism': that is, they present capitalism not 'as an international relation of exploitation [and competition] but as a relation between different sets of owners of sources of revenue *within* the state' (Pradella 2014, 190). As such, such research fails to conceptualise capitalist development as a (tendentially) globalising system where all developmental processes are shaped by (i) a world economy with a dynamic which tends to overdetermine local forms of economic growth and (ii) a states system where geopolitics severely impacts upon state policies. It is not surprising then that such research has tended systematically to overstate the case regarding the possibility of pursuing such preferential policy mixes—and offers little to no clues as to the (quite unique) structural contexts in which such developmental strategies are possible for states of the global south.

This dichotomy of neoliberal-globalist and methodologically nationalist theoretical perspectives on the political economy of development has plainly become strained in the post-2008 world, in which, while production has continued (though at a slower rate than previously) to become ever more internationalised through complex cross-border production networks (Henderson et al. 2002), the policy agency of states has remained as substantial as ever. The trial confronting political economists, then, is to deliver theoretical approaches that refuse to explore political economies in their isolation but as part of a world economy *and*, crucially, which can explain why and with what consequences the system of nation states is reproduced as an essential element of a world economy increasingly characterised by the 'geographical spread and functional integration of production activities' (Dicken 2014).

This introductory chapter proposes Trotsky's notion of UCD as one theoretical orientation capable of living up to this challenge, but also highlights some critical deficiencies associated with recent scholarship in this area. An extensive debate on the value of UCD for developing an integrated analysis of states and capital has developed over the last decade (for a critical overview, see Rioux [2015, 482–486]). While I believe a UCD perspective can assist in developing an understanding of the materiality of the capitalist states system as a 'dimension of the capitalist mode of production' (Callinicos 2009, 83; Pozo-Martin 2007;

Desai 2012; Davidson 2012), and this literature has significantly advanced our historical understanding of global process by which the feudal states system was transformed into a capitalist one (cf. Anievas and Nişancıoğlu 2015), it is yet to satisfactorily account for why, and with what consequences, the plurality of states remains 'a constitutive expression and component of capitalist relations of exploitation and competition' (Hirsch and Kannankulam 2011, 22) in an era when the transition to capitalism is complete. In attempting to account for why capitalist value relations continue to be expressed through a system of multiple nation states and with what implications for our understanding of the world system this can present, the purpose is to develop UCD as a framework capable of understanding the dramatic and mutually interactive transformation of China and the global political economy since the 1970s as a singular process.

2.2 The Revival of Uneven and Combined Development

Justin Rosenberg (2006, 312), in his pioneering reassessment, argues that the classical social theorists principally conceived societies in the singular, rather than in their interactive multiplicity: 'in the classical tradition, the interactive multiplicity of social development as a historical process does not enter into the formal theorization of development'. Building on his (Rosenberg 1994) critique of Realist international relations (IR) theory, he goes on to contend that Russian revolutionary and theorist Leon Trotsky's (Trotsky 2007, 2009) analysis of Russia's socio-economic development was singularly successful in incorporating the fact of political multiplicity into social theory (Rosenberg 2013), supported as it was by the concept of the ***uneven and combined development*** (UCD) of world capitalism. At the same time, debates among Marxists over contemporary US imperialism (Harvey 2003; Callinicos 2003), the birth of the capitalist world system (Wood 2002; Teschke 2003); and the nature of the states system under contemporary capitalism (*CRIA* 2007, 2009) led Barker (2006) and Ashman (2010)—among others—to suggest UCD not only (as per Trotsky) as a theoretical orientation capable of integrating the fact of multiple states into analysis of social development, but have also identified it as the most important' source of a powerful centrifugal drive which helps keep states multiple' (Callinicos 2009, 92). So UCD not only holds the promise of providing an elusive social theory of multiple states and describing its effects of increasingly integrated economies, but also explains *why*—in the context of increasingly universal market society—capitalist states remain multiple.

Trotsky, since the failed revolution of 1905, had sought to push the Russian Social Democratic Labour Party (RSDLP) towards a direct seizure of power on the basis of the strategy of permanent revolution (which would eventually transpire in October 1917, following its 1912 split into Bolshevik and Menshevik parties). The orthodox Second International Marxism of the period, however, which predominated among the party's leadership figures like Georgi Plehkanov and Karl Kautsky, adhered to what became known as 'stagism': the notion that Russia (and similarly poor states) should have to first experience a bourgeois revolution in order to eradicate feudal social relations from the Russian countryside, which encompassed approximately 90% of the population, and industrialisation in the cities. This bourgeois revolution would eventually develop the material basis for socialism. Even after the split of 1912, the (more radical) Bolshevik leadership under Lenin adhered to a modified form of two-stage theory in which a coalition of workers and capitalists would achieve these tasks of the bourgeois revolution before moving towards socialism. Trotsky's concept of permanent revolution, by contrast, located the failure to overthrow Tsarism in the weakness of Russian capitalism and the bourgeoisie, and its concomitant dependence on the authoritarian state. This state, in turn, had its social base in the semi-feudal Russian countryside. As such, a weak and politically dependent capitalist class could not be expected to lead a French-style bourgeois revolution against its political guarantor. Instead, land reform and industrial development could only be achieved via a permanent revolutionary process which moved directly from Russia's contemporary form of semi-feudalism towards socialism. Only in April 1917 were Trotsky's prescriptions accepted by the Bolshevik party (represented by Lenin's famed 'April Theses' directing an immediate seizure of power by workers' soviets).

The radical novelty of this political contribution (despite its antecedents in Marx and Engels' work: see Löwy [2010]) was matched by the ferocity of contemporary debates. But underlying permanent revolution as a strategic orientation, though, was the equally innovative but far less discussed concept of the uneven and combined development (UCD) of global capitalism (Trotsky 2007). *Uneven* development became a widely accepted component of the Bolsheviks' theoretical canon, particularly after Lenin (1916) defined imperialism as the upshot of a world system now dominated by capitalism: in which the 'uneven and spasmodic development of individual enterprises, individual branches of industry and individual countries is inevitable'. The dynamism and fundamental unpredictability of global economic development (as represented by the dramatic rise of German economy under Bismarck) meant that any permanent, 'ultra-imperialist' accord between the great powers had been rendered impossible. The concept of uneven development would subsequently be subsumed under Stalin's project of building 'socialism in one country': because the 'advantages of backwardness' provided the possibility of skipping ahead of rivals through catch-up development.

Challenging this latter notion, while expanding upon Lenin's, Trotsky accentuated the *twin* tendencies inherent in capitalism, of both differentiation as well as equalisation of levels of economic development over geographical space: through perpetual expansion, capital 'brings about their *rapprochement* and equalises the economic and cultural levels of the most progressive and the most backward countries'. He stressed the global nature of capitalism, a system defined by the development of its parts in combination, not isolation. The result is 'on the one hand, unevenness, i.e., sporadic historical development… while, on the other hand, the organic interdependence of the several countries, developing toward an international division of labor' (Trotsky 1928). Interconnectedness of the world economy rendered impossible any delinking of socialist Russia, as *per* Stalin, but also introduced complicating factors into Lenin's understanding of uneven development.

Specifically, Trotsky grasped far better than Lenin how unevenness was not only distributed among states, but also *inside* social formations. In Russia, elements of sophisticated industrial capitalism coexisted with semi-feudal agrarian social relations. More importantly, not only did they share a single political territory, but these different productive forms were profoundly entangled with one another. The modern munitions factories in St Petersburg and Moscow provided the anachronistic Tsarist state with the means to defend itself against colonial encroachment and the further spread of capitalist relations:

> The backward nation, moreover, not infrequently debases the achievements borrowed from outside… The very process of assimilation acquires a self-contradictory character. Thus the introduction of certain elements of Western technique and training, above all military and industrial, under Peter I, led to a strengthening of serfdom as the fundamental form of labor organization. European armament and European loans – both indubitable

> products of a higher culture – led to a strengthening of tsarism, which delayed in its turn the development of the country. (Trotsky 2009, 4–5)

Stalinist understandings of catch-up development through technology transfer are not compatible with this analysis. As Trotsky argues, Russia's gradual entry into the world economy neither set it on the same road to capitalism as Britain and France had followed, nor entirely inhibited its development into a major capitalist power (Trotsky 2007). Instead, it modulated the direction of this development resulting in the emergence as a 'peculiar' national form of capitalism, distinct from both early and late prior developers. This developmental path preserved the late developing features of the Russian social formation in its form of state and peasant economy, while creating extremely advanced urban centres of industrial capitalism. Development is thus doubly 'combined': as capitalism links (combines) all corners of the world into an integrated totality for the first time, techno-economic advances ricochet around all other societies, producing social combinations of progressive and regressive elements in late developers depending on the form of their adoption.

Using the concept of 'insertion' into the global economy and the hierarchy of imperialist states at a particular point in its economic development, Trotsky also highlights how geopolitical pressures and rivalries engendered by the existence of the capitalist states system act as a constitutive factor, shaping national development trajectories (Trotsky 2009, 7). While global capitalism is a 'single economic and political organism' (Trotsky 2007, 12), its political and economic structure is also territorially fragmented into the system of nation states which arose in tandem with the capitalist world system. This 'coeval' (in Ashman's terminology [2006, 95]), rather than contradictory, development of a world economy and a competitive system of nation states, mean that economic and technological advances in competitor states confront capitalists and state managers as 'external' challenges. Such 'external influences differ not only in (socio-spatial) origin but also in kind from their internal political, material and ideational equivalents. Because they traverse more than one political jurisdiction, they add a strategic, geopolitical dimension to social development' (Rosenberg 2013, 583). So, the states system—as it systematically differentiates social space under capitalism—plays a causal role in influencing states' development trajectories.

Trotsky's theory of UCD, then, pinpoints the distinctive role that capitalist geopolitics play in hampering development in some parts of the world system, while acknowledging the possibility of development (Harman 2010). Capital, he argues, operates through 'anarchistic methods... developing some parts of the world economy while hampering and throwing back others', through 'tiger leaps and such raids on backward countries'. As such, the 'unification and levelling of the world economy is upset by [geopolitics] even more violently and convulsively than in the preceding epochs' (Trotsky 1928). While uneven development is the most 'general law of the historic process', then, the combined development which the global reach of capitalism entails reproduces this unevenness according to a new dynamic, driven by novel class formations and state forms (Trotsky 2009, 4).

Compare Marx's (1990, 91) occasional anticipation that each state would repeat the developmental trajectory of earlier states ('the country that is more developed industrially only shows, to the less developed, the image of its own future'). Trotsky, by contrast, theorises a nonlinear global history—in which late developers can leap ahead much more quickly by appropriating technologies and capital from advanced economies, but must embed these borrowed social forms in very different socio-economic contexts. This is some distance from static conceptions of a world system which locks the global south into permanent forms of 'underdevelopment'—but neither does it render catch-up in any way inevitable or simple (Harman 2010). Instead, Trotsky's understanding of catch-up development is only one potential outcome of highly specific historical conjunctures and strategic agencies to which the world system may give rise.

Drawing on Trotsky's work and the growing secondary literature, we can summarise the theoretical significance of the theory of UCD by identifying three sociological propositions at its core:

(1) The 'whip of external necessity' obliges all states to take developmental initiatives, due to economic and military threats from more developed states (Trotsky 2009, 4). In Trotsky's time, most states which could not meet these obligations were subjected to formal colonisation, but today are considerably more likely to experience informal subjugation and poverty.
(2) However, the 'privilege of historical backwardness' grants those late developing states which *can* successfully take developmental initiatives the possibility of temporally compressing their economic growth processes: leapfrogging the stages of development passed

through by first movers by importing industrial technologies, organisational and institutional forms (Trotsky 2009, 5).

(3) During catch-up development, though, late developers are likely to experience 'contradictions of sociological amalgamation' (Allinson and Anievas 2010) as an upshot of combining new and old. This is because the 'new' (be they technologies, firm types, or state institutions) are very rarely adopted universally across the territory of a state—but, rather, contained within economic sectors and subnational regions. The risk, then, is that the idiosyncratic social structures which emerge possess intense contradictions, sharpened by the fusion of new and old—which Trotsky (2009) colourfully terms 'debased adaptation' (for a summary, see Davidson 2006, 12).

Effects (1) and (2) are both forms of combined development which operate *between* states and have been widely observed by the literature on catch-up development (discussed further in Chapter 3). Effect (3), however, operates *inside* states. To this extent, it can be understood as representing a geopolitical theory of the social—a means of integrating the causal effects of geopolitical competition between states with the trajectory of social development within a state. This opens the door to a multiscalar theory of development which can illuminate several conceptual and empirical difficulties confronting those studying development in the global south which too often remains trapped at either the national or international scale of analysis.

Three axioms emerge from these propositions that can help orient our study of geopolitical economy: First is that the capitalist world economy constitutes a totality, not the space where essentially autonomous states sometimes interact; and so its transformations are cumulative and not iterative (see also McMichael 2001; Harris 1986). Second is that the states system shapes and upholds uneven development, which is not a purely 'economic' process—since advanced states (except in unusual conditions, as explored in Chapter 4) are likely to attempt to maintain their own advantage and block rival developers, while the agency of peripheral states pursuing strategies of catch-up development fuels combined development and interstate competition.[1] Third, states' geopolitical interactions are informed by their constantly changing developmental trajectories as state-society complexes. As new forms of state crystallise from processes of combined development and subsequently engage politically and economically with other states, disruptive international competitive effects (theorised as 'anarchy' in the International Relations literature) are highly likely to emerge as an outgrowth of societal change.

UCD, then, represents an orientation which helps give theoretical weight to the aphorism that global and domestic politics and economics are intrinsically interconnected. As Antonio Gramsci (1971, 176) writes in suggestive comments on Fordism (which were subsequently used by neo-Gramscian IR theorists):

> Any organic innovation in the [national] social structure, through its technical-military expressions, modifies organically absolute and relative relations in the international field too.

Similarly, Trotsky's argument (with which Gramsci was familiar) begins with 'modifications' in the international political economy and locates the impact of these on national social structures. As Green (2014) notes, then, UCD is methodologically *inter*nationalist. But its orientation, unlike International Relations theory, is towards understanding the specificities of *national* social formations.

2.3 The Limits of UCD?

Despite its apparent promise for grasping current developments, the scholarly interest in UCD has instead led to historically focused debate on the transition to capitalism. Rosenberg (2008), Shilliam (2009), Matin (2013), and Anievas and Nişancıoğlu (2015) (see also the symposium on their book: cf. Anievas and Nişancıoğlu 2018) have engaged in a constructive and contentious debate surrounding the (specifically *international*) historical sociology of the transition to capitalism. Because, as Anievas (2014) points out, the existence of the states system was

[1] This competition does not of necessity take military form. In fact, it is far more likely to take the form of tariffs, protectionism and the formation of regional trading blocs—which are best understood as part of a continuum of international relations (Davidson 2012).

assumed rather than historically accounted for by theories of imperialism like Lenin's and Bukharin's, examining the mixture of historical and structuralist logics at play in the persistence of this states system has injected new life into older debates on the transition to capitalism (see Wood 2002; Teschke 2003).

The overwhelmingly historical focus of this debate, however (and its focus on what the Annales School of history term the *longue durée* of capitalist development) has inhibited deployment of UCD as a framework for examining contemporary case studies. As such, only a small handful of studies seek actually to apply these concepts to contemporary cases (e.g. Rosenberg and Boyle 2019; Dunford and Liu 2017). More significant yet is the absence of any further significant theoretical development. So Rioux (2015, 507–508) notes the 'lack of proper theorisations of why capital's dynamics produce uneven and combined development', across this work, which has lead to a 'perennial failure to theorise historically and spatially specific processes of U&CD'. The outcome is that recent UCD literature has not engaged with dependency theory, world systems theory, or uneven geographic development: all of which share the problematic of the perpetuation of geographic unevenness, political multiplicity, and catch-up development. It has also not explained precisely why capitalist UCD should reproduce a system of states (for more on this question, see the next chapter). This literature has, in short, had surprisingly little to say about contemporary capitalism.

Partly to blame for this shortcoming is Rosenberg's (2010) contention that UCD should function as a transhistoric theoretical abstraction, equally valid for historical periods prior to capitalism, which significantly shaped the terms of the subsequent debate (cf. Ashman 2009 for a critique). But Trotsky's own contributions complicate matters, since his focused specifically on the effects of sociological amalgamation *across* modes of production—that is, between feudalism and capitalism. There seems little reason, however, why this analysis cannot be extended to the contradictory effects of sociological amalgamation *inside* the capitalist mode of production but across variegations of it—i.e. between the predominantly neoliberal global north and the predominantly state capitalist global south, for instance.

This is so because the core concepts of UCD in fact revolve around the law of value. Indeed, removed from the capitalist law of value, which give advancement, 'backwardness' and late development their meaning, UCD risks becoming merely 'descriptive rather than explanatory' (Kiely 2012, 234) insofar as it doesn't identify any specific social mechanisms driving unevenness or enforcing combination. Rioux (2015) locates the source of the problem in the fact that Trotsky's scattered writings on UCD only haphazardly explain how it relates to the economic dynamics of capitalism as a social system. Herod (2006, 156) thus observes that Trotsky 'does not develop a formal conceptual outline' of UCD, while Hardy (2014, 145) also notes that Trotsky 'did not offer an explanation of the drivers or causes of unevenness'. The concept is elaborated with reference to the specificities of the Russian (and Chinese) social formations, but not generally. As such, the historical debate alluded to above has turned on whether the 'international', or Marx's laws of accumulation, should take priority.

Colin Barker (2006, 80) offers one attempt, via the latter route, to specify the functioning of UCD as a theoretical abstraction tied to the laws of motion of capital. He suggests the capitalist law of value, defined by the universal obligation of laggard capitals to either improve their productivity or to fail, 'expresses the capitalist form of combined and uneven development in a summary manner'. Because leading firms 'shape the *validation* of products via socially necessary labour time... [all other] producers are *compelled* to try to match the latest technique'. Development, then, measured by the labour productivity of firms (or clusters of lead firms) across a national territory, provides an empirically observable proxy for identifying economically advanced and late developing states. And the ability of laggard firms, regions, and states to make 'leaps' towards the most advanced through the importation of the latest productive techniques, organisational and institutional forms firmly identifies UCD as an outgrowth of the capitalist law of value, which could not have operated systematically under any prior mode of production.

But while this forms a starting point, such an abstract formulation, however, cannot tell us much about existing patterns of UCD in the contemporary world economy or their relationships with the system of nation states. And—as argued throughout this book—the advent of global production networks means that 'socially-necessary' labour time becomes less of a homogenous and more of a geographically relative measure of value than before, with quite complex ramifications for understanding a state's location in the world system. Having identified this failure of the UCD literature to live up to its promise, the remainder of this chapter seeks to reconstruct, from the first principles of Marxist political economy, why the states system remains a constitutive 'dimension of the capitalist mode of production' (Callinicos 2009, 83), how it interacts with uneven development, and how it continues to form a critical vector of the global political economy and its UCD.

2.4 Karl Marx and Uneven Geographical Development

Marx has often been portrayed as a 'hyper-globaliser', notoriously recognising the ability of capital to 'batter down all Chinese walls' and integrate far flung corners of the world into a single economy (Desai 2002). But his political economy did not preclude territorial fragmentation, differentiation and spatial competition within a fully capitalist world economy. For instance, in a notebook produced prior to the publication of *Capital*, Marx (1973, 887–888) observes the 'monopoly of concentrated English capital and its dissolving effect on the smaller national capitals of other countries'. Discussing the development of tariff-based protectionist competition between the United States and the UK, he further claims that:

> These world market disharmonies are merely the ultimate adequate expressions of the disharmonies which have become fixed as abstract relations within the economic categories [...] which have a local existence of the smallest scale.

In fact, a cursory examination of his journalism (cf. Marx 2007) alongside important recent contributions to scholarship (Pradella 2015) reveal Marx conceived the relationship between the world economy and the system of states as a set of contradictory and conflictual 'internal relations', far from the perspective of *external* relations between states and markets that dominates orthodox international political economy today (Bieler and Morton 2014; Bruff 2012; cf. Ollman 1970).

However, despite this predisposition to understand and theorise the capitalist system as a totality, but one fractured into competing blocs of capital, in *Capital* itself—where he most completely elaborates his conception of the laws of motion of capital—Marx quite definitively abstracts from questions of territorial difference, foreign trade, and state power. At the critical juncture of Volume I of *Capital* where he outlines his theory of the reproduction of the total social capital, Marx (1990, 727, fn2) states:

> In order to examine the object of our investigation in its integrity, free from all disturbing subsidiary circumstances, we must treat the whole world of trade as one nation, and assume that capitalist production is established everywhere and has taken possession of every branch of industry.

This treatment of the capitalist world as a single, borderless entity underpins *Capital's* theoretical perspective. In discussing the role of gold as money in the context of simple capitalist reproduction in Volume II of *Capital*, Marx (1992, 546) grapples with the problem of its production in distinctive concrete social formations, which sits in contradiction with its universalising role. He concludes that that while 'capitalist production never exists without foreign trade', because trade 'replaces domestic articles only by those of use or other forms... [analysing it] can therefore only confuse things, without supplying any new factor'. Finally, in Volume III, when Marx (1991) discusses the various forms that surplus-value takes (profit, rent, interest), 'he quite ignores one form: *tax*. Any further development of the critique of political economy most decidedly requires the development of that category, for tax collection is the presupposition of all state intervention' (Barker 2009, 22).[2]

Neil Smith (2010, 128) contends that Marx's inability to systematically integrate uneven geographical development and state power into his analytical framework was not 'arbitrary... [but] consistent with his logico-historical method, this assumption reflects his conviction that capital would progressively level these geographical differentiations'. If correct, this would represent a damning indictment of Marxist theory's capacity to theorise contemporary patterns of UCD in a global political economy which remains riven by profound territorial and political boundaries.

Smith's logic may be misleading, however. Outlining his proposed method in the *Grundrisse* (1973, 101), Marx proposes to ascend 'from the simple, such as labour, division of labour, need, exchange value, to the level of state, exchange between countries and the world market'. *Capital*, unfinished text as it was, never reached this level of theoretical exposition of the state and world economy. So while the published volumes did exclude consideration 'of foreign trade, of geographical expansion', and the states system—as these 'merely complicated matters' at the high

[2] Compare Marx's more or less scattered remarks on taxation, with the 100+ pages each devoted to: the conversion of surplus value into industrial profit, merchant capital, interest bearing capital, and ground rent, respectively.

level of abstraction at which his work began (Harvey 2001, 308)[3]—it does not at all mean that his theoretical framework was incompatible with such extension to incorporate these as core concepts of capitalism as a social system (cf. Callinicos 2009, 2014). The failure, then, may be more our own than Marx's: Lasslett (2015, 642) consequently notes how 'reluctance among [Marx's] students to widen the boundaries of *Capital* – with honourable exceptions – has blunted efforts to theorize the specific way state power is organized under capitalism, and how it mediates the processes and tendencies conceptualized in *Capital*'s first three volumes'.

It is my aim here, in a limited sense, to take up this challenge and develop an explanation of how processes of geographical articulate with Marx's (incomplete) theory of the state. Starting with those geographers—Harvey (2007), Smith (2010), and Massey (1995)—who have best engaged with the spatiality of capitalist accumulation, I develop a critique of their work for emphasising capital's 'economic' logic without effectively incorporating states into the analysis. Second, I scrutinise Jessop's (1982, 1990, 2008) strategic-relational approach, which represents the most coherent body of Marxist state theory, highlighting its propensity towards an overly political analysis of capitalist development. Both these traditions, I argue, implicitly counterpose and prioritise economic and political logics which a fuller understanding of UCD can help to integrate.

2.5 Uneven Geographical Development and States

Uneven development and the world of unequally powerful and wealthy nation states plainly bear a relationship with one another, but the direction of causality is unclear. Does 'economic' uneven development give rise to the political superstructure of an imperialist states system, or does the imperialist states system amend capitalism's natural levelling tendencies to

[3] Pradella's (2013) recent contention that Marx was here theorising a globally expansionary system and thus did to some extent aim to incorporate political mediations into his theory of accumulation in *Capital*—as, for instance, in the chapter on primitive accumulation—does not resolve the problem that he deliberately chose not to incorporate the competitive dynamic of multiple nation states into the scope of his analysis. As she notes (2013, 124), 'in Volume I Marx does not take into account the relations in circulation and the multiplicity of nations'.

give us uneven development? World systems theorists have long taken the latter path, constructing a theoretical orientation which explains how the states system undergirds capitalism's uneven development (Arrighi et al. 2003). Rosenberg (2009, 109), however, favours the former explanation; arguing that 'uneven development gives rise to political multiplicity; and through this multiplicity, that same unevenness super-adds a class of anarchical causes to the nature of social development'. In this view, the states system and the 'anarchic' relationship between states is an outcome of the uneven development of the productive forces (though this interstate system may then, through secondary causation, amend this uneven development). Werner Bonefeld (2014, 152, my italics) agrees, favourably quoting Marx's *Grundrisse* in support of this position: the system of interstate relations is *founded on* the 'international relations of production. International division of labour. International exchange and import. Rate of exchange'. I also find this second position more convincing. Here, I develop an explanation of why the global capitalist economy continues to be divided into a system of differentiated sovereign states by examining how the universal processes of capital accumulation results in uneven development across geographic space.

The principle contribution of uneven development theory in economic geography has been to specify the existence a *fixity-motion* dialectic intrinsic to the process of capital accumulation. Capital, as value in motion, contains opposing tendencies to concentrate and centralise, developing certain spaces of the world economy, alongside a tendency to move and disperse across space, underdeveloping many others (Harvey 2007; Smith 2010; Massey 1995). Mobility is easily accounted for by the hunt for the best possible return on capital advanced. But for capital to move requires an ever-greater quantity of physical infrastructures to be fixed in space: both within the production process in new growth areas, as in increasingly high-tech plant and equipment, but also and increasingly in logistics and physical infrastructures (airports, highways, and rail) across old and new areas. Capitalist competition results in technological and organisational dynamism, which by necessity emerges in particular locations and firms before becoming generalised—raising the possibility of rising returns to capital as the gains from investment are corralled within certain cities, regions or states. Meanwhile, the tendency of profit rates to fall over time as competition cheapens output is and all firms adopt new techniques ensures the permanent spectre of capital flight from established regions.

The 'concentration and centralisation' of capital, a tendency observed by Marx (1990) in the first volume of *Capital*, has both social and spatial forms. While capital's *social* concentration and centralisation under the control of fewer and larger firms is Marx's focus, Smith (2010) records corresponding *spatial* concentration and centralisation of capital in particular cities and regions. This takes place due to:

- A generally increasing ratio of capital to labour over investment cycles.
- The effect of economies of scale and scope.
- Productivity gains from multi-firm agglomeration economies/ clustering.
- Increasing significance of ancillary and logistics services and infrastructure for firms' productivity.
- The benefits of population density for the productivity of collective consumption (hospitals, schools, swimming pools).

These forces draw capital together in particular spaces at the expense of others. Without the existence of centripetal forces, the spatial concentration and centralisation of capital would become absolute:

> Centralisation of the means of production and socialization of labour at last reach a point where they become incompatible with their capitalist integument. (Marx 1990, 625)

Spatial concentration and centralisation of capital, however, 'brings only a limited equalization of levels and conditions of development', because of equally significant and opposing forces towards dispersal and mobility (Smith 2010, 196). These forces exist because of:

- Shifts in production location brought about by technological innovations outside of existing centres of production (Storper and Walker 1989, ch 9).
- A tendency towards overaccumulation of capital and falling profits.
- An expansionary urge to develop spaces where profits remain high and markets not yet saturated.
- Shifts in firms' organizational forms (from joint stock to multinationals to production networks) and the consequent establishment of new spatial divisions of labour (Massey 1995, 2005).

- Absolute and relative increases in the liquidity of deterritorialised forms of capital—precious metals, money, and (overwhelmingly, today) credit and fictitious capital.

Collectively, these forces inhibit absolute spatial concentration and centralisation of capital, and encourage 'portions of the original capital [to] disengage themselves and function as new capitals' (Marx 1990, 625). The credit system plays a critically important role in directing surplus capital towards profitable but capital scarce places during crises of overaccumulation in already developed regions (Harvey 2010).

Moreover, it is possible to identify patterns emerging from these fundamental and opposing economic forces. Smith (2010) famously observes the dynamic whereby a particular space is developed through capital accumulation, followed an exodus of capital at a certain point in its development resulting its subsequent underdevelopment and capital flight. Once overaccumulation strikes again in the new location, capital may abandon it and return to the original space of development—now devalued by the exodus of capital and so prepared for another round of accumulation. The overall picture becomes one of a system of space economies of differentially productive, and capital intensive, agglomerations of fixed capital (Sheppard and Barnes 1990). The geographical elaboration of Marx's categories suggests that capital survives 'by occupying space, by producing a space', but that in spite of capital's universalising drive, its spatial corollary in fact 'has nothing homogenous about it' (Lefebvre 1976, 21; 1991, 308).

At any time-point, we might identify relatively static regional, national, and international divisions of labour as an outcome of this process. Within the world economy's absolute space, concrete national spaces of capital exist in a relative relation to each other—being either more or less productive than the world average. Agglomeration of capital in these particular spaces logically demands those economically dependent on these agglomerations (specifically, coalitions of state managers and capitalists and, sometimes, organised labour) to work collectively in ameliorating the negative consequences of competition with other such aggolmerations. This may be done through establishing favourable general conditions of production such as legal system, a stable economic environment (infrastructure, monetary stability, a skilled labour force), or more directly through industrial policy, tax-breaks, subsidies and tariffs. It may further entail attempts to externalise the fallout from economic competition (for instance, through currency wars or dumping cheap commodities in foreign markets).

Regardless, a natural outcome of this interdependency between states and capital is the emergence of what Harvey (2001) calls 'structured coherences' of accumulated capital—in which firms of various kinds, employing capital investments with radically different turnover times and extra-economic requirements, are brought into a functional unity under the authority of a capitalist state. Consequently, as Bukharin (1917) could observe even a century ago when looking at the congruence between growing state investments and the global spread of capitalist relations: 'the internationalisation of capital is simultaneously its nationalisation'. The states system can, in this way, be understood as a crucial means of mediating the sharp contradiction between fixity and motion inherent in the process of capitalist development (Holloway 1995), and thus *enabling* globalisation rather than inhibiting it. Uneven geographical development determines the shape of the states system and the varying forms and functions of its constituent states. As Pradella (2013, 130) comments on Marx's method, 'the logic of the state is internal to the logic of capital. For this reason, although historically state intervention was primary for the genesis of industrial capital, its analysis logically follows the analysis of accumulation'.

2.6 The Limits to Uneven Development Theory

Capital's natural tendency towards uneven development contains the *potentiality* of a hierarchically organised and territorially differentiated system of states, on the basis of the laws of capital accumulation outlined by Marx in *Capital*. This vindicates our rejection of the world systems theory explanation, since it explains uneven development as the outcome of competitive battles between capitals and states in production, rather than in exchange, relations (Shaikh 1979, 1980; cf. Frank, 1967; Amin 2010).

However, uneven development theory's functionalist view of the state leads it to highly abstract and unsatisfactory explanations for the role states play in governing the unevenly developed world economy. Bearing parallels with orthodox International Relations (IR) thought, uneven development theory has tended to either to present states as unified representatives of pre-given national interests, or to refuse to theorise them at all. This is a serious weakness, however, because distinctively political forces—which cannot be understood as mere 'expressions' of underlying economic dynamics—significantly shape state action. I illustrate this issue here with reference to major studies of uneven development.

Neil Smith's classic study of uneven development recognises this problem but offers no solution. Aiming to 'offer a skeletal account of the economic rationale for uneven development' (Smith 2010, 284), he considers how the fixity-motion dialectic in the capitalist production of space results in the emergence of distinctive urban, global and national scales of socio-economic life. As Smith (2010, 182–187) argues, the contradiction between the equalisation and differentiation of space tends to produce differentiation at the urban scale ('through the centralisation of capital, urban space is capitalized as an absolute space of production'), and equalisation at the global scale (through 'the attempt to level the world's labour power to the status of a commodity').

Once the analysis reaches the scale of the nation state, however, the theory of capital's 'economic' determinants shaping its uneven geography no longer holds:

> The actual determination of this [national] scale does not come directly from the dialectic of equalisation and differentiation, however much it is provoked by this relationship, but is politically determined by a series of historical deals, compromises, and wars. (Smith 2010, 190)

So: the dynamics of each spatial scale of organisation can be theorised as an expression of capital's value relations *apart from the states-system*—which, within the bounds of uneven development theory, appears as a product of pure historical contingency. Smith's conclusion, then, is that the existence of states bears no substantive relationship to the process of uneven development and, by implication, that the states system is only contingently necessary for capitalism to function (a position explicated in Smith [2006] and in Cowen and Smith [2009]).

This functionalism is prevalent across the economic geography literature on uneven development, much of which operates on the understanding that states relay the pre-existing interests of capitalists unmediated. Harvey (2001, 2007, ch 13) conceives state institutions as direct expressions of capitalist interests within a given territory (a view he has since recognised as inadequate, noting that he has yet to discover any theory of the state which avoids this pitfall). Cox's concept of local 'growth coalitions' likewise represents policies as the result of the particular fraction of capital which has captured a given state (cf. Cox and Wood 1997). And Amin and Thrift's (2010) complementary concept of 'institutional thickness' in the relations between firms and states fails to identify any distinctively political dimensions to regional development patterns. The result is an austere understanding of politics as form of spatial battles over the fruits of uneven development. Actors (fractions of classes directly tied to capitals they represent) are understood to possess coherent interests and to bear these concerns directly against those representing contending spaces. Critically, the *form* taken by states is generally assumed to correspond directly to the general interests of capitals operating inside the territory.

Consequently, scholarship in this tradition regularly attempts to explain specific patterns of uneven development in the world economy through a direct elaboration of the categories developed by Marx in *Capital*. Weeks (2001) explains contemporary uneven development as an outcome of struggles between geographical agglomerations of fixed capital with productivity differentials; while Starosta's (2010a, b) critique of the global value chains literature similarly elaborates on Marx's categories to explain unequal development without reference to states' mercantilist or imperialist practices. Selwyn (2014) further suggests that the exploitation of global production networks by transnational firms debars late entrants from competing with firms in the core countries, but without considering how states might be intertwined with these firms and their competitive capacities.

By theorising (or, failing to theorise) states in this way, uneven development theorists abandon any substantive attempt to incorporate political and geopolitical factors into their theory construction, which instead appear as addendums or caveats to the theory-building effort. Many well understand the difficulty. Doreen Massey notes this problem in her own work (1995, 45), arguing that policymaking and regulation should principally be understood as an expression of 'politics, set – obviously – within the wider constraints of economic conditions but not simply relaying them unmodified, and as a function of the construction of that particular political hegemony'—though she does not further develop the implications of this insight for her theory of the spatial division of labour.

But, if we accept that the existence of states is predicated on the uneven development of the capitalist world economy, then the reciprocal effects of this states system on the capitalist space economy (that is, how states themselves shape the geography of the world system) are surely contingent on the *form* that states take.[4] Since the form of any state is shaped by multiple factors (the specific political vehicles through which classes and class fractions organise themselves as social forces; the success or failure of hegemonic projects on the part of state managers and dominant classes; and the specific instruments and methods of state intervention available and mobilised in any given period). These all entail their own unique sets of determinations, none of which the capital theoretical perspective of uneven development theorists seriously attempts to analyse. As Poulantzas (2014, 128–129) puts it, the state, 'like 'capital'... is rather a relationship of forces, or more precisely the material condensation of such a relationship among classes and class fractions, such as this is expressed within the State in a necessarily specific form'.

Insofar as they remain firm-centric, these various strands of uneven development theory do not permit any agential role for states in upholding or transforming patterns of uneven development. Industrial policies, global trade regimes, and the politics of multilateral organisations are absent from such accounts (Gordon and Webber 2020). But, as Peter Gowan (2010, 135) notes, recent decades have witnessed a substantial increase for states' (already significant) roles in 'constructing secure market bases for their companies, training workforces, supplying transport and communication infrastructures — and, of course, the exercise of geopolitical influence to open and protect overseas markets'. A fuller explanation of capitalism's actually existing uneven geography must surely attempt a theorisation of the role of competition between states and the extensive support provided by advanced capitalist states for firms located within their borders (Harman 1991; Gowan 1999).

How to explain uneven development theory's reluctance to engage with such problems? Desai (2013, 14) puts this down to a failure to examine empirically 'the multiple instances of combined capitalist development' in the postwar period. Smith (2006, 185) articulates this, arguing that the qualifier 'combined' is outdated—because Lenin's 1916 statement ('the colonial policy of the capitalist countries has *completed* the seizure of the unoccupied territories on our planet') suggests that 'combinations' of modes of production (feudalism and capitalism, principally) no

[4]In a different context, Marx discusses how the rise of joint stock companies (a new form of firm organisation) alters the accumulation process by permitting a greater concentration of capital (Marx 1990, 310–311).

longer exist in any significant sense. But this draws attention away from Trotsky's two most prescient points of analysis, as well as illustrating the importance of the kind of elaborated definition of UCD presented here. First, that 'combined development' represents a feature of a mature capitalist system characterised by generalised commodity production: both in terms of the universal pressure exerted by the most productive capitals over all others in the world economy (unlike earlier modes of production, where competitive pressures between states were sporadic rather than systematic), and in terms of repeated cases of states' skipping stages of development by importing aspects of these most advanced productive methods and technologies. Second, that unevenness is itself definitively *not* simply an 'economic' question (the geographically uneven development of the productive forces), but also profoundly *political*, insofar as imperialism plays a determinate role in 'throwing back' some parts of the world and preserving a hierarchy of states tied to an imperialist chain (cf. Sakellaropoulos and Sotiris 2015).

In summary, uneven development, if understood as a purely economic feature of capital, cannot theorise how capital's economic dynamics are mediated by political factors. While uneven development theory elaborates the fixity/ motion dialectic, insofar as it examines the impact of the political mediation of this dynamic, it does so in profoundly functionalist terms. Extending uneven development theory and integrating its insights with a political theory of the state as a material component of capitalist development is, I argue, one of the most promising aspects of UCD as an avenue of theory-building.

2.7 A State Theoretical Extension

Functionalist approaches to the state assume that the state acts in the *general interests* of capital accumulation, rather than the (potentially destructive) short-term interests of capitalists themselves. But state theorists have long since demonstrated that the 'aggregate requirements' of capital accumulation do not exist. This is because a polyvalent society and capitalist class could not possibly settle on a single strategy suited to all forms of accumulation. Instead, state policies represent the outcome of the exercise of *hegemony* by a fraction of the capitalist class, which privileges the material interests of a specific set of capitalists while attempting to align these with the material interests of other class fractions. To the extent that this project proves successful, the state 'realizes the function of political hegemony which the [atomised] bourgeoisie is unable to achieve' (Poulantzas 2014, 284). This section aims to open a space to consider how these political determinations can be integrated, in theory and in practice, into an analysis of uneven development.

Bob Jessop (1982, 221; see also 1990, 2008) has developed the most expansive materialist theory of the state to date. His work coheres around three core concepts (developed in dialogue with the Regulation School, discussed below): the accumulation strategy, the hegemonic project, and the form of the state. In his view, 'the state' does not really exist as unitary actor, but instead represents a relationship between a heterogenous set of institutions which 'cannot, *qua* [an] institutional ensemble, exercise power' without the successful exercise of hegemony by a particular class or class fraction, 'which must be constituted politically'. This emphasises the most complex aspect of Poulantzas' understanding of the heterogeneity of societal interests, since it does not just encompass capitalist *economic* interests, but also competing (and relatively autonomous) *bureaucratic* interests. When successfully constituted, a hegemonic project—by definition, given that it is exercised by only one or more fractions of the capitalist class—favours a particular kind of capital accumulation over others. This, when generalised across the policies of varied state institutions, is identifiable as an accumulation strategy. If successfully incorporated into hegemonic project, of course, the accumulation strategy must maintain an environment in which various kinds of capital can successfully accumulate across the economy. Finally, the interaction of hegemonic projects and accumulation strategies over time is path-dependent, leading to the emergence of a particular kind of state form quite distinct from others—a 'structured terrain' of institutions favouring some kinds of capitals over others (the historic predominance of the Treasury in British politics, for instance, has tended to favour accumulation strategies privileging various economic activities associated with the City of London).

The state does not merely *function* for capital, then. Any function, if appropriately exercised, is contingent on the capacity of a particular faction of the capitalist class to present its sectoral interests as universal, binding a heterogeneous economic territory into 'structured coherence' in which plausible prospects of economic growth exist for a sufficiently large coalition of capital. It is consequently necessary to identify the means by which the 'general interests' of capital are formed, articulated and pursued in response to existing patterns of uneven development—alongside how these interests are moderated by their conflict with alternative possible strategies (Jessop 1990, 215). And this reveals the significance of integrating domestic and international theory, since political actors bidding to exercise state power must confront develop an accumulation strategy which not only mediates between conflicting domestic interests, but also serves as a viable strategy in the global economy. As Adrian Smith (2015, 300) puts it, 'the particular configuration of the state and the accumulation regime, involving the organization of forms of insertion into the world economy… is contingent and associated with the wider social struggles involved in establishing the form of the state'. With this in mind, approximating an analysis of any concrete pattern of accumulation without a political analysis of class conflict, social struggles, and hegemonic strategies holds inadequate explanatory power.

Evidence of Althusserian structuralism is present in Jessop's argument that there is no necessary correspondence between the separate 'chains of causality' implied by economic, political and ideological analyses. For Jessop, though these spheres may intersect, the autonomous logics of economics, politics and ideology operate according to distinct causal pathways (1982, 213). A rigid analytical separation is thus maintained between the political level of the state, and the economic level of capitalist development, because of the impossibility of reconciling these logics due to the unpredictability of state forms:

> While the combination or interaction of different causal chains produces a determinate outcome (necessity), there is no single theory that can predict or determine the manner in which such causal chains converge and/or interact (contingency). (Jessop 1982, 213)

Holloway and Picciotto (1977, 96) similarly allow a distinction between economics and politics with their claim that 'the state is not capital' and should be understood outside of the strictures of the value form, narrowly conceived. But they maintain there nonetheless exists a 'generality implicit in [the state's] form', though they don't clarify its source. Jessop (2008, 8), by contrast, maintains that there can be no general theory of capitalist states. Political institutions may ultimately be founded on the capitalist value form, but function at a profoundly different level of social life:

> A state could operate principally as a capitalist state, a military power, a theocratic regime, a representative democratic regime answerable to civil society, an apartheid state, or an ethico-political state… [while there] is

no unconditional guarantee that the modern state will always (or ever) be essentially capitalist.

Jessop's approach is consequently critical of attempts to extend Marx's value theory to encompass the state (in the tradition of German state derivationists: cf. Clarke 1991; ten Brink and Nachtwey 2008) is to mistakenly appeal to 'one plane or axis of theoretical determination to explain everything about the state and politics' (Jessop 1982, 212). This state-derivationist effort to derive the existence of the capitalist state from the logical preconditions established in Marx's economic writings *did* prove to be untenably reductive (cf. Bieler et al. 2010). And the state theoretical emphasis on understanding the profusion of state forms capitalism throws up represents an advance on the austere political optic of uneven geographical development, and complements Trotsky's (2007, 132) insistence that 'economic [and political] peculiarities of different countries are in no way of a subordinate character' to the determinants of the world market in analysing their social content.

But two substantive barriers constrain the utility of the state theoretical approach. First, with the stark distinction drawn between politics and economics and the forefronting of state forms and actions as objects of analysis, state theory essentially abstracts from uneven geographic development and the global division of labour as both the material basis for the states system and a (partial) determinant of state form (Budd 2008). Jessop's state theory is thus vulnerable to charges of both methodological nationalism and politicism, insofar as it grants states undue autonomy in shaping their 'own' economies.[5] Instead, national economies are better conceived as components of a global division of labour (Bryan 2001). As McNally argues (2014, 25) a national economy is already a 'space of world money, a hyper-complex space, to borrow a term from Lefebvre, which resides inside the state itself – and thus operates as an internal power, rather than merely as an external constraint'. Second, by treating the state in the singular as Jessop does—rather than as one component of a multiplicity of interacting states—interactions between units are not considered to possess determinate effect on the composition of the individual units themselves (cf. Rosenberg 2013). As Barker (1991, 210)

[5] Jessop's more recent work (2014) has moved away from a focus on national states and begun to explore questions of world economy and its relation with the states system.

points out, state theory separates the individual state from the states system—and consequently from the discipline of interstate competition:

> The strict demarcation line drawn between "state" and "capital" rests on an account of the state form in which the state is treated in the singular… the bounds of capitalism are treated as coterminous with the national frontiers. That is, rather than seeing capitalist society as a *global* 'social formation', as a real totality, the world is seen as a set of capitalist *societies*, a mere agglomeration and not a unity.

It thus abstracts from a crucial source of political-economic pressure experienced by every state in the world system (though unevenly). The UCD perspective accounts for the production of a multiplicity of states as an outgrowth of the value form, but also conceives the value form as itself reproduced through the pressures states place upon one another through geopolitical and geoeconomic competition. State power, then, can be understood as the responsibility of managing a particular fragment of the world economy. Catch-up, combined development must internalise the logic of the value form in its state strategy, and contend with the geopolitical strategies of other states. These two demands instil a generality within the capitalist state form which state theory fails to recognise.

2.8 Uneven and Combined Development: Towards a Research Programme

This chapter has so far identified *logical-theoretical mechanisms*, rooted in the uneven geographical dynamics of capitalism, which produce UCD. I have further stressed the significance of examining the political mediation of such economic/geographical tendencies, while also criticising the separation state theorists posit between the state and its sitedness in the global division of labour.

From this UCD perspective, national 'accumulation regimes', 'modes of regulation' and forms of state can be comprehended as outcomes of the interaction between uneven geographical developments and the determinate effect of the political 'moment' of regulating capitalist development. State regulation and intervention cannot then be divorced from the coercive operation of the law of value in the world economy, or the discipline of competition with rival states. Hegemonic projects are, at root, *competitive* strategies—shaped in relation to other states' strategies. In Trotsky's elaboration of the operation of UCD in Russia, a major theoretical contribution was to successfully integrate this political moment of accumulation with its broader context in the uneven geographical development of capitalism—avoiding the twin pitfalls of 'voluntaristic' (Bonefeld 1994) and functionalist understanding of politics. As Davidson (2006, 23) puts it, 'Trotsky, who emphasised more than any of his contemporaries the reality of the world economy, was also the thinker who refocused attention from 'the international' in general to its impact on individual nation states'.

I want here to elaborate Trotsky's implicitly stated theory by proposing a means of operationalising his approach as a method for analysing concrete manifestations of UCD in the global political economy. The study of a process of UCD can be approached as follows:

1. Outline geopolitical-economic *unevenness* in the world system.
2. Explore how a late developing social formation inserts itself into the world capitalist economy, *combining* its economic development with advanced capitalist states by appropriating their progressive elements.
3. Explore the *uneven* impact of advances inside the late developing society—including its impact on class formation, urban/rural divisions, political contests, ideological forms unique to the social formation in question.
4. Consider how the *combination* of these uneven types of development within the spatio-temporal matrix of the national state results in unique social tensions, with a specific focus on how these unevennesses are combined within the form of state and its regulatory/interventionist activities.
5. Examine the reciprocal effects which this process of economic development reacts back upon the world system through geoeconomic and geopolitical pressure.

Section 2.2 noted the three major dynamics enforced by UCD upon late developers:

- The 'whip of external necessity';
- The 'privilege of historical backwardness';
- The 'contradictions of sociological amalgamation'. (cf. Davidson 2006; Trotsky 2009)

The model suggested above integrates these three dynamics into a research framework as follows. First, uneven development and a global division of labour are identified, as corresponding to the economic and spatial dynamics of capital. UCD's recognition of a centrifugal drive emanating from the capital relation helps account for capitalism's 'integrated but differentiated… clumpy and territorialised' character (Ashman 2006, 101). This uneven development thus constitutes a material basis for the hierarchical international states system, which is superimposed upon uneven development while containing the possibility of transforming it. This is especially so since each state in this system experiences permanent relations of competitive tension with the economic and military capacities of every other state. For weaker and poorer states, this is experienced as the stark imperative to modernise (the 'whip of external necessity') or lapse into dependency (Trotsky 2009, 5; Mann 1993).

Research should then examine the specific processes by which this competition is mediated by forms of state and state actors (politicians, bureaucrats, the judiciary and security officials) who hold distinct interests. While capital (at least in its money form) is highly mobile, state managers remain bound to their territory. State actors aim to overcome structural constraints imposed by global uneven development by seeking out advantages for their capitals—through tariffs and regulatory standards embodied in trade agreements, treaties and, more rarely, military interventions. Because the limits imposed by global uneven development are not absolute, and can be transformed by state intervention, peripheral states hold at least the possibility of pursuing combined capitalist development and achieving rapid growth through technology transfer, the importation of organisational techniques, social practices and ideologies—potentially breaking with existing patterns of inequality between states. This is Trotsky's 'privilege of historical backwardness' (Trotsky 2009, 20–21; Gerschenkron 1966). But, in pursuing combined development, social formations tend to experience the 'contradictions of sociological amalgamation' (Allinson and Anievas 2010) associated with the import of more developed technologies and social forms. Precisely because these technologies and organisational techniques cannot be imported wholesale but are implanted into a social formation with a unique class and state structure, they serve to alter processes of class formation, class struggles, state forms, peripheral social in unpredictable ways.

This final point highlights the attention future research should pay to what geographers variously term 'bounded complexes of production and circulation', 'territorial production complexes', 'structured coherences' or 'territorial assemblages' of fixed capital: in other words, the social and technological mixes making up national economies (von Braunmühl 1978; Storper and Walker 1989; Harvey 2001; Swyngedouw 1992). Classic theories of 'catch-up' development such as Gerschenkron (1966) and Veblen (2003) have conceived these in purely economic terms. But the emergence of such territorial assemblages of capital is, as we have seen, in no way a merely economic process—but critically reliant on the agency of the state. As Swyngedouw (1992, 425) argues:

> The uniqueness of territorial assemblages as a force of production, compared with technology, is the combination of the *indivisibility of its use value* on the one hand, and its rootedness in space on the other. This double characteristic defines the unique nature of the socialized character of territorial organization as a force of production [my italics].

Because the state provides an organising role for labour markets, and a multiplicity of fixed capitals and infrastructures with differential turnover times, catch-up development is intrinsically political insofar as it draws antiquated forms of production together with the most advanced and mediates their entanglement. Since then private sector alone is highly unlikely to pursue the substantial infrastructural and basic research investments required to orchestrate catch-up, the process of combined development to some extent *requires* the intervention of a state in order construct a territorial assemblage, able to compete with more advanced productive forces in leading capitalist economies. Under present circumstances, this has plainly empowered fractions of the capitalist class that are hostile to (elements of) neoliberalism and Washington consensus policy prescriptions.

This adds a new dimension of complexity to the simple notion of importing technologies in order to catch up with more developed social formations. What happens when a technological innovation is torn from its context in an 'indivisible' complex of use values in an advanced capitalist society, and implanted into a late developer? Trotsky's answer was a rapid pace of change, 'national peculiarities' of class formation and development embodied in entirely new forms of state, and explosive political struggles. In this way, a new level of 'unevenness' is arrived at, shaped by the 'political' and the destabilising, path-dependent effects of combined social development on a state driving towards the most advanced capitalist economic and social forms. Internal geographical, social, institutional and cultural unevenness is a feature characteristic of such societies undergoing catch-up under conditions of UCD, combined and coexistent as features of an idiosyncratic society.

The states system has long been subsumed under the imperatives of capitalist accumulation; as Marx (1990, 919) writes, 'national debts, i.e., the alienation of the state—whether despotic, constitutional or republican—marked with its stamp the capitalistic era'. But this 'subsumption' under the law of value is an *active process*: states' strategic agency, and their territorial competition, ultimately serves to reproduce the capital relation by enforcing compliance on weaker states on pain of subjugation. The novel, non-teleological patterns of development that unevenness and combination produce, as developing states strive to escape this competitive trap by—on rare occasions it becomes possible—transforming their economies and driving towards the levels of development enjoyed by advanced economies, forms the basic theoretical framework for a consideration of China's rise developed in this book.

References

Allinson, Jamie C., and Alexander Anievas. 2010. The Uneven and Combined Development of the Meiji Restoration: A Passive Revolutionary Road to Capitalist Modernity. *Capital & Class* 34 (3): 469–490.

Amin, Ash, and Nigel Thrift. 2010. Living in the Global. In *Globalisation, Institutions and Regional Development in Europe*, ed. Ash Amin and Nigel Thrift, 1–22. Oxford: Oxford University Press.

Amin, Samir. 2010. *The Law of Worldwide Value*. New York: Monthly Review Press.

Anievas, Alex. 2014. A World After Its Own Image? The States-System, Capitalism and Unevenness. In *International Relations: Continuity and Change in Global Politics*, ed. William Brown, Olaf Corry, and Agnes Czajka. Milton Keynes: Open University Press.

Anievas, Alexander, and Kerem Nişancıoğlu. 2015. *How the West Came to Rule: The Geopolitical Origins of Capitalism*. London: Pluto.

Anievas, Alexander, and Kerem Nişancıoğlu. 2018. Lineages of Capital. *Historical Materialism* 26 (3): 167–196.

Arrighi, Giovanni, Beverley Silver, and Benjamin Brewer. 2003. Industrial Convergence, Globalization, and the Persistence of the North-South Divide. *Studies in Comparative International Development* 38: 3–31.

Ashman, Sam. 2006. From World Market to World Economy. In *100 Years of Permanent Revolution: Results and Prospects*, ed. Bill Dunn and Hugo Radice. London: Pluto.

Ashman, Sam. 2009. Capitalism, Uneven and Combined Development and the Transhistoric. *Cambridge Review of International Affairs* 22 (1): 29–46.

Ashman, Sam. 2010. Capitalism, Uneven and Combined Development and the Transhistoric. In *Marxism and World Politics: Contesting Global Capitalism*, ed. Alexander Anievas. London: Routledge.

Barker, Colin. 1991. A Note on the Theory of Capitalist States. In *The State Debate*, ed. Simon Clarke, 204–213. Hampshire: Macmillan.

Barker, Colin. 2006. Beyond Trotsky: Extending Combined and Uneven Development. In *100 Years of Permanent Revolution: Results and Prospects*, ed. Bill Dunn and Hugo Radice, 78. London: Pluto.

Barker, Colin. 2009. Value, Force, Many States, and Other Problems. Paper presented at Historical Materialism conference, London, November 2009. Available online at https://sites.google.com/site/colinbarkersite/7—publications-and-papers-2006-. Accessed 1 February 2016.

Barrow, Clyde W. 2005. The Return of the State: Globalization, State Theory, and the New Imperialism. *New Political Science* 27 (2): 123–145.

Bhagwati, Jagdish. 2004. *In Defence of Globalization*. Oxford: Oxford University Press.

Bieler, Andreas, and Adam Morton. 2014. Uneven and Combined Development and Unequal Exchange: The Second Wind of Neoliberal 'Free Trade'? *Globalizations* 11 (1): 35–45.

Bieler, Andreas, Ian Bruff, and Adam David Morton. 2010. Acorns and Fruit: From Totalization to Periodization in the Critique of Capitalism. *Capital & Class* 34 (1): 25–37.

Bonefeld, Werner. (1994). Aglietta in England: Bob Jessop's Contribution to the Regulation Approach. In *Ecole de la régulation et critique de la rai- son économique*, ed. F. Sebaï & C. Vercellone, 299–330. Paris: L'Harmattan.

Bonefeld, Werner. 2014. *Critical Theory and the Critique of Political Economy: On Subversion and Negative Reason*. Bloomsbury: Oxford.

Bruff, Ian. 2012. The Relevance of Nicos Poulantzas for Contemporary Debates on 'the International'. *International Politics* 49 (2): 177–194.

Bryan, Dick. 2001. Global Accumulation and Accounting for National Economic Identity. *Review of Radical Political Economics* 33 (1): 57–77.

Budd, Adrian. 2008. Politics Without Enough Economics. *International Socialism* 2: 119.

Bukharin, Nikolai. 1917. *Imperialism and World Economy*. Available at http://www.marxists.org/archive/bukharin/works/1917/imperial. Accessed 10 October 2018.

Callinicos, Alex. 2003. *The New Mandarins of American Power: The Bush Administration's Plans for the World*. Cambridge: Polity.

Callinicos, Alex. 2009. *Imperialism and Global Political Economy*. Cambridge: Polity.

Callinicos, Alex. 2010. *Bonfire of Illusions: The Twin Crises of the Liberal World*. Cambridge: Polity.

Callinicos, Alex. 2014. *Deciphering Capital: Marx's Capital and Its Destiny*. Bookmarks Publications.

Cambridge Review of International Affairs. 2009. Various authors. 22 (1): 1–193.

Cambridge Review of International Affairs [CRIA]. 2007. Various authors. 20 (4): 523–709.

Clarke, Simon. 1991. The State Debate. In *The State Debate*, 1–69. Palgrave Macmillan, London.

Cowen, Deborah, and Neil Smith. 2009. After Geopolitics? *From the Geopolitical Social to Geoeconomics. Antipode* 40: 2–48.

Cox, Kevin R., and Andrew Wood. 1997. Competition and Cooperation in Mediating the Global: The Case of Local Economic Development. *Competition & Change* 2 (1): 65–94.

Davidson, Neil. 2006. From Uneven to Combined Development. In *100 Years of Permanent Revolution: Results and Prospects*, ed. Bill Dunn and Hugo Radice. London: Pluto Press.

Davidson, Neil. 2012. The Necessity of Multiple Nation-States for Capital. *Rethinking Marxism: A Journal of Economics, Culture & Society* 24 (1): 26–46.

Desai, Meghnad. 2002. *Marx's Revenge: The Resurgence of Capitalism and the Death of Statist Socialism*. London: Verso.

Desai, Radhika. 2012. Marx, List and the Materiality of Nations. *Rethinking Marxism: A Journal of Economics, Culture & Society* 24 (1): 47–67.

Desai, Radhika. 2013. *Geopolitical Economy: After US Hegemony, Globalization and Empire (The Future of World Capitalism)*. London: Pluto Press.

Dicken, Peter. 2014. *Global Shift: Mapping the Changing Contours of the World Economy*. London: Sage.

Dunford, Michael, and Weidong Liu. 2017. Uneven and Combined Development. *Regional Studies* 51 (1): 69–85.

Evans, Peter. 2014. The Capability Enhancing Developmental State: Concepts and National Trajectories. In *The South Korean Development Experience: Beyond Aid*, ed. Eun Mee Kim and Pil Ho Kim, 83–110. Basingstoke: Palgrave.

Frank, Andre Gunder. 1967. *Capitalism and Underdevelopment in Latin America*. New York: Monthly Review Press.

Gerschenkron, Alexander. 1966. *Economic Backwardness in Historical Perspective: A Book of Essays*. Cambridge: Harvard University Press.

Gordon, Todd, and Jeffery R. Webber. 2020. Complex Stratification in the World System: Capitalist Totality and Geopolitical Fragmentation. *Science & Society* 84 (1): 95–125.

Gowan, Peter. 1999. *The Global Gamble: Washington's Faustian Bid for World Dominance*. Verso.

Gowan, Peter. 2010. Industrial Development and International Political Conflict in Contemporary Capitalism. In *Marxism and International Politics*, ed. Alexander Anievas, 125–145. Oxford: Routledge.

Gramsci, Antonio. 1971. *Selections from the Prison Notebooks*. London: Lawrence and Wishart.

Green, Jeremy. 2014. Beyond Coxian Historicism: 19th Century World Order and the Promise of Uneven and Combined Development. *Millennium: Journal of International Studies* 42: 286–308.

Hardt, Michael, and Antonio Negri. 2000. *Empire*. Cambridge: Harvard University Press.

Hardy, Jane. 2014. Transformation and Crisis in Central and Eastern Europe: A Combined and Uneven Development Perspective. *Capital & Class* 38 (1): 143–155.

Harman, Chris. 1991. The State and Capitalism Today. *International Socialism* 2 (51): 3–54.

Harman, Chris. 2010. *Zombie Capitalism: Global Crisis and the Relevance of Marx*. London: Verso.

Harris, Nigel. 1986. *The End of the Third World: Newly Industrialising Countries and the Decline of an Ideology*. London: I.B. Tauris.

Harvey, David. 2001. *Spaces of Capital: Towards a Critical Geography*. London: Routledge.

Harvey, David. 2003. *The New Imperialism*. Oxford: Oxford University Press.

Harvey, David. 2007. *The Limits to Capital*. London: Verso.

Harvey, David. 2010. *The Enigma of Capital and the Crises of Capitalism*. Oxford: Oxford University Press.

Henderson, Jeffrey, Peter Dicken, Martin Hess, Neil Coe, and Henry Wai-Chung Yeung. 2002. Global Production Networks and the Analysis of Economic Development. *Review of International Political Economy* 9 (3): 436–464.

Herod, Andrew. 2006. Trotsky's Omission: Labour's Role in Combined and Uneven Development. In *100 Years of Permanent Revolution: Results and Prospects*, ed. Bill Dunn and Hugo Radice, 152–165. London: Pluto.

Hirsch, Joachim, and John Kannankulam. 2011. The Spaces of Capital: The Political Form of Capitalism and the Internationalization of the State. *Antipode* 43 (1): 12–37.

Holloway, John. 1995. Global Capital and the National State. In *Global Capital, National State and the Politics of Money*, ed. Werner Bonefeld and John Holloway. Basingstoke: Macmillan.

Holloway, John, and Sol Picciotto. 1977. Capital, Crisis and the State. *Capital & Class 1* (2): 76–101.

Jessop, Bob. 1982. *The Capitalist State: Marxist Theories and Methods*. Oxford: Martin Robertson.

Jessop, Bob. 1990. *State Theory: Putting the Capitalist State in Its Place*. Cambridge: Polity.

Jessop, Bob. 2008. *State Power: A Strategic-Relational Approach*. Cambridge: Polity.

Jessop, Bob. 2014. Capitalist Diversity and Variety: Variegation, the World Market, Compossibility and Ecological Dominance. *Capital & Class* 38 (1): 45–58.

Kiely, Ray. 2012. Spatial Hierarchy and/or Contemporary Geopolitics: What Can and Can't Uneven and Combined Development Explain? *Cambridge Review of International Affairs* 25 (2): 231–248.

Klassen, Jerome. 2014. Hegemony in Question: US Primacy, Multi-polarity, and Global Resistance. In *Polarising Development: Alternatives to Neoliberalism and the Crisis*, ed. Lucia Pradella and Thomas Marois, 74–85. London: Pluto Press.

Lasslett, Kristian. 2015. The State at the Heart of Capitalism: Marxist Theory and Foucault's Lectures on Governmentality. *Critical Sociology* 41 (4/5): 641–658.

Lefebvre, Henri. 1976. *The Survival of Capitalism: Reproduction of the Relations of Production*. Macmillan: London.

Lefebvre, Henri. 1991. *The Production of Space*. Chichester: Wiley.

Lenin, Vladimir Ilyich. 1916. *Imperialism: The Highest Stage of Capitalism*. Available at http://www.marxists.org/archive/lenin/works/1916/imp-hsc/. Accessed 1 August 2013.

Löwy, Michael. 2010. *The Politics of Combined and Uneven Development: The Theory of Permanent Revolution*. Chicago: Haymarket.

Mann, Michael. 1993. *The Sources of Social Power: Volume 2, The Rise of Classes and Nation States 1760–1914*. Cambridge: Cambridge University Press.

Marx, Karl. 1973. *The Grundrisse*. Harmondsworth: Penguin.

Marx, Karl. 1990. *Capital*, vol. I. London: Penguin.

Marx, Karl. 1991. *Capital*, vol. III. London: Penguin.

Marx, Karl. 1992. *Capital*, vol. II. London: Penguin.

Marx, Karl. 2007. *Dispatches for the New York Tribune: Selected Journalism of Karl Marx*. London: Penguin.

Massey, Doreen. 1995. *Spatial Divisions of Labour: Social Structures and the Geography of Production*. London: Macmillan.

Massey, Doreen. 2005. *For Space*. London: Sage.
Matin, Kamran. 2013. *Recasting Iranian Modernity: International Relations and Social Change*. London: Routledge.
McMichael, Philip. 2001. World-Systems Analysis, Globalization, and Incorporated Comparison. *Journal of World-Systems Research* 1 (3): 68–99.
McNally, David. 2014. The Blood of the Commonwealth: War, the State, and the Making of World Money. *Historical Materialism* 22 (2): 3–32.
Nowak, Jorg, and Ekrem Ekici. 2018. The Return of the National Imperialist State. *Rupture*. Issue 1. Available online at https://rupturemagazine.org/2018/01/25/113/. Accessed 28 December 2019.
Ollman, Bertell. 1970. *Alienation: Marx's Concept of Man in Capitalist Society*. Oxford: Oxford University Press.
Poulantzas, Nicos. 2014. *State, Power, Socialism*. London: Verso.
Pozo-Martin, Gonzalo. 2007. Autonomous or Materialist Geopolitics? *Cambridge Review of International Affairs* 20 (4): 551–563.
Pradella, Lucia. 2013. Imperialism and Capitalist Development in Marx's *Capital*. *Historical Materialism* 21 (2): 117–147.
Pradella, Lucia. 2014. New Developmentalism and the Origins of Methodological Nationalism. *Competition & Change* 18 (2): 180–193.
Pradella, Lucia. 2015. *Globalisation and the Critique of Political Economy: New Insights from Marx's Writings*. London: Routledge.
Rioux, Sébastien. 2015. Mind the (Theoretical) Gap: On the Poverty of International Relations Theorising of Uneven and Combined Development. *Global Society* 29 (4): 481–509.
Robinson, William I. 2005. Global Capitalism: The New Transnationalism and the Folly of Conventional Thinking. *Science & Society* 69 (3): 316–328.
Rosenberg, Justin. 1994. *The Empire of Civil Society: A Critique of the Realist Theory of International Relations*. Verso.
Rosenberg, Justin. 2005. Globalization Theory: A Post Mortem. *International Politics* 42 (1): 2–74.
Rosenberg, Justin. 2006. Why Is There No International Historical Sociology? *European Journal of International Relations* 12 (3): 307–340.
Rosenberg, Justin. 2008. Anarchy in the Mirror of Uneven and Combined Development: An Open Letter to Kenneth Waltz. Paper presented at the *British German IR conference BISA/DVPW*, Arnoldshain, Germany, 16–18 May.
Rosenberg, Justin. 2009. Problems in the Theory of Uneven and Combined Development. Part I: Introduction. *Cambridge Review of International Affairs* 22 (1): 107–110.
Rosenberg, Justin. 2010. Basic Problems in the Theory of Uneven and Combined Development. Part II: Unevenness and Political Multiplicity. *Cambridge Review of International Affairs* 23 (1): 165–189.

Rosenberg, Justin. 2013. The 'Philosophical Premises' of Uneven and Combined Development. *Review of International Studies* 39 (3): 569–597.
Rosenberg, Justin, and Chris Boyle. 2019. Understanding 2016: China, Brexit and Trump in the History of Uneven and Combined Development. *Journal of Historical Sociology* 32 (1): 32–58.
Sakellaropoulos, Spyros, and Panagiotis Sotiris. 2015. From Territorial to Nonterritorial Capitalist Imperialism: Lenin and the Possibility of a Marxist Theory of Imperialism. *Rethinking Marxism* 27 (1): 85–106.
Selwyn, Benjamin. 2014. *The Global Development Crisis*. John Wiley & Sons.
Shaikh, Anwar. 1979. Foreign Trade and the Law of Value: Part I. *Theory and Society: An Independent Journal of Marxism* 43 (3): 281–302.
Shaikh, Anwar. 1980. Foreign Trade and the Law of Value: Part II. *Theory and Society: An Independent Journal of Marxism* 43 (4): 27–57.
Sheppard, Eric, and Trevor Barnes. 1990. *The Capitalist Space Economy: Geographical Analysis After Ricardo, Marx and Sraffa*. London: Routledge.
Shilliam, Robbie. 2009. The Atlantic as a Vector of Uneven and Combined Development. *Cambridge Review of International Affairs* 22 (1): 69–88.
Smith, Adrian. 2015. The State, Institutional Frameworks and the Dynamics of Capital in Global Production Networks. *Progress in Human Geography* 39 (3): 290–315.
Smith, Neil. 2006. The Geography of Uneven Development. In *100 Years of Permanent Revolution: Results and Prospects*, ed. Bill Dunn and Hugo Radice, 180–195. London: Pluto Press.
Smith, Neil. (2010) [1984]. *Uneven Development: Nature, Capital, and the Production of Space*. Georgia: Georgia University Press.
Starosta, Guido. 2010a. Global Commodity Chains and the Marxian Law of Value. *Antipode* 42 (2): 433–465.
Starosta, Guido. 2010b. The Outsourcing of Manufacturing and the Rise of Giant Global Contractors: A Marxian Approach to Some Recent Transformations of Global Value Chains. *New Political Economy* 15 (4): 543–563.
Storper, Michael, and Richard Walker. 1989. *The Capitalist Imperative*. Oxford: Blackwell.
Swyngedouw, Erik. 1992. Territorial Organization and the Space Technology Nexus. *Transactions of the Institute of British Geographers* 17 (4): 417–433.
ten Brink, Tobias, and Oliver Nachtwey. 2008. Lost in Transition: The German World-Market Debate in the 1970s. *Historical Materialism* 16 (1): 37–70.
Teschke, Benno. 2003. *The Myth of 1648: Class, Geopolitics, and the Making of Modern International Relations*. London: Verso.
Trotsky, Leon. 1928. *The Third International After Lenin*. Available online at https://www.marxists.org/archive/trotsky/1928/3rd/ti01.htm. Accessed 11 January 2015.

Trotsky, Leon. 2007. *The Permanent Revolution & Results & Prospects*. London: IMG.

Trotsky, Leon. (2009) [1932]. *The History of the Russian Revolution: Volumes I, II & III*. Chicago: Haymarket.

Veblen, Thorstein. 2003. *Imperial Germany and the Industrial Revolution*. Kitchener: Batcohe.

Von Braunmühl, Claudia. 1978. On the Analysis of the Bourgeois Nation State within the World Market Context: An Attempt to Develop a Methodological and Theoretical Approach. In *State and Capital: A Marxist Debate*, ed. John Holloway and Sol Picciotto, 160–177. London: Edward Arnold.

Weeks, John. 2001. The Expansion of Capital and Uneven Development on a World Scale. *Capital & Class* 25 (2): 9–30.

Wolf, Martin. 2005. *Why Globalization Works*. New Haven: Yale University Press.

Wood, Ellen. 2002. *The Origin of Capitalism: A Longer View*. London: Verso.

CHAPTER 3

From Varieties of Capitalism to Uneven and Combined Development: A New Perspective

3.1 Introduction

This chapter moves on to consider how middle-range theory—in particular, orthodox and heterodox comparative capitalisms research—has approached the 'China question'. It outlines how latent conceptual limitations have often fed into impoverished empirical research strategies, before suggesting why UCD (outlined at an admittedly high level of abstraction in the last chapter) may fare better as a means of both conceptualising contemporary Chinese capitalism in comparative fashion. The chapter first spells out a critique of Varieties of Capitalism theory informed by the theoretical elaboration of Chapter 2, and highlights how this approach—while fertile in some regards—has failed to capture well the Chinese case. I highlight three distinct characteristics of China's growth which pose major problems for VoC theory: 'bad' institutions, the significance of global production networks (GPNs), and profoundly uneven internal geographical development. Next, I consider heterodox 'comparative capitalisms' approaches (represented here by the most influential and theoretically coherent of these, 'Variegated Capitalism'). While this work addresses most of the shortcomings of VoC theory, it also suffers from its own self-imposed ontological restrictions—most significantly, a simultaneous *supranational* and *subnational bias*, which successfully analyses local differences in the context of the global political economy, but

S. Rolf, *China's Uneven and Combined Development*,
Studies in the Political Economy of Public Policy,
https://doi.org/10.1007/978-3-030-55559-7_3

does not succeed in reintegrating the national state as a significant political economic actor (an especially significant flaw for those wishing to understand the Chinese experience). Factors of geopolitical economy, class formation, and political hegemony—staples of historical materialist analysis—are consequently excluded from the optic of such research.

With this critique sketched out, I return again to UCD. I outline why I consider it an improvement on the comparative capitalisms theories discussed at this lower level of concrete institutional political economy analysis, insofar as its careful deployment permits the study of subnational variegation without abandoning the analytical core of a historical materialist research programme. In this way, the chapter seeks to prepare the ground for Chapter 4's analysis of China's 'mode of integration' into the world economy.

3.2 Varieties of Capitalism and China

For political economists seeking an antidote to the ascendant hyperglobalising convergence theory of the mid 1990s, Hall and Soskice's (2001) foundational *Varieties of Capitalism* (VoC) proved a lodestone. It upheld a non-teleological and path-dependent conception of capitalist development; emphasised the continuing significance of geographical differentiation over a 'flat earth' perspective; and held to understanding the causal role in economic development played by institutions and politics (against the extreme *laissez-faire* of Washington Consensus' prescriptions). Symbolically, VoC represented a celebration of alternatives to the doctrinal Anglo-American model of neoliberal capitalism sweeping orthodox political science and began to dislodge the stultifying intellectual environment induced by Western post-Soviet triumphalism.

Weaknesses in Hall & Soskice's approach fast became evident, however—any concise rehearsal of which would include: methodological nationalism; the assumption of institutional stasis and coherence; apolitical firm-centrism; a bogus ideal typical characterisation of 'liberal market economy' (LME) and 'co-ordinated market economy' (CME) poles (with little room for middle-cases) which wrote out commonalities and emphasised minor distinctions; an orientation towards Western economies (paradigmatically, the United States and Germany) which excluded the developing world; and a lack of attention to the novel and idiosyncratic unifying and differentiating forces of global financial flows

(Dixon 2014). Despite its avowed catholicism, VoC reproduced many of the worst aspects of the 'microeconomics imperialism' to which it opposed itself by privileging firms as the central agents of economic life (Milonakis and Fine 2009; Ashman and Fine 2013). Such flaws were exposed in practice by the 2008 crisis and its aftermath, as the major facts of the previous two decades (persistent growth, incremental institutional change) gave way to the cataclysmic 'exogenous' shock of (almost) global recession (Coates 2015). Fixated by incremental and technocratic adaptations of statecraft under assumed conditions of capitalist stability, VoC struggled to either anticipate or adequately conceptualise the rupture—disconnected as it was from analysing the very fabric it professed to be differentiated in the first place: capitalism. Bruff (2011, 482) captures this neatly, arguing: 'institutions are of considerable importance for how capitalist societies evolve, but such institutions are clearly also grounded in capitalist conditions of existence'—conditions which are, by implication, global, crisis-ridden, and highly varied at spatial scales beyond the national.

Economic crisis and intellectual critique notwithstanding, *VoC* and associated comparative capitalisms literatures continue to flourish. *VoC* approached the categorization of political economies through exploring five major institutional variables:

- Interfirm relations
- Modality of labour relations
- Welfare
- Training and education
- Corporate governance and finance

Unsurprisingly, given the critical account sketched above, employments of this conceptual VoC map have consistently struggled to bear the weight of China's political economy. In a critical meta-analysis, Peck and Zhang (2013) note how Witt (2010), McNally (2007), and Fligstein and Zhang (2011), come—with great difficulty—to contradictory conclusions in locating China on the CME–LME spectrum. To this list, one could add the scholarship of Ahrens and Junemann (2010), Wilson (2007), Popov (2011), Rutten (2013), Pieterse (2015), and Nölke et al. (2015): all of who share a commitment to typifying Chinese capitalism according to the checklist above, and regard the VoC framework as broadly productive, but come to basically regard the CME–LME binary as an inadequate means to this end. Various post hoc modifications of the original research programme are duly suggested. But while the CME–LME binary is typically considered an expendable aspect of the framework at this point, curiously, few authors working with the VoC paradigm are willing to concede the potential for economic growth in the absence of institutional complementarity (Peck and Zhang 2013, 362). McNally (2007, 197–198) is representative when he contends that 'institutions must to a certain extent be compatible with each other to advance capitalist accumulation and establish international competitiveness'.[1]

Whatever its general merits, in the Chinese case, the search for institutional complementarity presents only dead-ends, since contradictory findings in each of the core research areas of VoC listed above are easily observed. For instance: (1) *Interfirm relations* comprise small locally oriented capitals governed by reciprocal (*guanxi*) relations, state capitalist enterprises with significant operational autonomy and cushioning from market imperatives, and ferociously market-competitive foreign-invested firms embedded in captive production networks. (2) *Labour relations* are profoundly variegated, from Guangdong's exploitative 'dormitory labour regime' (Pun and Smith 2007), to well-remunerated professional white-collar work at transnationally owned or connected software firms (Lüthje et al. 2013), and a declining but relatively privileged state sector workforce (Lan et al. 2015). (3) *Welfare* benefits remain unevenly distributed due to restrictions imposed by the *hukou* (household registration) system, remnants of workplace provision in the state sector, and uneven rollout of new programmes (especially in central and western provinces) (Lee 2007). (4) *Training and education* vary immensely along the lines of labour relations: in state-owned enterprises, some investment in training takes place as the 'iron rice bowl' secures lifelong employment, while workers in private sector factories struggle to gain skills (Fu and Gabriel 2012). (5) *Corporate governance* contrasts strongly between state-owned enterprises with easy access to (state bank) credit which are torn between the profit imperative and securing dominion of CCP control over the commanding heights of the economy; and small private firms sourcing capital from

[1] More recently, McNally (2012) has embraced 'variegated capitalism' and renounced the need for complementarity: see below.

retained profits and operating according to a more purely market logic (cf. Nee and Opper 2012).

The bifurcated nature of China's political economy is further considered in Chapters 4–6. For now, and as this too-brief account illustrates, a boilerplate application of the VoC framework to China invariably proves inconclusive, whatever its (highly contested) merits in other contexts. And the literature is further marked by a dearth of constructive dialogue given its conflicting findings, underwhelming given Peck and Zhang's (2013, 366) earlier hope that the 'frictions caused by importing the VoC framework [into China] can be potentially productive' in spite of these weaknesses. Perhaps most damningly, Tsai and Naughton (2015, 15–20) elaborate on how VoC's commitment to firm-centrism 'obscures the defining role of the state in China's reform process', rendering its potential for dialogue with the wealth of scholarship on China's political economy that sits outside of Western institutionalist literature by definition limited. To this extent, applying the VoC framework to China has in some ways revealed more about the theory's own observance of microeconomic conceptions of rationality than it has about China's recent political-economic history.

Beyond the paradoxes generated by constraints specific to the VoC framework, we might identify three further difficulties in representing Chinese capitalism for comparative political economy. These are the related problems of 'bad' institutions, global production networks, and uneven development, which are taken here in turn. Alongside the question of institutional complementarity, the history of China's reform period questions the (commonly assumed) correlation between institutional quality and economic growth. Ang (2016) emphasises the total absence of Weberian bureaucratic rationality during the takeoff period of China's boom. The semi-legal, undirected nature of China's early reform period accumulation process is captured well by Nee and Opper's (2012) fieldwork exploring rural entrepreneurship in Zhejiang. But even today, China's institutions remain of relatively low 'quality'—from the perspective of foreign investors and international organisations. This is reflected in China's poor performance across a range of World Bank (n.d.) 'doing business' measurements. Of a total 289 states, in 2017, China ranked in position 134 for 'protecting minority investors' and 136 for 'ease of starting a business'. China's overall ranking was a rather underwhelming 89: surprising for the world's largest recipient of foreign direct investment. And despite a sweeping anti-corruption drive, revenues continue to bleed to corrupt cadres on an industrial scale (Pei 2016). The deficiencies of Chinese statecraft, considered from the angle of global investors, belie the notion that good governance—or even its perception—are necessary components of catch-up growth. The most convincing explanation for this is the devolution of political patronage to local governments competing for recognition from the central state, which acts to moderate the scale of cronyism and channel it in productive, rather than extractive, directions (Bai et al. 2014). Regardless, China's 'bad' institutions have proved no deterrence to the accumulation of capital over the long-run.

Nor has this has inhibited China's deep integration into the global economy. Chinese growth has been significantly dependent on global economic engagement since, at the latest, the early-to-mid 1990s. By 2007, the export sector contributed 42% to annual GDP growth, while China held US$1tn in US treasury bonds as its surpluses were recycled into the US economy (what Ho-Fung Hung [2015, 125] calls a 'tribute payment through which Asia's savings were transferred into Americans' consumption power'). This problem is now widely grasped by the economics press as one of 'global imbalances' (Roach 2014), but such entanglements are perhaps better understood from a production networks perspective: which recognises the complexities of national measurements of value-added trade data in global production networks (Xing 2016; see Chapters 4 and 5 for more detail). But the transnational economic interdependencies which have come to characterise China's economy do not figure well into methodologically nationalist, 'billiard ball' understandings of self-contained varieties of capitalism. Given its profound external orientation, can China's period of growth—as intrinsically and intensely reliant on integration with external economies as it was—be convincingly isolated and analysed as a 'national' model of capitalism?

Finally, China's profoundly uneven geographical development raises fundamental problems with a national perspective that subsume subnational differences under a homogenous form of capitalism (Fan 1995; Wei et al. 2011). Zhang and Peck (2016) demonstrate the inadequacy of the traditional distinction between China's rustbelt and sunbelt industrial zones (cf. Lee 2007) and identify a rich tapestry of variegated economic geographies, marked by different labour forms and degrees of international connectivity. Whether China is considered an 'LME' or a 'CME' matters to a significant degree upon whether one looks, for example, at Heilongjiang's state-owned heavy industries or Zhejiang's mass of small-scale private factories. Given its geographical and sectoral unevenness—coupled with China's immense size and the pace of change of its institutions—it is not surprising that the PRC's political economy simply defies categorisation in unreconstructed VoC terms.

3.3 Variegated Capitalism and Its Critique

Aiming to transcend the methodological nationalism of VoC, 'variegated capitalism' theorists begin not with a horizontal comparison of nation states, but instead treat the world economy as an integrated—but differentiated—totality.[2] On this basis, they explore how the global economy, or sections of it, are subject to 'cross-cutting and connective processes, such as neoliberalization', which remain unintelligible if understood as endogenous to individual states (Peck and Zhang 2013, 359). They further elaborate on how capitalism is territorialised and governed at urban and macro-regional (as well as national) scales, so incorporating into their analysis spatial hierarchies of production, distribution, and institutionalisation beyond that of the nation state (Peck and Theodore 2007). The perspective employs a topological approach to space, which understands economic relationships not to be determined solely by geographical distance, but instead by (perpetually redefined) cost–benefit calculations based on evolving transportation and communications technology.[3] And finally, tensions, inconsistencies, and incoherence of and between institutions and across scales are considered part and parcel of capitalism as a contradiction-laden socioeconomic system, without assuming these to be necessarily disruptive of capital accumulation.

Given the above critique of VoC approaches, these conceptual advances are especially germane for addressing China's idiosyncratic brand of capitalism—as recent important contributions under the variegated capitalism rubric testify (Peck and Zhang 2013; Zhang and Peck 2016; McNally 2012; ten Brink 2013; Mulvad 2015). Of these, the two widely cited contributions of Zhang and Peck are the major focus of

[2] Variegated capitalism is of dual heritage: it has roots in both economic geography Peck and Theodore (2007) and economic sociology/political economy (Streeck 2009; Jessop 2014).

[3] To illustrate this point: London may be considered 'closer' to New York than to Sunderland, in this reading, due to the depth of their financial interconnectedness. Sheppard (2016) refers to such connections as 'wormholes'.

this section.[4] We have noted already these authors' innovative mapping of China's six major urban-regional production systems: the offshore 'Greater Chinese' hubs of Taiwan and Hong Kong, Guangdong's factory economy, Sunan's high-tech industrial parks, Chongqing's (ostensibly) egalitarian revanchist Maoism, Zhonguancun's Silicon Valley-esque innovation hub, and Wenzhou's clusters of family-owned SMEs. Drilling below the national scale, they follow—but significantly deepen—earlier analyses of China's uneven regional development, by demonstrating the existence of fundamental and polymorphic regional divergences in labour relations, training systems, interfirm relations, and forms of corporate governance & financing (the core VoC categories). Further, for Zhang and Peck (2016, 59–60), these models occupy 'unique relative positions both within the domestic political sphere and with respect to global production chains'. These six instances of uneven geographical development are conceived as (mediated) geographical expressions of a China's tripartite industrial structure, as outlined by Ernst and Naughton (2008). This model is characterised by large state enterprises in heavy goods industries, small private firms in low value-added export industries, and a dynamic but small 'middle' of high-tech foreign and domestic invested firms in areas like ICT.[5] And, for Zhang and Peck, local governance structures are understood to be significant actors in shaping how this tripartite structure is concretised into pluriform geographical regions, as in the case of Suzhou's pioneering activist local government in attracting Taiwanese capital for high-tech manufacturing (Zhang and Peck 2016, 70). Significantly, the centre-local tensions, significant ambiguities and overlappings of state and private authority, and intense interurban competition are treated as—hitherto—productive, rather than damaging (as VoC would have it), features of China's political economy, especially by encouraging local experimentation with new policy mixtures.

[4] Their work, presented as two articles, is treated as a unified piece of scholarship. Peck and Zhang (2013) is more dialogical, aiming toward a synthesis of multiple contradictory perspectives, while Zhang and Peck (2016) is more a dialectical application of a perspective (synthesised from this process of critique) which aims to model China's capitalist system. Their combination of theoretical and empirical work has inspired the writing of this thesis.

[5] Much hinges on the perceived strength and character of this middle—particularly in terms of innovation capacity—when considering whether China is likely to avoid succumbing to the 'middle-income trap', as discussed later in this thesis.

Ten Brink (2013, 37) also points to the (fragile) dynamism generated by this institutional incoherence, in what he terms China's 'fragmented multi-level governance'. He develops the framework to argue, convincingly, that China's integration with the global political economy and exposure to international competition makes redundant any understanding of China as somehow 'non-capitalist' (perhaps along the lines of Arrighi [2007], who views China as a 'non-capitalist market economy'). Even state-owned enterprises (SOEs) are, after all, ultimately forced to compete in capitalist markets, however distorted by state incentives. China is fruitfully dubbed a 'state-permeated yet competition-driven capitalism' (ten Brink 2013, 37). Similarly, for McNally (2012), 'Sino-Capitalism' is characterised as *guanxi* networked, state-directed, and globally integrated hybrid form of capitalist development—with institutional *incoherence* ('institutional arrangements compensate for each other's weak points rather than pushing incentives in the same direction') a significant and productive feature of its political economy. He notes the weaknesses of the central government vis-a-vis local interests, but sees this 'balancing' between a late-developing and strong Gerschenkronian state, and a vibrant grassroots entrepreneurialism, as the key to China's success (McNally 2012, 755).

Unique to McNally's analysis however is a focus on the geopolitics of China's rise: Sino-Capitalism is conceived as a potential future challenger to US hegemony. While this geopolitical orientation is an important advance, the Sino-Capitalism concept abounds with ambiguities. If China is far more deeply economically integrated into the global economy and institutions of global governance than previous catch-up developers like McNally argues (2012, 749), precisely which forces and mechanisms might cause it to diverge from, say, Japanese and Korean acquiescence to the US-led global order? And can Sino-Capitalism plausibly be treated as 'outside' (765) the global political economy which, as McNally acknowledges (755), birthed it by way of FDI and export markets? Worse, McNally highlights Waltz's (1979) problem of a 'second-image' conception of geopolitics that reduces geopolitical interactions to 'domestic' causality—but then proceeds without granting any determination whatsoever to distinctively 'geopolitical' causalities in his account of China's emergence and future development. Instead, Sino-Capitalism appears as an almost purely domestic, territorially bounded phenomenon—the growing strength of which is likely to have some impact on the global order—but the shape of which is itself apparently unafflicted by the manifold geopolitical tensions which have surrounded its emergence. Take the example of renminbi internationalisation as illustrative of this point. McNally (2012, 757) identifies Sino-Capitalism as a form of capitalism with distinct characteristics (a 'network-based mode of informally dealing with contradictions between capitalist accumulation and continued party-state hegemony', an 'only partially formalized' regulatory regime, and 'vibrant interpersonal networks'), before considering how these fixed traits shape its strategies for achieving currency internationalisation. No attention is paid to how the very fact of China's prior entry into a liberal, rules-based multilateral order might have had some hand in shaping the Sino-Capitalism which is now engaging it more fully.

As should be evident from this overview, variegated capitalism lacks the rigid parsimony of VoC analysis and is open to a wide range of creative deployments and theoretical incorporations. But in the absence of much collaborative dialogue in this emergent literature, there is little consensus on the nature of the specific economic dynamics or underlying macro-forces shaping particular instances of capitalist variegation, beyond rather opaque allusions to 'neoliberalisation', 'globalisation' and 'regionalisation'. Indeed, of the authors cited, only ten Brink (2013) unambiguously defines China as capitalist, emphasising the competitive pressures to accumulate facing private and state firms alike. Other analyses remain ambiguous about the ultimate character of China's (presumably not-quite?) capitalism and prefer the epithet 'hybridity'. Nor, given the radical discontinuities in the form and functions of China's governance structures since 1978 (cf. Naughton 2016), is it clear that the Chinese case 'affirm[s] at least one of the central tenets of VoC scholarship, concerning the entrenched nature of institutional path-dependence' (Peck and Zhang 2013, 386). Beneath the façade of a stable Communist Party there has taken place a revolution in political structures and procedures of governance at all levels (Yang 2004).

All authors listed also give rather short shrift to big questions of global political economy like overaccumulation in global manufacturing markets (cf. Hung 2008), the modularization of production (Breznitz and Murphree 2011), or the constraints imposed by trade multilateralism (Moore 2002), which have major implications in structuring the 'limits of the possible' facing Chinese state managers. Stated theoretically, as Tilley (2015, 220) argues, tackling these broader issues would amount to quite fundamentally reversing the aim of VoC scholarship towards 'a consideration of how capitalist forces produce spatial forms including the nation (rather than how the nation produces forms of capitalism)'. Though I prefer a dialectical approach which acknowledges a two-way directionality to the relationship between capital and institutions, her criticism does lay bare the extent to which theorists—even of variegated capitalism—have overwhelmingly focused their attention on how states shape capital, and not vice versa.

And, last but not least, Tilley's argument cited above alludes to two deeper ambiguities in Peck & Zhang's work, which are not theoretically elaborated. First, Zhang and Peck argue (2016, 74–75)—and I agree—that 'exploring causally significant differentiation at the regional or sub-national scale is, of course, but one of the methodological manoeuvres necessary for a truly multi-scalar analysis of capitalist variety', and should not be read 'as a deconstructionist's charter'. But no overarching explanation for China's dramatic urban-regional differentials is provided: Are they an inevitability, given the sheer scale of China's continental economy (2016, 61)? A product of the simultaneous 'internationalization and regionalization' of the world economy and the rescaling of national state functions (2016, 74)? Or the outcome of a peculiarly Chinese modality of practising political power which 'combines centralized party discipline and entrepreneurial localism' (2016, 66)? They do not say, and so the conceptual assumptions underpinning their research programme is not explicated, at least in the works referenced here. As the authors themselves acknowledge (2016, 74), '"finding" such regional differences is merely a prelude to seeking *explanations* for their (re) production in the context of ongoing scalar transformation of capitalism, though this is a task that must remain for future work'.

And secondly, for their commendable commitment to multiscalar analysis, Peck & Zhang do in one sense grant implicit primacy to the national scale by choosing to explore *China's* variegated capitalism, rather than that—for instance—of 'Guangdong' or 'East Asia' (both spatial categories which would also reveal profound heterogeneity if disaggregated into their constituent localities). It is perhaps unsurprising that this tension goes largely unacknowledged, given the framing of their research as a critique of methodologically nationalist VoC. But there are indeed strong reasons to believe that nation states continue to play a uniquely privileged role in the reproduction of global capitalism. China's national government is of especial significance, moreover, given the centralised nature of its party-state. Heilmann (2009), who grasps better than most the complex central-local dynamic at work in China's political system, insists upon the "shadow of hierarchy" under which the party centre superintends even the apparently autonomous work of local governments. And Rithmire (2014, 188–189), reviewing recent literature on China's regions, notes the need for a 'multilevel theorizing… taking seriously both local heterogeneity and the central power dynamics that promote or inhibit it', in order to avoid the risk of 'methodological localism'.

Had Zhang & Peck conceded some ground on the privileged role of the national state, the next plausible step of their analysis might have been to examine how subnational unevenness is in practice routinely 'held together' (in Yang and Naughton's [2004] informative metaphor) by the daily business of central statecraft: structures of taxation, welfare provision, the national currency, infrastructural provision, geopolitical practices, and the (re)production of nationalist ideology—functions overwhelmingly preserved by national governments. Acknowledging the operation of this scalar hierarchy would open the door for an examination of this process of holding together: what Mike Davis (2015, 50) calls the 'political *chemistry*… of transmuting sectoral into national interests'—or creating national interests to reconcile competing sectoral interests. That is, how the dialectical interrelationship between the exercise of political hegemony at the apex of the central state, and the polymorphic reality of (globally interconnected) political economic life across the Chinese territory, is perpetually reproduced, would become the object of empirical analysis. And furthermore, geopolitical pressures—still vectored largely (though not exclusively) through the states system—might then be more firmly integrated as factors constitutive of these 'local' forms of development, which, despite increasing international economic linkages, remain formally subordinated to the authority of the central state.

In my view, all these steps can be taken without adhering to the methodologically nationalist fiction—of a flat, self-contained economic territory corresponding rigidly to the boundaries of the state—which so hampers otherwise productive VoC thinking. And such a direction of thinking goes some way to addressing Mulvad's (2015) recognition of the ideological component of political contestation intrinsic to hegemonic projects. Instead of a rigid emphasis on struggles between supposedly fixed interest groups (exporters vs. domestic producers) being mechanically played out within the state, such class fractional pressures might be read as state actors seek to perceive, decipher and cohere pluralistic interests into a (partially) coherent national agenda which is also consonant with the imperative of generalised economic growth. This process even takes on a heightened form in a formally Leninist party-state, where—despite formal restrictions on democratic politics and the operation of a 'mass-line' among party cadres (Heilmann and Perry 2011)—various class fractions plainly coalesce around different branches of government, creating divisions which must be permanently renegotiated by the political centre. And it explains why, despite the complex heterogeneous local realities discovered by Zhang & Peck, China's dominant national mode of economic governance still appears on balance to be a neoliberal 'Guangdong' model of labour exploitation and the radical commodification of every area of social life—rather than a neo-Maoist 'Chongqing' vision premised upon more classically social democratic norms.

Establishing why China's political economy seems to cohere in this way demands a further investigation of the theoretical and practical mechanisms by which diverse and developing urban-regions are assembled and reassembled into a national state—in an open, non-deterministic fashion which should be fully expected to evolve along with the organisation of global capital.

3.4 States, Cities and Capital

In order to build on the advances of Variegated Capitalism for understanding China's political economic system, the remainder of this chapter elaborates on the conceptual grounds for proposing such a privileged role for the national state—especially given our prior critique of methodological nationalism. Beyond the Chinese case, a great deal of research in economic geography has catalogued profound variegation between localised territorial production complexes (or, more simply, 'cities')—and their increasing significance as loci of capital accumulation. Neoliberalism is widely seen as being synonymous with the re-territorialisation of state functions at urban-regional (alongside the macro-regional) scale. Most conspicuously, the world-cities literature depicts (using a topological spatial imaginary) how urban regions have become profoundly interconnected even as they appear increasingly detached from their attendant 'national' economies (Sassen 2001). For many, this shift signifies a fundamental transformation in the political geography of global capitalism. Scott (2012) is representative of a trend when he registers a preference for viewing the contemporary world as a 'mosaic of city-regions', rather than one of national states. And Krätke (2014) extends the world-cities framework beyond its origin in 'service sector' cities (London, New York, Tokyo) to usually overlooked but highly networked 'manufacturing' cities (Milwaukee, Nagoya and Torino) which he views as equally globally networked and detached from their host nation state. Inconsistencies in the precise nature of the new scale to be understood notwithstanding (Urban? Regional? Local? see Agnew 2013), the picture, overwhelmingly, is of cities floating free from their national moorings—relocated in a global, urbanised division of labour.

There are strong empirical reasons to object to aspects of this picture. Some significant functions of central states (urban planning policies, [limited] powers of taxation, industrial policies and collective bargaining institutions) have certainly been devolved in the neoliberal period, as summarised by Brenner (2004, 218–219). And the urban process and city governments have come to play an increasing role in the accumulation process (cf. Harvey 2012). But—and equally empirically observable—the well-established role played by national states continues, despite this rescaling. This argument was dramatically substantiated in the case of London (the archetypical 'world city'), where financial institutions were bailed-out by central government in the aftermath of the 2007–2008 crash (Therborn 2011), and it is obviously true that the central state remains critical for the Chinese case (as we observed above). This has also been the message of much statist political economy, responding to a very different set of fallacies regarding the notion of a stateless globalisation that predominated early in the last decade (Weiss 2012). These authors have pointed to a wealth of functions played by national states that could probably never be reproduced at urban-regional scales. Indeed, urban industrial districts are hardly new phenomena in the history of capitalism, and have not previously been positioned as antagonists of national state power. Crucially, nation states retain the principle of sovereignty—however compromised this is in practice—from which these unique social functions (such as money creation, tariff-setting and tax policies) flow.

While scholars in the Variegated Capitalism tradition—geographers as they mostly are—do not fall prey to such flat earth delusions regarding the end of nation states, they have maintained a silence on a question of crucial significance: why a networked and highly dynamic system of urban regions, operating under a more or less global division of labour which plainly overspills national boundaries, should continually cohere under the political authority of a rigid and formally anachronistic system of national states?[6] It was in fact this question, posed in a different form (that of the non-emergence of Robinson's [2005] 'transnational state'), to which uneven and combined development (UCD) was initially revived to help answer (Callinicos 2007). Recall that this debate concluded by highlighting the inherent 'clumpiness' of capitalist production, formed by the uneven development of the productive forces and the potential of rising returns to scale and monopoly rents (Ashman 2010). Agglomeration economies are seen to form the material basis for political multiplicity as a phenomenon of capitalist modernity, as states are bound to competitively attempt to valorize the fixed capital formations within their territorial borders in the world economy. This account of territorial states as capitalist phenomena (rather than a hangover of feudal social relations) is certainly historically apposite: as Agnew (2006, 529) notes,

> [T]he idea that absolutism's strong territoriality laid a template for later capitalism is fanciful. Only after 1815 did Europe's state boundaries solidify; even then it was only in the twentieth century that they became the policed barriers we now think of them as.

But there remain important unresolved theoretical issues here, which were only touched upon in Chapter 2. In Harvey's (2001, 329) well-known elucidation on a 'structured coherence' (his term for a capitalist state), he seeks to provide an economic basis for a nation state as, first and foremost, a space where 'capital can circulate without the limits of profit within socially-necessary turnover time being exceeded by the cost and time of movement... the space within which labour power can be substituted on a daily basis—the commuter range', and a space 'formally represented by the state'. This, he claims, offers a 'conceptual bridge... [with which] to integrate Marx's history with Lenin's geography of capitalist dynamics [and imperialism]' (Harvey 2001, 333). Davidson (2012) cites this exposition positively, which in his view forms an adequate material basis for the national state (though he rightly insists that states also require a sufficiently strong national identity in order to be able to function, a political factor underplayed by Harvey and others).

[6] Indeed, Jamie Peck's (with Nik Theodore 2007, 763) initial statement of intent in the variegated capitalism perspective recognised that geographers have had far more to say about 'factors endogenous to local and regional economies... than it has about the relations between such economies, interlocal and international "rules of the game", and macroinstitutional ensembles'.

Harvey is surely correct to identify potent tendencies towards agglomeration as a function of a global division of labour, which inevitably produce—in Gough's (2014) terminology—*local* capitalisms, based around urban labour markets, politics and patterns of daily life. But Harvey's formulation contains an incongruity: while his explanation holds for cities, labour power is plainly *not* substitutable within most national economies on a daily basis. Depending on the size and form of state in question, intranational labour mobility between such localities may take years or even generations to adjust to new market conditions (consider Germany's problem of chronic, intergenerational labour immobility). Nor is there any particular logical reason why socially-necessary turnover time should assume a geographically national form, beyond the (circular) argumentation that national states themselves create the infrastructural geographies within which capital may circulate. Harvey's effort to provide a link between agglomerations of fixed capital at the urban scale and political multiplicity crucially elides the distinction between national states and city governments.

That there could be no straightforwardly economic rationale for the radical heterogeneity in the size and form of states surely necessitates some level of historicisation if we are to understand their concrete forms, which should not be reduced to purely functionalist elements of a capitalist superstructure. When Harvey (2007, xvii) argues that 'capital accumulation necessarily produces and transforms spatialities and territorial structures (showing that if something like states did not exist capitalists would have to create them)', this plainly should not be interpreted as an argument that—for example—a hypercomplex state-society composite like China's might be created at the whim of blind competition between capitals. Better instead to view states as part of what Callinicos (2009) terms an 'articulated structure' of capitalist social relations, with distinct but interdependent economic, political and ideological spheres. Historically, we can posit that an unevenly developed network of capitalist urban regions seizes upon an already-existing states system, subjecting it to the logic of competitive accumulation and restructuring it—as far as possible—according to its needs by delegating 'political' authority and the monopoly of violence required to give birth to capitalist social relations to state managers.

But in so doing capital necessarily separates out a distinct set of social actors—politicians—who are ultimately dependent on, but not directly accountable to, capitalists. As Wood (2003, 11) argues, capital thus 'completes' a social form (sovereignty) inherited from a precapitalist epoch:

> Although the sovereign territorial state was not created by capitalism, the distinctively capitalist separation of the 'economic' and the 'political' has produced a more clearly defined and complete territorial sovereignty than was possible in non-capitalist societies.

And as a system of states becomes crystallised, the pressures of interstate competition become 'activated', ensuring that highly diverse state forms are subjected to universal pressures of competition. This is what motivates Allinson and Anievas (2009, 64) to argue that although the nation states system historically predates capitalism, the globalising thrust of capitalist expansion—combined with capitals' tendency to utilise and transform existing territorial structures as part of their competitive strategy—means international relations' 'distinct causal determinations, articulated and expressed through inter-societal competition, are, as a general abstraction, only fully activated under the specific socio-historical conditions of generalized commodity production'. While the distinction that Wood poses between the political and the economic is more a tendency rather than an absolute condition (Mieville 2006, 221), it nevertheless has determinate, material effects insofar as it 'activates' these geopolitical determinations and sets territorial states into competition with one another.

This explanation transcends either 'contingency' or 'necessity' in explaining why the states system maintains its relationship to contemporary capitalism, and drives home the importance of the *geopolitical* qualifier in the geopolitical economy perspective this book takes. The particular connections that develop between territorially located capitals and cities and national states may appear quite artificial and contingent (why should tax revenues from the City of London's profitable banks subsidise unproductive capitals in Wales?) But the capitalist impulse to escape competition through protection, security and political representation on the world market is a universal one. Making use of existing state infrastructures (however unsuited to the particular interests of particular capitals) nearly always outweighs the immense difficulty of establishing *new* national states, infrastructures, etc. This binds particular capitals to particular states in a historically path-dependent and messy fashion—leaving state managers, in turn, with some autonomy to exercise their own judgement regarding how best to cohere the territorial production complexes falling under their jurisdiction.

Agnew (2009, 33) expresses this contradiction between 'glocal' cities and national states when he describes national territories as 'ensembles of places linked together dynamically and unevenly by territorialized networks as well as by areal governance'. The means by which a state's spatial governance is practised in relation to 'its' cities is evidently profoundly intertwined with the predominant form of capitalism (cf. Soja 1989). For instance, the wartime rise of nationalised industries meant urban regions became closely integrated with their national economies and functioned less part of a global division of labour in the immediate postwar period. The neoliberal period may be viewed as one of reversion to the mean in the relationality between cities and states: nurtured back to health by states, capital became again both powerful and restless enough to seek profitable opportunities beyond its existing national environments.

There is an implicit hierarchy of determinations in this method of explaining the relations between cities as economic nodes and national states as combinatory formations; one which privileges the agency of capital in creating uneven development but does not discount the role of states in reshaping this geography. This strongly supports the account of UCD given in the previous chapter. As Lenin (1916) argues, it is first and foremost capital that produces geographical differentiation: '*abstract* theoretical reasoning may lead to the [mistaken] conclusion... [that] magnates of capital will unite on a world scale in a single world trust... [overcoming] competition and struggle between sums of finance capital nationally isolated'. This 'profoundly mistaken idea... [assumes] that the rule of finance capital lessens the unevenness and contradictions inherent in the world economy, whereas in reality it increases them' (Lenin 1916). Thus 'unevenness' is the consequence of capital understood narrowly as an economic force. And this persistent *economic* transformation manifests in permanent political upsets in the balance of power between states, which further magnify already-existing tendencies towards unevenness and discounts the possibility of states creating permanent stability in international relations:

> The *even* development of different undertakings, trusts, branches of industry, or countries is impossible under capitalism. Half a century ago Germany was a miserable, insignificant country, if her capitalist strength is

> compared with that of the Britain of that time; Japan compared with Russia in the same way. Is it "conceivable" that in ten or twenty years' time the relative strength of the imperialist powers will have remained unchanged? It is out of the question. (Lenin 1916; see also Callinicos 2009)

The order of determination is clear: capital develops unevenly, and states intervene as second order determinations trying to reshape this unevenness in their favour. Insofar as the global division of labour is an urban one, and this network of urban regions develops unevenly, cities will continue to rely upon and to reproduce a system of national states precisely because of the shifting economic-geographic pressures they constitute. And these states will remain heterodox creatures, riven between geopolitical pressures which enforce competitive mechanisms upon them, and their very different sizes and forms which grant them quite different capacities for intervening and combining capitals into national systems of accumulation.

The purpose of this brief digression is to support Radice's (2000) case for a *historical* political economy to account for the divergent path dependencies of national institutions; particularly under conditions of globalisation, in which monetary and financial flows deeply interlink national economies into a global web of interdependencies (Pettis 2013). The way state managers choose to bind together unevenly developed regions and economic sectors into never-uniform national states rests profoundly upon their history—nowhere more so than in China, where contemporary market forces and institutions with millennia of history have collided (Faure 2006). Such historicity is absent from VoC, which provides a purely functionalist perspective on national path dependency based on an abstraction—the ideal typical CME–LME binary. Variegated capitalism, in contrast, treats national models of capitalism as fictions, dispensing with the VoC binary through a ruthless process of disaggregation. But while states are, ultimately, abstractions, they are *real* abstractions insofar as their work of national governance serves to flatten and homogenise social space inside their borders (Lefebvre 1991; Scott 1998). This process is both continuous and always prone to failure, of course, but to simply ignore the state—treating it as an abstraction or a wholly 'artificial' construction (cf. Ince and Barrera de la Torre 2016)—is to misrepresent its material effects.

The Variegated Capitalism instinct to disaggregate states into their constituent urban regions and highlight their differential links with the global economy forms a vital precondition for analysing the pattern of contemporary capitalist development. But only by ***reintegrating*** these observations—through a specific explanation of how such subnational variegation becomes cohered into a functional national state—can we develop a cogent method for undertaking comparative political economy. This is precisely the argument made in Ron Martin's (2015, 258–259) recent critique of regional studies, where he tasks geographers of urban-regions with ignoring 'how the particular cases and instances of regional development we study relate to the wider system(s) of which they are a part—how uneven regional development is a ***combined***, relational process'. And Lim (2016, 83, original italics) is, I think, driving towards much the same conclusion in the Chinese case when argues that 'the theoretical challenge is to ***explain how and why territorially fragmented logics of socioeconomic regulation function at the national scale to preserve CPC power***'. This discussion has remained somewhat abstract, but the following chapters concretise it with regards to the Chinese experience.

3.5 Conclusion

The previous chapter presented an a priori sketch of the theory of uneven and combined development, before developing the theory in dialogue with the theoretical approaches predominant in economic geography and Marxist state theory. This chapter has sought further to develop UCD by bringing it into contact with the meso-level institutionalist political economy of VoC and Variegated Capitalism. I have argued that VoC theory—developed as it was in the particular time-place of advanced capitalist economies during the great moderation—has proven quite unsuited to conceiving China's political economy under radically different conditions (a developing economy with highly idiosyncratic political institutions experiencing rapid but geographically uneven economic growth). Variegated capitalism, while more promising, suffers from some specific difficulties in incorporating the dynamics of geopolitical economy, national political hierarchies, and class formation into its analytic purview.

By contrast, the UCD approach neither separates states from their contexts in the global political economy, nor abstracts away subnational geographical differentiation. But it does foreground the role of class relations, politics and history in shaping national systems of accumulation. Discussing the failure of the Russian capitalist class to mount a democratic revolution and the very peculiar hybrid political economy which consequently emerged in Russia, Trotsky (2009, 8–9) presents a profoundly neat summary of his powerful analytical approach:

> The social character of the Russian bourgeoisie and its political physiognomy were determined by the condition of origin and the structure of Russian industry... The extreme concentration of this industry alone meant that between the capitalist leaders and the popular masses there was no hierarchy of transitional layers.... the proprietors of the principal industrial, banking, and transport enterprises were foreigners, who realized on their investment not only the profits drawn from Russia, but also a political influence in foreign parliaments, and so not only did not forward the struggle for Russian parliamentarism, but often opposed it: it is sufficient to recall the shameful role played by official France. Such are the elementary and irremovable causes of the political isolation and anti-popular character of the Russian bourgeoisie.

Economics plays a determining role, then, but one refracted through the agency of social classes and the political form of state. And the theory goes one step further than Variegated Capitalism by demonstrating how economic regions or localities that appear radically disjointed with the national economic territory at large (the technologically advanced metal factories of St Petersburg vs the agrarian hinterland) are made nonetheless to cohere through the political agency of the national state's hegemonic practices. UCD thus strives towards conceptualising how variegated subnational systems of accumulation are combined into social formations. Key, as I have argued, is to develop an approach which identifies the economically and politically dominant fractions of capital at the national scale.

Capitalist history is replete with instances of catch-up development, beginning with the USA, Germany and Japan, followed by East Asian NICs in the postwar period, and now encompassing China. Each process produced vast geographical and social dislocations that impacted on the development process. Each late developer required increasing quantities of capital investment to be outlayed by the state. And in every case, the geopolitical economy into which the late developer emerged structured the internal constitution of each society in determinate ways, with very different consequences regarding class formation, the form of the state, and future economic development. The following chapters develop these insights to show how UCD offers the possibility of comprehending

China's reform period as an example of a recurrent and theorisable process.

Here, I want to conclude by arguing that the 'systems of accumulation' (SOA) approach, as developed by Ben Fine and collaborators, forms a complementary addition to the more abstract analytic categories of UCD in approximating concrete analysis of national political economies, especially when a set of particular growth dynamics are (temporarily) locked into place. In short, the SOA approach seeks to identify 'core' economic sectors (the most productive and profitable segments of a national economy), and to locate these in their broader sets of social class and institutional relations. Work along these lines has already produced valuable rereadings of the developmental trajectories of industrialising social formations in the global south like South Africa and Brazil, though typically without extensive reference to the broader dynamics of UCD (Fine and Rustomjee 1996; Ashman and Fine 2013; Saad-Filho 2010). This approach also draws on Weiss' (2014, 165) incisive critique of VoC which argues that the task is not explaining '[capitalist] diversity itself, but rather how it is conditioned and by what factors… by grounding the study of institutions in the analysis of the economic surplus that they both consume and help to reproduce'. Thus it follows that profitable 'core sectors'—those producing the economic surpluses which sustain political institutions through tax or other revenue streams—can be identified. Ashman et al. (2013, 249) further note that 'core sectors need to be located in relation to the state, finance, class relations and value creation, and how these impact across society as a whole'. In sum, a system of accumulation is a means of understanding a national economy as a differentiated totality, in which surpluses from profitable sectors might circulate through the institutions of state and be transferred to less productive sectors through a variety of fiscal and monetary transfers.

References

Agnew, John. 2006. The English Road to Modern International Relations: Benno Teschke, The Myth of 1648: Class, Geopolitics, and the Making of Modern International Relations. *International Politics* 43: 526–530.

Agnew, John. 2009. *Globalization and Sovereignty: Beyond the Territorial Trap*. London: Rowman & Littlefield.

Agnew, John. 2013. Arguing with Regions. *Regional Studies* 47 (1): 6–17.

Ahrens, Joachim, and Patrick Jünemann. 2010. Transitional Institutions, Institutional Complementarities and Economic Performance in China: A 'Varieties of Capitalism' Approach. *Ordnungspolitische Diskurse*, No. 2010–11. Available online at: http://hdl.handle.net/10419/55399. Accessed 11 June 2019.

Allinson, Jamie, and Alexander Anievas. 2009. The Uses and Misuses of Uneven and Combined Development: An Anatomy of a Concept. *Cambridge Review of International Affairs* 22 (1): 47–67.

Ang, Yuen Yuen. 2016. *How China Escaped the Poverty Trap*. New York: Cornell University Press.

Arrighi, Giovanni. 2007. *Adam Smith in Beijing*. London: Verso.

Ashman, Sam. 2010. Capitalism, Uneven and Combined Development and the Transhistoric. In *Marxism and World Politics: Contesting Global Capitalism*, ed. Anievas Alexander. London: Routledge.

Ashman, Sam, and Ben Fine. 2013. Neo-liberalism, Varieties of Capitalism, and the Shifting Contours of South Africa's Financial System. *Critical Perspectives on Southern Africa* 81 (82): 144–178.

Ashman, Sam, Ben Fine, and Susan Newman. 2013. Systems of Accumulation and the Evolving MEC. In *Beyond the Developmental State: Industrial Policy into the Twenty-First Century*, ed. Ben Fine, Jyoti Saraswati, and Daniela Tavasci, 245–268. London: Pluto.

Bai, Chong-En, Chang-Tai Hsieh, and Zheng Michael Song. 2014. Crony Capitalism with Chinese Characteristics. Working Paper, University of Chicago. Available online at: https://pdfs.semanticscholar.org/aadb/87c81db7223b50f1bbb608796bf2b92cb32b.pdf. Accessed 29 March 2020.

Brenner, Neil. 2004. *New State Spaces: Urban Governance and the Rescaling of Statehood*. Oxford: Oxford University Press.

Breznitz, Dan, and Michael Murphree. 2011. *Run of the Red Queen: Government, Innovation, Globalization, and Economic Growth in China*. New Haven: Yale University Press.

Bruff, Ian. 2011. What About the Elephant in the Room? Varieties of Capitalism, Varieties in Capitalism. *New Political Economy* 16 (4): 481–500.

Callinicos, Alex. 2007. Does Capitalism Need the State System? *Cambridge Review of International Affairs* 20 (4): 533–549.

Callinicos, Alex. 2009. *Imperialism and Global Political Economy*. Cambridge: Polity.

Coates, David. 2015. Varieties of Capitalism and 'the Great Moderation'. In *New Directions in Comparative Capitalisms Research: Critical and Global Perspectives*, ed. Matthias Ebenau, Ian Bruff, and Christian May, 11–28. Basingstoke: Palgrave.

Davidson, Neil. 2012. The Necessity of Multiple Nation-States for Capital. *Rethinking Marxism: A Journal of Economics, Culture & Society* 24 (1): 26–46.

Davis, Mike. 2015. Marx's Lost Theory: The Politics of Nationalism in 1848. *New Left Review* 93: 45–66.
Dixon, Adam. 2014. *The New Geography of Capitalism: Firms, Finance, and Society*. Oxford: Oxford University Press.
Ernst, Dieter, and Barry Naughton. 2008. China's Emerging Industrial Economy: Insights from the IT industry. In *China's Emergent Political Economy: Capitalism in the Dragon's Lair*, ed. Christopher A. McNally, 39–59. London: Routledge.
Fan, C. Cindy. 1995. Of Belts and Ladders: State Policy and Uneven Regional Development in Post-Mao China. *Annals of the Association of American Geographers* 85 (3): 421–449.
Faure, David. 2006. *China and Capitalism: A History of Business Enterprise in Modern China*. Hong Kong: HK University Press.
Fine, Ben, and Zaveher Rustomjee. 1996. *The Political Economy of South Africa: From Minerals-Energy Complex to Industrialisation*. London: Hurst.
Fligstein, Neil, and Juanjun Zhang. 2011. A New Agenda for Research on the Trajectory of Chinese Capitalism. *Management and Organization Review* 7 (1): 39–62.
Fu, Yuming, and Stuart A. Gabriel. 2012. Labor Migration, Human Capital Agglomeration and Regional Development in China. *Regional Science and Urban Economics* 42 (3): 473–484.
Gough, Jamie. 2014. The Difference Between Local and National Capitalism, and Why Local Capitalisms Differ from One Another: A Marxist Approach. *Capital & Class* 38 (1): 197–210.
Hall, Peter, and David Soskice (eds.). 2001. *Varieties of Capitalism*. Oxford: Oxford University Press.
Harvey, David. 2001. *Spaces of Capital: Towards a Critical Geography*. London: Routledge.
Harvey, David. 2007. *The Limits to Capital*. London: Verso.
Harvey, David. 2012. The Urban Roots of Financial Crises. In *Socialist Register 2012: The Crisis and the Left*, ed. Leo Panitch, Greg Albo, and Vivek Chibber. Pontypool: Merlin.
Heilmann, Sebastian. 2009. Maximum Tinkering Under Uncertainty: Unorthodox Lessons from China. *Modern China* 35 (4): 450–462.
Heilmann, Sebastian, and Elizabeth J. Perry. 2011. Embracing Uncertainty: Guerilla Policy Style and Adaptive Governance in China. In *Mao's Invisible Hand: The Political Foundations of Adaptive Governance in China*, ed. Sebastian Heilmann and Elizabeth J. Perry, 1–29. Cambridge, MA: Harvard University Press.
Hung, Ho-fung. 2008. Rise of China and the Global Overaccumulation Crisis. *Review of International Political Economy* 15 (2): 149–179.

Hung, Ho-fung. 2015. *The China Boom: Why China Will Not Rule the World*. Chichester: Columbia University Press.

Ince, Anthony, and Gerónimo Barrera de la Torre. 2016. For Post-Statist Geographies. *Political Geography* 55: 10–19.

Jessop, Bob. 2014. Capitalist Diversity and Variety: Variegation, the World Market, Compossibility and Ecological Dominance. *Capital & Class* 38 (1): 45–58.

Krätke, Stefan. 2014. Cities in Contemporary Capitalism. *International Journal of Urban and Regional Research* 38 (5): 1660–1677.

Lan, Tu, John Pickles, and Shengjun Zhu. 2015. State Regulation, Economic Reform and Worker Rights: The Contingent Effects of China's Labour Contract Law. *Journal of Contemporary Asia* 45 (2): 266–293.

Lee, Ching Kwan. 2007. *Against the Law: Labour Protests in China's Rustbelt and Sunbelt*. Berkeley, CA: University of California Press.

Lefebvre, Henri. 1991. *The Production of Space*. Chichester: Wiley.

Lenin, Vladimir Ilyich. 1916. *Imperialism: The Highest Stage of Capitalism*. Available at: http://www.marxists.org/archive/lenin/works/1916/imp-hsc/. Accessed 1 August 2013.

Lim, Kean Fan. 2016. On the Shifting Spatial Logics of Socioeconomic Regulation in Post-1949 China. *Territory, Politics, Governance* 5 (1): 65–91.

Lüthje, Boy, Siqi Luo, and Hao Zhang. 2013. *Beyond the Iron Rice Bowl: Regimes of Production and Industrial Relations in China*. Frankfurt: Campus Verlag.

Martin, Ron. 2015. Rebalancing the Spatial Economy: The Challenge for Regional Theory. *Territory, Politics, Governance* 3 (3): 235–272.

McNally, Christopher. 2007. China's Capitalist Transition: The Making of a New Variety of Capitalism. In *Capitalisms Compared* (Comparative Social Research, Volume 24), ed. Lars Mjøset and Tommy H. Clausen, 177–203. Bingley: Emerald.

McNally, Christopher. 2012. Sino-Capitalism: China's Reemergence and the International Political Economy. *World Politics* 64 (4): 741–776.

Mieville, China. 2006. *Between Equal Rights: A Marxist Theory of International Law*. London: Pluto Press.

Milonakis, Dimitris, and Ben Fine. 2009. *From Political Economy to Economics: Method, the Social and the Historical in the Evolution of Economic Theory*. London: Routledge.

Moore, Thomas G. 2002. *China in the World Market: Chinese Industry and International Sources of Reform in the Post-Mao Era*. Cambridge: Cambridge University Press.

Mulvad, Andreas. 2015. Competing Hegemonic Projects Within China's Variegated Capitalism: 'Liberal' Guangdong vs. 'Statist' Chongqing. *New Political Economy* 20 (2): 199–227.

Naughton, Barry. 2016. Inside and Outside: The Modernized Hierarchy That Runs China. *Journal of Comparative Economics* 44 (2): 404–415.

Nee, Victor, and Sonja Opper. 2012. *Capitalism from Below: Markets and Institutional Change in China*. Cambridge: Harvard University Press.

Nölke, Andreas, Tobias ten Brink, Simone Claar, and Christian May. 2015. Domestic Structures, Foreign Economic Policies and Global Economic Order: Implications from the Rise of Large Emerging Economies. *European Journal of International Relations* 21 (3): 538–567.

Peck, Jamie, and Jun Zhang. 2013. A Variety of Capitalism… with Chinese Characteristics? *Journal of Economic Geography* 13 (3): 357–396.

Peck, Jamie, and Nik Theodore. 2007. Variegated Capitalism. *Progress in Human Geography* 31 (6): 731–772.

Pei, Minxin. 2016. *China's Crony Capitalism: The Dynamics of Regime Decay*. Cambridge: Harvard University Press.

Pettis, Michael. 2013. *The Great Rebalancing: Trade, Conflict, and the Perilous Road Ahead for the World Economy*. Princeton: Princeton University Press.

Pieterse, Jan Nederveen. 2015. China's Contingencies and Globalisation. *Third World Quarterly* 36 (11): 1985–2001.

Popov, Vladimir. 2011. Is Chinese Variety of Capitalism Really Unique? February 18. Available online at: https://ssrn.com/abstract=1764094 or http://dx.doi.org/10.2139/ssrn.1764094. Accessed 12 August 2017.

Pun, Ngai, and Chris Smith. 2007. Putting Transnational Labour Process in Its Place: The Dormitory Labour Regime in Post-Socialist China. *Work, Employment & Society* 21 (1): 27–45.

Radice, H. 2000. Globalization and National Capitalisms: Theorizing Convergence and Differentiation. *Review of International Political Economy* 7 (4): 719–742.

Rithmire, Meg. 2014. China's "New Regionalism": Subnational Analysis in Chinese Political Economy. *World Politics* 66 (1): 165–194.

Roach, Stephen. 2014. *Unbalanced: The Codependency of America and China*. New Haven: Yale University Press.

Robinson, William I. 2005. Global Capitalism: The New Transnationalism and the Folly of Conventional Thinking. *Science & Society* 69 (3): 316–328.

Rutten, Koen. 2013. Authoritarianism, Capitalism and Institutional Interdependencies in the Chinese Economy: Implications for Governance and Innovation. PhD dissertation, The London School of Economics and Political Science (LSE). Available online at: http://etheses.lse.ac.uk/827/. Accessed 2 February 2017.

Saad-Filho, Alfredo. 2010. Neoliberalism Democracy and Development Policy in Brazil. *Development and Society* 39 (1): 1–28.

Sassen, Saskia. 2001. *The Global City*. Princeton: Princeton University Press.

Scott, Allen J. 2012. *A World in Emergence: Cities and Regions in the 21st Century*. Cheltenham: Edward Elgar.

Scott, James. 1998. *Seeing Like a State: How Certain Schemes to Improve the Human Condition Have Failed*. New Haven: Yale University Press.

Sheppard, Eric. 2016. *Limits to Globalization: Disruptive Geographies of Capitalist Development*. Oxford: Oxford University Press.

Soja, Edward. 1989. *Postmodern Geographies*. London: Verso.

Streeck, Wolfgang. 2009. *Re-forming Capitalism: Institutional Change in the German Political Economy*. Oxford: Oxford University Press.

ten Brink, Tobias. 2013. Paradoxes of Prosperity in China's New Capitalism. *Journal of Current Chinese Affairs* 42 (4): 17–44.

Therborn, Göran. 2011. End of a Paradigm: The Current Crisis and the Idea of Stateless Cities. *Environment and Planning A* 43 (2): 272–285.

Tilley, Lisa. 2015. Decolonizing the Study of Capitalist Diversity: Epistemic Disruption and the Varied Geographies of Coloniality. In *New Directions in Comparative Capitalisms Research: Critical and Global Perspectives*, ed. Matthias Ebenau, Ian Bruff, and Christian May, 207–223. Basingstoke: Palgrave.

Trotsky, Leon. 2009 [1932]. *The History of the Russian Revolution: Volumes I, II & III*. Chicago: Haymarket.

Tsai, Kellee, and Barry Naughton. 2015. Introduction: State Capitalism and the Chinese Miracle. In *State Capitalism, Institutional Adaptation and the Chinese Miracle*, ed. Barry Naughton and Kellee Tsai, 1–24. Cambridge: Cambridge University Press.

Waltz, Kenneth. 1979. *Theory of International Politics*. London: Addison-Wesley.

Wei, Yehua Dennis, Danlin Yu, and Xiaojing Chen. 2011. Scale, Agglomeration, and Regional Inequality in Provincial China. *Tijdschrift Voor Economische En Sociale Geografie* 102 (4): 406–425.

Weiss, Linda. 2012. The Myth of the Neoliberal State. In *Developmental Politics in Transition: The Neoliberal Era and Beyond*, ed. Chang Kyung-Sup, Linda Weiss, and Ben Fine, 27–41. Basingstoke: Palgrave.

Weiss, Oliver. 2014. Economic Surplus and Capitalist Diversity. *Capital & Class* 38 (1): 157–170.

Wilson, Jeanne. 2007. China's Transformation Towards Capitalism. In *Varieties of Capitalism in Post-Communist Countries*, ed. David Lane and Martin Myant, 239–257. Basingstoke: Palgrave.

Witt, Michael A. 2010. China: What Variety of Capitalism? INSEAD Faculty & Research Working Paper, no. 2010/88/EPS. Available online at: https://papers.ssrn.com/sol3/papers.cfm?abstract_id=1695940. Accessed 11 November 2016.

Wood, Ellen. 2003. *The Empire of Capital*. London: Verso.

World Bank. n.d. *Indicators*. Available online at: data.worldbank.org/indicator. Accessed 12 June 2019.

Xing, Yuqing. 2016. Estimating the Upper Limits of Value Added in the People's Republic of China's Processing Exports. In *Uncovering Value Added in Trade: New Approaches to Analysing Global Value Chains*, ed. Yuqing Xing. Singapore: World Scientific.

Yang, Dali. 2004. *Remaking the Chinese Leviathan: Market Transition, Political Leadership, and Economic Governance in China*. Stanford: Stanford University Press.

Yang, Dali, and Barry Naughton. 2004. *Holding China Together Diversity and National Integration in the Post-Deng Era*. Cambridge: Cambridge University Press.

Zhang, Jun, and Jamie Peck. 2016. Variegated Capitalism, Chinese Style: Regional Models, Multi-scalar Constructions. *Regional Studies* 50 (1): 52–78.

CHAPTER 4

China's Boom (I): The Geopolitical Economy of Reform and Opening, 1978–2000

4.1 Introduction

This chapter presents an overview of the geopolitical economy of China's entry into the world economy after 1978, showing how this *mode of integration* contributed to the social and industrial patterning of China's domestic political economy. When considering the structural determinants of economic liberalisation, accounts of China's reform period typically focus on the domestic economic growth imperative and political constraints of stability, governance, and maintaining Party rule—such as incorporating the political interests of neoconservatives (or ex-Maoists), retooling the party administrative apparatus, empowering local governments, and so on (e.g. Shirk 1993; Yang 2004; Shambaugh 2008). While important, my argument here is that geopolitical-economic factors inflected just as significantly the pattern of Chinese development: through dictating its very possibility, its historical timing and its terms of access to global markets. In turn, the influence of international political economic influences left determinate traces on the class and economic incentive structures of Chinese society.

Breslin (2007, 24) exaggerates matters when he argues that until 'as late as Deng Xiaoping's "southern tour" in 1992, Chinese politics could be studied almost entirely in terms of domestic dynamics'. From 1978, negotiating myriad domestic and international constraints

S. Rolf, *China's Uneven and Combined Development*,
Studies in the Political Economy of Public Policy,
https://doi.org/10.1007/978-3-030-55559-7_4

and crises, while temporally compressing development, formed the broad strategic remit of state managers. Even before this, geopolitical conjunctures proved highly consequential for China's domestic political economy. Four major examples of international factors underpin this line of argument here: (1) The rise of cross-border trade, investment, and ultimately manufacturing networks—as an Asian regional, then as an a Transpacific phenomena involving US multinationals—underpinned by the US liberal imperialist project. (2) China's internally uneven development, enormously influenced by the 'Third Front' strategy, which shaped the industrial legacy which foreign investors encountered during reform and opening. (3) The 'strategic triangle' formed by the USA, the Soviet Union and China during late cold war geopolitics; and (4) the politics of China's WTO entry, which dramatically intensified China's manufacturing competitiveness. Collectively, these dynamics—all emanating from different facets of competitive political multiplicity—embedded themselves in China's 'domestic' polity, shaping investment and ownership structures and, consequently, class structures and the form of the Chinese state.

To preview our conclusions: the substantive outcomes of China's distinct modality of integration into the world economy were (1) to unleash the dynamics of catch-up development while forestalling the formation of a politically independent domestic capitalist class (Tsai 2005), and (2) to insulate the central state against the 'internationalisation' of its institutions. Outliers like Chin (2007) and Harris (2012) aside, few authors argue that transnational capital has deeply penetrated the Chinese state in the way it has elsewhere. For instance, Glassman (2004) explains how the integration of Thailand into GPNs led to shifts in the core functions of the national state towards mediating the relationship of transnational investors to local actors, representing a willing subordination of sovereignty and industrial policy to the demands of overseas investors. In China, by contrast, political responsibility for GPN-led accumulation was devolved to local party cadres. This engendered the emergence of a multilevel governance structure, under which local government actors came to form a 'bureaucratic capitalist' class in pursuing strategic coupling with GPNs. Localised bureaucratic capitalism (in its many regional variants) did become a defining structural feature of China's contemporary political economy (Au 2012), but this class fraction never became fully dominant at the national level, where a nationally oriented elite maintained political control and patronage relations with large state-owned enterprises—and arrangement which persists to date. In sum, China experienced an internationalisation of capital *without* the internationalisation of the state.

4.2 The Geopolitical Economy of Cross-Border Production

East Asian industrialisation can be understood as both a cause and outcome of an epochal phase shift in capitalist development, from the Keynesian-Fordist 'golden age' to a new geopolitical economy of neoliberalism. Following the Second World War and the successful reconstruction of European economies through the Marshall Plan, the US facilitated the creation of developmental states in East Asia (EA) as a bulwark against Soviet and Chinese expansion (Cumings 1997; Stubbs 2017). Japan, Hong Kong, South Korea, Singapore and Taiwan successfully pursued catch-up development, ultimately joining the ranks of advanced capitalist economies in terms of per capita incomes, institutions, and technological capacities. The initial motivations for EA industrialisation were as much geopolitical as economic, then, insofar as the nascent American hegemon bolstered its strength in East Asia through a security bargain reliant upon encouraging regional development, not least by opening its domestic market to imports (Arrighi 2009; Desai 2013). As Hung (2015, 53) puts it, this development was 'consciously cultivated by the United States as part of its effort to create subordinate and prosperous bulwarks against communism in East Asia'. And the strategy of import substitution industrialisation (ISI) pursued by developmental states before opening—particularly in Japan, Korea and Taiwan—was critical in providing the broad and deep industrial base on which later export success was predicated.

This eastward spread of industrial capital contributed already, by the late 1960s, to a deepening global manufacturing overcapacity. As Brenner (2006, 2009, 9) argues, postwar catch-up development in West Germany and East Asia represented stages in a singular 'extended process of uneven development' in which successive developers made 'huge, but often redundant, additions of manufacturing capacity': based more upon capturing existing shares of world export markets through price competition in a zero-sum fashion than on generating additional effective demand. And in Brenner's (2006) account, the recessionary bouts which subsequently spread across the world economy during the 1980s and

1990s functioned inadequately to clear out redundant plant and equipment as increasingly uncompetitive producers clung to market share, weighing on profitability and dragging down investment rates almost everywhere outside of China. The result was a slowdown in global growth; persistent profitability pressures across the world economy; the delinking of the dollar from gold; and the explosion of financialisation, speculation and bubbles across global north and south. A range of research now concurs on the existence of a generalised and protracted downturn in business profitability both in the US case and in the world economy more generally (Brenner 2006; Shaikh 2016; Roberts 2016; Li 2016).

In response to the crisis of 1973 a quadrant of interlocking processes emerged across the advanced economies—of which the continued eastward spread of industrial capital formed one—which are collectively referred to as neoliberal globalisation: industrial restructuring through outsourcing and consequent corporate vertical disintegration, wage repression, and a scalar dislocation of national capitalisms following their zenith in the 1950s and 1960s (Jessop 2008; Brenner 2004). While earlier EA development had been geopolitically motivated, during the 1970s, the flow of manufacturing capacity to Asia became firm-driven—as part of a generalised attempt by Western capitals to reduce the wage share through spatial relocation of production (a spatial shift also taking place *within* the advanced economies; Knox et al. 2014). And in parallel with the established role of FDI in the Asian Tiger economies undertaken by TNCs during the 1950s and 1960s arose a new system of fragmented production processes taking place across several national boundaries involving webs of small subcontractors organised by large lead firms.

The fragmentation of production often involved neither 'arm's length' pure market relations, nor formally integrated networks along the lines of intrafirm MNC subsidiary trade; but nominally independent, frequently medium- or long-term, 'repeated and trust-intensive' interfirm relationships (Kaplinsky 2015). Lead firms concentrated on 'core competencies' in brand management, advertising, cognitive and human capital development, R&D, and innovation; while subcontractors faced severe downward price pressure from their monopsonistic dependence on particular large customer relationships—but could nonetheless benefit compared with other exporters due to the enhanced possibilities for technology transfer and large-scale orders new production relations implied. Crucial to the new organisation of production is the capacity for groups of firms and states to monopolise high value-added activities and externalise low value-added fragments of production to other parts of the network. These arrangements have been variously theorised as 'global commodity/value chains' (GVCs; Gereffi 1994) and 'global production networks' (GPNs; Henderson et al. 2002).

Drawing on earlier examples of US consumer manufacturers' outsourcing and offshoring to East Asia by the likes of RCA, previously vertically integrated *keiretsu* in Japan pioneered a highly decentralised and transnational 'multilayered subcontracting system [which through the crisis of the mid 1970s] continued to increase in scale and scope through a spillover into select East Asian locations' (Arrighi 2009, 358). The consequence of regional Japanese investment was a putative 'flying geese' pattern of development, as successive states challenged the regional geography of unevenness and pursued strategic coupling with Japanese supply chains, drawing them into the incipient regional export boom. While outsourcing initially granted Japanese capital a global cost advantage, Western TNCs soon joined the fray. The rush was hastened as first innovators in new ICT industries—fruits of the microelectronics revolution—bypassed Western factories and sourced production from East Asia. And innovations springing from new computer communications technologies subsequently permitted the extension and management of long supply chains in longer established light goods industries such as textiles and garments (Henderson 1989; Gereffi 1994).

The geopolitical economy of neoliberalism, however, also imposed secular limits upon this East Asian developmental process—co-constituted as it was by significant wage repression in advanced capitalist economies. As Saad-Filho (2014, 70) writes, under flying geese, 'movements of capital, technology and manufacturing capacity within the region, and the upward mobility of countries, were predicated on access to AE [advanced economy] markets'. This preferential market access (granted on condition of geopolitical incorporation into the US sphere of influence), as already noted, infused regional catch-up development with a geopolitical logic from the outset. But this aside, the second primary motivation for outsourcing and offshoring from the advanced economies was to achieve a reduction in the wage bill in response to profitability problems, further delinking wage increases from productivity gains (Shaikh 2016, 730). So insofar as GPN-led restructuring successfully contracted the wage share in the advanced economies, making up the difference through credit provision (itself—especially in the US case—financed through the reinvestment of Asian surpluses in US Treasury bonds; Gowan 1999), the golden goose of Western consumer markets for manufactured exports became increasingly saturated. World market share was only capturable through intense price competition, resulting in a trend towards 'immiserizing growth' as a majority of developing economies attempting failed to achieve global competitiveness or even to develop at all (Kaplinsky 2015).

The advent of GPNs also entailed the decline of import substitution industrialisation strategies (ISI) and a transition to export oriented industrialisation (EOI) in the region. This shift was until rather late caricatured by institutions of global economic governance as one from 'state-led' to 'market-led' development (World Bank 1993). But ISI is better understood as a necessary precursor to EOI, where EA developmental states secured the world leading status of their export sectors through successful state-driven strategies of industrial upgrading (South Korea, for instance, successfully bucked the market and rationalised its automobile industry by driving out small producers; Chang 2002). And most such states continued to pursue industrial policies increasingly proscribed by the Washington consensus even during EOI. In the first postwar developers, then, the problem of global market saturation was initially ameliorated by the ability to compete directly on price and quality with advanced economy firms. Industrial policies consequently enabled broad, deep addition of national industrial capacities, where high-wage, high-skill and vertically integrated production provided sufficient employment and growth to stimulate domestic markets. And these economies possessed relatively small pools of labour on a global scale, which meant that the Lewis Turning Point of labour shortages came well before market saturation did, and sizeable segments of the population could benefit from sustained wage gains in line with accelerating productivity (Gray 2015). The endpoint in this early phase of development resembled the Rostowian high mass consumption phase.

By the 1990s, however, a combination of forces upset this trend. Ever intensifying price competition, the fast-increasing power of global original brand manufacturers (OBMs) instigated by the third industrial revolution, and the currency crisis of 1997–1998 all put developmental states under severe duress—bringing widespread speculation that South Korea and Taiwan may fall at the final hurdle posed by the middle-income trap and fail to create world leading firms (Bernard and Ravenhill 1995; Pirie 2013). These pressures, along with the new terms imposed by international organisations, finally consolidated EOI as the new development policy regime predicated upon comparative specialisation in particular segments of increasingly modularised industrial processes (Gereffi 2014, 17). Modularised production also fragmented the previous sectoral binary between 'high-value' and 'low-value' industries, as basic assembly processes across virtually all industrial sectors became increasingly susceptible to codification and outsourcing, while supply chain and brand management presented lucrative opportunities even in such previously low-margin industries as garments (consider the power of brands such as Nike, Gap, H&M, and Zara) (Sturgeon 2002). Yeung (2014) refers to this shift as a 'strategic decoupling' of firms from national political economies in favour of a 'strategic recoupling' with lead firms in global markets.

The shrinking policy space for developmental states was further confirmed during the 2000s, as—in different ways—archetypal developmental states in Japan, South Korea and Taiwan responded to the Asian financial crisis with political projects aimed at boosting competitiveness through reshaping their capitalisms (in however selective a fashion) towards the 'LME' Anglo-American model of capitalism.[1] This highly paradoxical outcome, given the superior handling of the 1997–1998 crisis by the most protectionist regional states (Henderson 1999), can only be explained as part of intensifying 'external' economic pressure towards competitiveness, and a consequent 'internal' eagerness of fractions of capital to tackle the wage gains made by labour during the democratisation struggles of the 1980s, via neoliberal structural reform (Gray 2011). This recomposition of state-capital relations bolstered the emergent division of labour across distinct city-regions, which upset national economies' location as the primary scalar loci of production, distribution and consumption (Sassen 2001; Scott 2012; Krätke 2014). This embryonic urban division of labour was pioneered in the tight-knit forms of state-business personnel interactions in particular cities of developmental states (Tokyo and Osaka in Japan, Seoul in South Korea, Taipei and Hsinchu in Taiwan) in (geographically speaking) reasonably small

[1] These state projects, however, were limited and often explicitly rejected IMF advice. But this does not negate the evidence of a broadly 'neoliberal' trajectory for these economies. For detailed discussions, see Gray (2011), Pirie (2007), Hsu (2009), and the essays collected in Witt and Redding (2014).

states, producing globally significant and deeply connected metropolises.[2] Under ISI, such cities existed primarily as (dominant) component parts of national economies: with states playing major roles across territories in managing wages, welfare, and consumption through Keynesian techniques—sociospatial arrangements evidently privileged by the geopolitical economy of 'embedded liberalism' (Ruggie 1982). Meanwhile, the outward orientation of EOI served to break 'local geographical bonds between production and consumption on which organised capitalism was based' (Knox et al. 2014, 279). So, while the urban scale has always played an important role for capitalist development, as noted in the previous chapter, under neoliberalism cities have tended to develop into more distinctively specialised units in a division of labour transcending the national scale.

A global process of state 'rescaling' ensued, from which emerged a new urban form—described by Sassen (2006, 54–55) as 'partly denationalized strategic territorializations with considerable regulatory autonomy'. The scalar corollary of deepened integration of the global economy and GPNs was, on the one hand, a geographical concentration of high value-added activities in particular advanced capitalist economy cities (such as London) based on intangible knowledge functions, skill sets and interpersonal relations ('social capital'); while on the other, industrial cities emerged with deep specialties in particular industrial processes (Krätke 2014). Replication of these territorialisations proved extremely difficult compared with the technology transfer in labour-intensive manufacturing industries: enabling rising returns to scale for the dominant regions in this global city network (Storper 2013). While Chapter 3 argued that this process was not completely novel nor antithetical to national state agency per se, it did render the postwar 'spatial Keynesianism' of geographically

[2] Two qualifiers are necessary here. The symbiosis between national states and economies in the postwar era is frequently exaggerated, conflating as it does characteristics of regional and sectoral specific labour regimes (e.g. high wages in car producing regions) with national economies as a whole (cf. Brenner and Glick 1991; Jessop and Sum 2006). Moreover, as Glassman (2016) has demonstrated, processes of state internationalisation played a major role from the beginning of East Asia's postwar catch-up development: Japan's developmental miracle, for instance, took place under the direction of a Pacific-oriented US ruling class, which supplied capital, personnel and technology to the state planning organisation, MITI—mirroring later processes across the region (Panitch and Gindin 2012).

even national development through redistribution and industrial dispersion far more difficult to pursue, fracturing the national state spatiality upon which the 'developmental' social compound rested.

In sum, by the late 1970s when Chinese state managers made a totemic set of decisions to modernise the economy, several regional neighbours—China's geopolitical rivals—were well advanced along the path of economic development. And while fragmented production chains dominated by large-scale R&D-intensive lead firms made *entry* into manufacturing for the world economy generally easier, they simultaneously restricted the possibilities for developmental states to achieve competitiveness through simple technology transfer and price competition. The scalar political economy of the postwar period had undergone a transformation: from nationally integrated Keynesian-Fordist economies engaging in trade in finished goods, towards a neoliberal globalisation of modularised production and innovation systems, with a division of labour grounded increasingly in city-regions. And unlike the other Asian tigers, China did not enjoy privileged access to US consumer markets (McNally 2012, 755). In sum, the highly favourable postwar geopolitical economy encountered by the East Asian developmental states was not open to China.

4.3 China's 'Historical Backwardness' and the 'Whip of External Necessity'

This increasingly hostile geopolitical economy notwithstanding, China also had distinctive problems of its own with which to contend after Mao's death and the downfall of the Gang of Four. In 1978, Deng Xiaoping inherited a vast geographical and administrative space which—scalar transformations of the capitalist world economy aside—discounted the possibility of developing of tight-knit forms of central state-business personnel interactions in one or two cities as a viable national model, and necessitated instead a sprawling, continental scale of industrial development. The absence of entrepreneurial culture resulting from three decades of Maoism, the devastation of the state's bureaucratic apparatus during the (only recently concluded) Cultural Revolution, and the absence of a legal framework of property rights, collectively presented what appeared as insuperable barriers to capitalist economic development. But, motivated by the 'whip of external necessity', China embraced the cause of catching up with the advanced capitalist economies.

The proximate trigger of China's reform period was a series of geopolitical conjunctures from 1976 which elicited intense anxiety that longstanding hostilities with the USSR would turn violent in the absence of US hegemony in East Asia, and that China was chronically underprepared to defend itself. During his final years, Mao Zedong expressed serious concern about the expansion of Soviet influence in Indochina following the North Vietnamese rout of US forces in Saigon (Garver 2016, 324–325). Carter's (short-lived) withdrawal of troops from South Korea in 1976 drummed home the risk of a potential total US abandonment of the Asia Pacific, prompting a confidential 1977 report by China's foreign minister to warn that 'revisionist Soviet social-imperialists are filling the vacuum left by the United States and are taking advantage of US weakness to make expansionist and infiltrative moves' (cited in Garver 2016, 326). The imperative of catch-up was further underscored by two major events in 1979: the weaknesses exposed in the People's Liberation Army (PLA) during China's short military adventure into Vietnam, and the Soviet invasion of Afghanistan. While victory in Vietnam was virtually assured by the sheer scale of the advance (300,000 troops across the length of Vietnam's northern border), the Chinese leadership was surprised by how weak their inferior weaponry and military technology proved against the Vietnamese troops' recently acquired Soviet supplies. The Soviet occupation of Afghanistan provided a further stark warning to China regarding the Russian capacity for full-scale land occupation of states it regarded as under its sphere of influence, prompting US-Sino cooperation in training resistance fighters (Garver 2016, 418). Deng's early period in power was, in sum, marked by a geopolitical conjuncture which prompted an existential crisis among Chinese elites, and his proposed response was a sharp strategic pivot towards the United States.

Why did catch-up take the form of 'reform and opening'? China's laggard economy was not a product of Maoism's planned economy per se. Some smaller Soviet economies fared comparably well under their plans, and China's own industrial output increased at a steady average of 11% from 1952 to 1978. But technical progress of industry was profoundly retarded by a specific set geopolitical dynamics which emerged from the late 1950s. During Mao's first decade the PRC enjoyed a close relationship with the Soviet Union: and the relatively economically advanced Stalinist state shared its technology and planning apparatus with the Chinese state managers. The rapid and socially convulsive industrialisation of the Great Leap Forward, for instance, borrowed heavily from the Gosplan of the USSR—a model of 'capital intensive investment in heavy industry' the ambiguities of which Anderson (2010, 84) captures in his description of it as a 'misfit, however necessary at the time'. Disastrous in its social consequences in the countryside (and declared fancifully by Mao as a means by which to 'catch up and overtake England in fifteen years'), it did undoubtedly serve its function in kick-starting heavy industrial development in China for the first time (Pantsov 2015, 189). Prior to the Great Leap, Deng himself had overseen Sino-Soviet technological transfers earlier in the 1950s and experienced their benefits for China's technologically backward economy (Vogel 2011, 120). The Sino-Soviet split, however, suspended transmission of technological innovations to China from the early 1960s—prompting Deng to remark in 1978 that 'compared with developed countries, China's economy has fallen behind at least ten years or perhaps 20, 30, or even 50 years in some areas' (cited in Garver 2016, 350). China's technological development slowed to a crawl, and state planners were reduced to using tight foreign exchange reserves to selectively import plants at very high cost for reverse engineering (Naughton 2007).

The protracted freeze in Sino-Soviet relations left China by 1978 profoundly impoverished. Annual per capita income was slightly over US$150—around 1.5% of the US level in dollar terms. The national economy was almost entirely self-sufficient and suffered from extremely restricted access to foreign goods and technology. SOEs dominated the industrial landscape, while the State Pricing Commission fixed the cost of hundreds of key goods. Lardy (2014, 74) describes China's Sixth Five Year Plan (1981–1985): 'over 250 pages in the English language version, it set a huge number of targets for output (again in detailed physical terms and more aggregated value terms) in agriculture, industry, and services' The centralised planning apparatus had functioned since the 1950s through sporadic national 'big pushes' towards industrialisation, but dysfunctional bureaucracies and the unwillingness of local cadres to follow incoherent instructions resulted in multiple self-contained regional planning centres (Naughton 2007; Lim 2017). What banking sector existed operated under the total control of the People's Bank of China (PBOC)—of which local banks were merely subsidiaries with no independent remit, making loans to SOEs only according to instructions in the central plan (de Rambures 2014). As such, opening was seen as a critical complement to the economic reform needed to drive a process of economic catch-up.

4.4 Politics of Reform and Opening

The significance of the Sino-US *entente* broached by Nixon and Mao in 1972 (under diplomatic the stewardship of Zhou Enlai and Henry Kissinger) became evident only in retrospect. Finally consolidated by Carter and Deng in 1979 in the Sino-US ratified *Joint Communique*, the new partnership established the United States' 'One China' policy transferring US recognition of Chinese sovereignty from Taipei's KMT to Beijing and the CCP. US diplomats had sought reprieve from the intense economic demands of maintaining a US forward presence in Asia following the calamitous defeat in Vietnam. The acquisition of viable nuclear weaponry during the mid-1960s by the PLA had also played no small role in this mutual recognition of sovereignty, while increasing Soviet success in Asia and across the third world pushed both sides towards a normalisation of relations which only deepened over the following decade. As Westad (2012, 449) writes, 'the Reagan administration offered China what it called a "strategic association" with the United States... a de facto alliance... As the Cold War grew colder in the early 1980s, Sino-American security cooperation expanded. US anti-Communist campaigns in Afghanistan, Angola, and Cambodia were closely coordinated with the Chinese'. This opened the door for China's re-entry into the world economic order, ending its deep and costly political economic isolation.

The potential economic benefits of this nascent security alliance with the United States could only be reaped through profound reform of the planned economy. But this took place against the backdrop of a highly inopportune domestic political context. Orchestrated by Deng Xiaoping in tandem with a leadership team headed by Hu Yaobang and Zhao Ziyang during the 1980s, economic reform was pitched as a double goal: a state- (and party-) building exercise in the unstable post-Mao era on the one hand, and a means of *jiegui*—'connecting tracks' with the global economic order in order to secure investment and growth—on the other (Chen 2009). Reconstructing party rule, Deng believed, necessitated the gamble that breaking China's isolation and ceding total central economic control would not threaten the CCP's monopoly on political power. But the bulk of the party leadership feared exactly this outcome, remaining firmly committed to the largely autarchic macroeconomic planning system as a consequence. On Deng and the reformers' part this necessitated, in Shirk's (1993, 6) metaphor, a protracted strategy of pushing 'against the stone wall of the Chinese bureaucracy. Where they found loose stones, they pushed through; when stones would not move, they did not waste energy pushing'. The mélange of possible reforms eventually settled on (detailed below) was consequently fashioned against the steadfast opposition of neoconservatives in the leadership, who fought hard to preserve the plan, and found political coherence around an 'anti-imperialist' opposition to Deng's normalisation of relations with the US (Fewsmith 2008, 46).

From the outset, then, reform and opening represented the articulation of a viable hegemonic project for maintaining the *form* of the party-state by permitting a significant drift in the *content* of the economic norms underpinning it. Deng's ode to political pragmatism in reform, 'crossing the river while feeling for the stones', obscures the extent to which reform was rooted in a relatively fixed set of political principles based upon meritocratic authoritarianism and economic liberalism, underpinned by the survival the CCP. As Naughton (2016, 404) notes, over the duration of the reform period, China's state evolved from a centralised but chaotic system into a 'capable, professional, and rule-bound system, but one that is still strongly authoritarian and hierarchical'. The trope of 'economic reform without political reform' is to this extent quite deceptive. Economic liberalisation was pursued in order that the logics of statist capitalist accumulation and the specific kind of political and economic crises it generated would no longer threaten party rule, as they perpetually had during Mao's final two turbulent decades (cf. Riskin 1987). Reform attempted to enshrine the (admittedly flexible) ideological principles of Maoism and perpetual CCP rule through a recomposition of both China's accumulation system and its institutions.

Reform moved Chinese society towards an ever-deeper commodification of land, labour, and capital (Walker and Buck 2007). Suspending the commitment to 'class struggle' and its legitimation of the state accumulation model, the Party focused instead on developing the means of production via the 'Four Modernizations' (agriculture, industry, defence and science)—which in practice meant the blossoming of markets and permission for some to 'get rich first', as the nascent private bourgeoisie was brought into the institutional framework of the state through the incorporation of private ownership recognition into the Party's constitution during the 1999 National People's Congress. However, if the pursuit of catch-up development was formulated in the language of preserving

China's relations of production by transforming its forces of production, perhaps inevitably, as we shall see, the eventual result was to upend both. China's 'mode of integration' with capitalist markets proved to be a socially transformative process—and the belief that Party rule and class structures could basically remain unchanged while overseeing a fundamental transformation of the accumulation system highly unrealistic.

4.4.1 *Reform and Opening in the 1980s*

The reform period is typically divided into two periods: the first decade of modest tinkering with the planned economy (especially in rural areas) and a small degree of opening to foreign investment from 1978, and the post-Tiananmen period—particularly from 1993—during which liberalisation and privatisation was accelerated (Naughton 2007, 90). The emergence of the 'Democracy Wall' protest movement of winter 1978–1979 shocked Deng and the reformers, who had so far wielded the public pressure for political reform to consolidate their power (vis-à-vis the neoconservatives) at the Third Plenum of December 1978. After the Plenum, and a crackdown on urban demonstrations, reformers decided to pursue market reform in the countryside rather than the more politically dangerous urban enterprises. Driving through economic reforms far away from Beijing also constituted a form of 'playing to the provinces': creating a bureaucratic constituency for market reform 'designed to turn provincial and enterprise officials into a pro-reform counterweight to the conservative center' (Shirk 1993, 335).

The following decade witnessed dramatic rural reforms: limited relief of the burden of forced grain transfers on the peasantry and rising prices for surpluses, a dismantling of the agricultural communes and return to private household farming, an easing of credit, and the establishment of Town and Village Enterprises (TVEs)—rural industrial firms—which together formed the future basis for rural entrepreneurialism. Though urban reform was slow, the rural transformation allowed the processing of marketised agricultural surpluses in TVEs, and then for urban SOEs to establish a subcontracting network for production inputs to the formerly repressed but increasingly booming consumer goods sector. Buck (2012) demonstrates just how crucial the TVEs were to China's early reform, avoiding the economic shock of big-bang style change by soaking up surplus rural labour and allowing restrained market competition to function inside the plan. In this way, despite their distinctive paces, rural (faster) and urban (slower) reforms can still be viewed as a singular process. Total TVE employment formed 135 million by 1996, while almost 60m of these were still genuinely 'collective' (state-owned) enterprises despite widespread privatisations during the mid-1990s (Huang 2008, 79). But during their first decade, the TVEs on the whole acted to transfer resources within the state sector, rather than representing any substantial economic privatisation. Deng described them as an accidental development, 'as though an army had appeared from nowhere' (cited in Ang 2016, 82). A great deal of the early success of the TVEs must be accounted for by the sellers' market in light manufactured consumer goods that Mao's 'big push' strategy of heavy industrialisation strategy and repressed consumerism had created (Naughton 2007, 332). Much of the TVE sector during these early days acted to bolster big SOEs in industrial cities, by supplying them with dirt cheap industrial inputs worked up by peasants in the surrounding countryside.

While TVEs took the economic pressure off urban-based state firms, political difficulties also rendered urban economic reforms more limited in scope, and private firms in the cities employed less than 10m by the end of the 1980s. Firms were restricted to hiring less than 8 workers (apparently due to Deng's interpretation of a passage in Marx's *Capital, Volume III*) and these—largely service-oriented firms like restaurants and shops given the scalar constraints—could not consequently form a basis for sustained industrial development. Instead, the special sanctions on enterprise given to TVEs interacted unexpectedly with another set of urban-oriented liberalisations considered 'safe' by Beijing: special economic zones (SEZs) for foreign investment established in the coastal cities of Shenzhen, Zhuhai, Shantou and Xiamen in 1979.

Geopolitical legacies profoundly structured the peculiar macroeconomic spatial matrix which these global investment flows encountered once China began to open its economy. The 1964 Gulf of Tonkin incident, the spark for the Vietnam war where the Vietnamese navy was accused of sinking a US warship, had alerted Mao to how industry was concentrated along China's coastal seaboards and its potential vulnerability to sea invasion. In response, he engineered a radical investment programme in China's geographically isolated inland provinces: from 1963 to 1975 over 40% of China's total national investment capital was sunk into inland defence and infrastructure projects (Naughton 1988)—an astonishing achievement for a deeply poor economy. At its height during the middle period of the Vietnam War, the Third Front project accounted for almost the entirety of new industrial capital investments—and involved the physical dismantling of numerous coastal plants and their transportation to and reassembly in China's interior.

In what can only be regarded as a fortunate historical accident, the economic starvation of once wealthy coastal regions engendered by the Third Front project unintentionally primed them for investment as the economy began to liberalise at the end of the 1970s—by freeing them from the burden of capital sunk into increasingly anachronistic state-owned capital goods and arms factories. This allowed their prime locational attributes to form the basis for a new round of investment based on foreign capital and imported advanced technology (Tsai 2005). Foreign-invested private firms were free to hire workers and manufacture for profit in these spatially delimited zones, which multiplied during the decade. But FDI, which first flowed mainly from Hong Kong garment firms to Shenzhen (and to a lesser extent the other three SEZs) began to overspill its bounds into semi-rural areas, leading to nearby TVEs being surreptitiously established as or converted into 'red hat' enterprises—ostensibly state-owned but effectively private firms producing goods for production networks or direct export (Tsai 2005). Already, these were far from the model of 'non-capitalist market economy' collectivism celebrated by Arrighi (2009, 361). Subcontracting networks formed rapidly and between 1980 and 1990, TVEs produced two thirds of all China's new export goods for world markets (Zweig 1997). In 1998, Guangdong—the most export oriented of China's provinces—was home to 1.3 million TVEs, a small minority of which earned US$18bn worth of foreign exchange through sales abroad (Sasuga 2004, 56).

On the basis of SEZs and TVE-led industrialisation, the interior bias of the 1960s–1970s Third Front industrialisation was completely reversed again by 1990 as 'the old industrial regions experienced slow growth, [and] several coastal provinces — Shandong, Jiangsu, Zhejiang, Fujian, and Guangdong... emerged as a new growth core' (Fan and Sun 2008, 12). It also produced what Au (2012) terms a 'bureaucratic capitalist' class at the local level of these regions—ostensibly independent of nominally private TVEs but incentivised to encourage their growth—both formally by growth targets and tax revenues, and informally by their illicit business interests in such ventures. Although the positive experience with SEZs surprised the Party leadership, overall reform remained contained during the 1980s—limited by the dominance of the reformists' rural focus. Westad (2012, 454) cautions against exaggerating the 1980s reforms. By the end of the decade, and despite the SEZ and TVE successes:

> The vast majority of workers were still employed in state-owned companies that functioned according to planned economy principles. After leaving school, people were assigned to a work unit where they were supposed to stay for life. Their wages were negligible... there was no labor market. There was no capital market. Bank loans were out of reach for ordinary people.

And the paradox of TVE-led rural industrialisation and the continuing legacy of socialist urbanism was manifest in the 'under-urbanisation' that still afflicted China by 1990, when nearly 75% of the population still resided in the countryside—a proportion basically unchanged since the founding of the PRC. Across China, in the spring and summer of 1989, demonstrations erupted again, partly in response to the inflationary pressures created by higher grain prices that negatively affected urban workers trapped in urban SOES facing deteriorating terms of trade with farmers and new rural industry. Further pursuit of reform required an urban bias that shifted the balance towards extracting surpluses from the countryside, and greater economic openness in order to technologically upgrade the still retrograde urban industrial base.

4.4.2 Reform and Opening in the 1990s

The Tiananmen Square killings sparked a protracted political confrontation at the apex of the CCP (Zhang et al. 2001). With the government facing international isolation and heavy sanctions, the successive downfall of Soviet states, and huge foreign capital flight, reform stalled. Economic collapse loomed and neoconservatives on the central committee—led by Chen Yun and Yao Yilin—responded to the crisis by mounting an intense challenge to reform and demanding a return to the plan. Capturing the leadership of the central bank, the propaganda department and other key ministries, they launched a public campaign blaming 'bourgeois liberalisation' for the political crisis, and directly targeted Deng's reforms (Zhao 1993).

Deng, however—drawing on success in creating local patronage groups for reform—mobilised the 'vehemence of the provincial opposition to fiscal recentralization' on central committee debates (Shirk 1993, 195) and successfully resolved the crisis in favour of the reformists in 1992. His February 'southern tour' of the export processing zones politically legitimated the new private economy and gained widespread positive media coverage. The greater danger, he argued, lay in retreating to the plan rather than deepening reform—and the embryonic formation of an export-oriented cadre-capitalist class proved sufficiently advanced and politically constituted at the national level to support his case. The 14th Party Congress in October approved measures to encourage foreign trade, raise growth targets, allow much greater private sector development, and to move towards the establishment of a 'socialist market economy' (Fan 2007, 100). This designation was highly controversial in China, but reformers' post-Tiananmen victory allowed membership talks with the GATT (soon to become the WTO) that had been launched in the 1980s to be renewed in November 1992. During first phase of China's combined development, then, the politics of a reformist hegemonic project defeated neoconservative economic interests. But Deng and his allies won only by presenting a vision of how catch-up development might rescue the party from the unfolding political and social crises in the postcommunist states—which meant his victory was always predicated upon making political concessions to the Party's proprietors.

Deepening reform was ineffectual without economic opening, however—also profoundly threatened by China's pariah status in the aftermath of 1989. But in spite of the proliferation of an international relations policy discourse of democratisation, human rights promotion, and associated 'post-sovereignty' norms during the 1990s, the events of Tiananmen Square did not ultimately derail the normalisation of Sino-US relations—though they remained on ice until 1997. Jiang Zemin's foreign minister, Qiang Qisheng, worked on a diplomatic charm offensive aimed at dismantling sanctions imposed in 1989 and had already scored significant successes with the US, Europe and Japan by the end of 1990 (Garver 2016). Diplomacy alone could not explain this success, and elements of the US state were clearly never enthusiastic about sanctions in the first place. Presidents Bush and Clinton's judgements, along with the Treasury and the Department of Commerce (cf. Breslin 2013, 94), was that trade and political channels should remain as open as politically possible since economic growth and commercial relations were the best antidote to authoritarianism. In an extraordinary op-ed published in the *Washington Post* just three weeks after the Tiananmen massacre, Henry

Kissinger—keen, perhaps, to rescue the legacy of his earlier diplomacy—argued that sanctions on China recently agreed by the US Congress were counterproductive, because 'punishing a country for past actions is bound to backfire'.

Despite tough talk from Clinton in the runup to his first presidential victory, an effective thawing of US-Sino relations coincided with the near meltdown of the Japanese economy in 1994–1995. This crisis prompted the United States to abandon its attempts to revive domestic manufacturing and enact a 'reverse' Plaza Accord—revaluing the dollar against the yen and so reviving East Asian export competitiveness. While Japan was the trigger, the result was 'de facto abandonment of any real attempt on the part of the United States to stand up to ever more powerful competition from East Asia, ultimately centered in China, and its all out embrace instead of integrated international production by way of supply chains, foreign direct investment and the re-location of industry to lower wage venues, not least China' (Brenner 2009, 19; cf. Desai 2013). China duly continued to receive 'Most Favoured Nation' status from the United States (formally decoupled from 'human rights issues' in 1994), significantly lowering tariffs for manufactured exports and paving the way for its export boom of the 1990s and 2000s. In this way, the geopolitical economy of the US' shifting accumulation strategy towards finance, legal services and high-tech R&D based manufacturing intersected with China's internal politics to accord China a vital second chance at integration into global manufacturing networks.

Despite the successful overtures made to foreign governments, the political liberalism that had accompanied economic relaxation in 1980s China perished. In its wake came a system of renewed and austere authoritarian rule, now flexibly refitted to accommodate further private investment from the increasingly dynamic and globally networked capitalist economy of the 1990s—which China's leaders became serious about joining. But given the reformists' increasing cognisance of China's primary comparative advantage, cheap labour, they could not afford for the negative social impact of reforms to go persistently challenged by a restive civil society aiming to defend the social compact developed under Maoism.

The significance of Tiananmen in this regard, argues Wang Chaohua (2015, 28), was that it:

> Relieved the burden of debt that Deng had owed to popular support since 1976. He could now proceed with a programme of reform that would pose no challenge to the party's authority — especially not on the terrain of socialist principles. Tiananmen thus paved the way for China's integration into the global capitalist system.

In this context, Jiang Zemin and Zhu Rongji's subsequent decade of rule represented the closest approximation to Washington Consensus-type neoliberalism China has experienced. Corporate governance at SOEs was devolved to the company level as central plan withered to a few essential goods, and profit, rather than fulfilment, became the key performance metric. Over fifty million SOE workers were laid off during the decade to 2000—an astonishing near one-third of the total urban labour force (Naughton 2007)—as part of an effort to 'smash the iron rice bowl' and introduce state firms to the strictures of market discipline. SOEs, previously responsible for the consumption and welfare needs of their employees under the *danwei* system (cf. Andreas 2019), were permitted to grant time-limited (rather than lifetime) contracts, and a raft of state-owned *danwei* housing was sold off during the late 1990s. The agricultural bias of the 1980s reforms was decisively reversed, as farmers were persistently squeezed by lower grain prices to provide cheaper inputs and a migrant labour pool for the cities. Hung (2015), for instance, calculates a near doubling of the urban-rural income inequality ratio between 1980 and 2009 (from 1.8 to 3.3), mostly accounted for by the decade of the 1990s. The system of dual-track pricing (that allowed SOEs to retain earnings from goods produced surplus to the plan and sold on the open market) effectively ended as the state stopped setting procurement prices for most goods. And from 1997, TVEs—the protagonists of the 1980s growth spurt—and small urban state firms were privatised *en masse* in a radical programme of 'grasping the large, letting go of the small' (Garnaut et al. 2006). Finally, China's banking system was twice reformed in 1994 and 1998, from its Soviet model towards one based on 'international methods of corporate governance'—though this process was never completed (Walter and Howie 2011, 34).

Still lacking the domestic capital, technology and managerial expertise to pursue a major industrialisation drive, the necessity of securing foreign investment, exchange, technology and know-how lay behind much of this economic liberalisation (Gallagher 2005). Boosting the export sector seemed the most assured means of dealing with 1993's balance of payments crisis (Hung 2015, 69), so the renminbi was sharply devalued from 5.76 to 8.62 US$ and tax rebates offered for exports (Zhu and Kotz 2011, 21). This proved hugely successful, with FDI accounting for 17% of gross fixed capital formation in 1994, and exports consistently generating more than 18% of China's GDP from 1994 onwards (this figure would increase even more dramatically after 2000). These aggregate figures, moreover, significantly underestimate the significance of FDI to China's emergent export hubs. In 1993, China's coastal cities received 87% of total FDI inflows (Yeh 2000, 49), quickly rendering their economies almost totally dependent on export-oriented manufacturing. By 2000, a third of China's total manufacturing was carried out by foreign-invested enterprises (FIEs) (Andreas 2008, 130). And this new, foreign capital-permeated private sector enjoyed a considerably higher return on assets than the state sector, which suffered from chronically low profits and persistent overcapacity troubles (Lardy 2014; Hung 2008, 166).

The ready availability of FDI—a product of rising outsourcing practices in other East Asian states and the existence of a large regional Overseas Chinese population with surplus capital to invest—further incentivised the Chinese leadership in the direction of overseas investment (Gallagher 2005). But the motivations for turning to specifically foreign investment were unlikely purely economic. The focus on the mobilisation of foreign, rather than domestic, capital, also allowed rapid private sector-led industrial development to continue while having the politically advantageous effect of forestalling the formation of a politically independent domestic capitalist class (cf. Heartfield 2005). As Harvey (2005, 123) writes: this 'heavy reliance upon foreign direct investment... has kept the power of capitalist class ownership offshore'. And from the mid-1990s, concerted efforts were made to incorporate what new (onshore) private capitalists that did emerge into the political parameters of Party rule—allowing direct membership of the Chinese Communist Party, various official resolutions on representing entrepreneurs (Jiang's 'Three Represents') who were allowed to form chambers of commerce, and encouraging local governments to form direct ('crony') relationships with significant private economic players in their localities (Dickson 2008). This small-scale, offshore capital-dominated and politically subordinate capitalist class could not sink state-led development efforts by threatening the autonomy of state industrial policy, as did powerful national bourgeoisies in emerging economies like India, Turkey and Brazil (Chibber 2003).

Another reason the textbook version of economic liberalism did not materialise was the second major political development of the 1990s: a political reconstitution of the economic conservative faction on the national leadership, following their defeat in 1992. Influenced by a miscellany of 'New Leftist', economic nationalist, and rehabilitated Maoist political thought, conservatives abandoned their failed earlier attempts to restore the plan, and instead oriented themselves around a critique of the economic decentralisation which had occurred during the 1980s. This, they argued—drawing on a study of China's failing 'state capacity' first published in 1992 by Wang Shaoguang and Hu Angang (1993)—now precipitated a potential fiscal collapse of government revenues and threatened 'stability', the new legitimation discourse pressed by Deng (cf. Fewsmith 2008). Given that further privatisations and liberal reforms appeared inevitable, their main objectives shifted to strengthening the fiscal health of the central state (especially in the aftermath of the Asian currency crises of 1997/1998), protecting the interests of the state sector (as far as possible within the obvious constraints of Zhu's liberalisation drive), and ensuring economic reform did not slide again towards democratisation. Each successive step towards liberalisation was fiercely contested by an increasingly consolidated faction of conservatives in the central government, conscious of the growing risk to them and their patronage networks in the state sector.

Walter and Howie (2011) demonstrate how this logic played out within the banking sector. A wave of non-performing loans led to the creation of asset management companies in 1997–1998 which took on the failing loans, while the big four state banks were recapitalised and floated on international markets. Attracting 'blue chip strategic investors as Bank of America and Goldman Sachs.... brought in less for their money than for the expertise', banks appeared to be converging on an Anglo-Saxon model (Walter and Howie 2011, 54). But conservatives resisted what they perceived as the 'imperialist' takeover of national assets, ultimately derailing Zhu's planned restructuring by restricting flotations to well below global norms and creating a 'fortress banking system'. The result was a set of far more efficiently governed and corporatised banks, but still owned by the state and often (though now *less* often) forced to lend with little commercial consideration to state-owned enterprises. While the conservatives could not win, they remained sufficiently powerful to stalemate successive reform drives and shore up financing for SOEs, their personal 'cash machines' (Walter and Howie 2011, 24).

A major concession the conservatives extracted early in the Zhu-Jiang leadership period was the establishment of a new fiscal contract between central and local governments. The explosion of FDI during the 1990s deepened the extraordinary decentralisation of power that had begun during the 1980s, by further increasing the economic significance of the coastal regions. Because the central state was primarily financed by remittances from SOEs under the plan, the rise of private and semi-private firms allowed local governments to retain tax revenues they generated during the 1980s—incentivising subnational governments to encourage private sector economic growth. These had consequently competed to attract manufacturing clusters into their jurisdictions with tax breaks and rebates, proactively finding suppliers and customers, and developing industrial park infrastructure (Oi 1995). But the conservatives' reaction to this—drawing on Wang and Hu's aforementioned text—resulted in the institution of a new fiscal system in 1994. The 1994 Tax Sharing Reform aimed to upset this arrangement by instituting a more standardised taxation system, based upon Local Taxation Bureaus established at every scale of the state (accountable to the central government), which remitted all collected funds upwards to Beijing and reallocated them in accordance with new centrally stipulated ratios (Li and Yang 2014).

However, this transition between taxation regimes was far from smooth—since it stripped local governments of around a third of their total revenues overnight. A 1993 subnational government surplus of 6bn yuan was turned into a deficit of 172.6bn yuan in 1994 (Li and Yang 2014, 5). The intention was to plug the gap with transfer payments from central government, but these proved chronically irregular in practice and frequently failed to cover the funding hole over the following years. Adding to this difficulty was the absence of a centralised social security net, with local governments responsible for virtually all social spending. The result was what Kroeber (2016) terms 'unfunded mandates': the growing social service bills facing local governments in the post-*danwei* era, which now possessed little means to fund them. The outcome (almost surely not the intention of conservative champions of 'state capacity') was an explosion of extra-budgetary revenue collection by local governments scrabbling for cash. This acted to deepen competition by authorities to attract manufacturing firms into their jurisdictions, but now in order to levy semi-licit fees and charges on them. And this ultimately scuppered recentralisation efforts in some aspects—by 2012, 85% of total government spending was undertaken by provincial and lower tier governments

(Kroeber 2016), offering the central state little direct control over social security and industrial policy spending.

A second unintended effect of the tax reshuffle was to further reinforce the 'urban bias' of future reform. Looking for revenues, local states learned that their monopoly of urban land-use rights (saleable on lease since the separation of [state] ownership from usage rights in 1988) meant they could extract huge rents from developing land and turning it over to private leasers. Industrialisation in cities had secondary effects in boosting economic activity in the services, construction, and consumption sectors, further enhancing revenue growth for city governments. Urban development thus came gradually to replace the prior industrial corporatism of local governments, and by the late 2000s, as Hsing (2010, 9) puts it, 'urban land-use planning has replaced economic planning as the main vehicle of state intervention in the local political economy'. The legacy of the rural TVEs was especially significant in (still formally) rural areas like much of Guangdong province, since the special permission required to rezone agricultural land for industrial usage was not required by villages possessing enterprises—enabling the widespread emergence of 'urban villages' in formerly agricultural areas.[3]

Together, these developments (economic decentralisation, and local governments hungry for fee payments from either manufacturers or land-use sales) helped further congeal the distinctive bureaucratic capitalist class that had begun to form in the export-oriented areas. This class—comprised of both 'embourgeoised' local party cadres and 'politicized' capitalists (political only insofar as they were guided by patronage relations with local government; So 2003), and based primarily in coastal areas—became incentivised to deepen reform and opening in order to sustain economic openness and thus export growth. But because cadres and capitalists were overwhelmingly small firms tied to particular local governments (a Hong Kong investor with a factory in Shenzhen, for instance, was most likely to enjoy *guanxi* relations with the local village or township government), the system enforced territorial competition at the lowest levels and delimited this class fraction's influence over national-level politics (in Korea, by contrast, exporters in giant *chaebols* enjoyed a

[3]While urban land was privileged by reform, then, rural land in geographically prime areas with existing commercial enterprises could be quickly converted for industrial usage in places like Shenzhen and Dongguan, with the interesting side-effect of massively enriching local villagers (see Saich and Hu 2012).

close working relationship with the national government and considerable influence over national policymaking). Despite the perverse effects of tax reform, then, decentralisation was not total. Central state revenues improved significantly, and local governments became in practice legally subordinated to and incentivised by central policy edicts in a way that had not been the case in the 1980s (Lim 2016)—though this power shift was not particularly conspicuous while the growth imperative dominated policy at all levels and central–local interests largely aligned. As Wang (2016, 34) writes, local governments became judged by Beijing mostly on their economic performance 'with specific criteria for attracting outside investment (*zhaoshang yin zi*). Tellingly, there were no equivalent criteria for either education or healthcare'.

This points to the third major factor that enabled the takeoff process of China's combined development: the formation of a migrant working class. While in the early 1990s the *hukou* household registration system, which restricted migration (effectively criminalised until 2002) and tied social security payments to birthplace, might have appeared as an anachronism of the plan in an export-industrialising economy, it increasingly came to form a structural feature of China's accumulation system. As the demand for labour in coastal cities boomed, and the urban bias placed the agrarian economy under immense strain, workers arriving in the new factories found themselves without access to any form of welfare and—at least initially—precarity engendered by the threat of deportation and police harassment. Low wages and lack of social protections led to the phenomenon of the 'dormitory labour regime' where workers live on factory premises; while often spending significant periods of the year during unemployed spells returning to the family farm in the hinterland—what Lu and Pun (2010) term 'incomplete proletarianization'.

For export manufacturers, the appearance of this labour force seemed a virtual lucky accident; while local governments were little incentivised to pursue welfare rollouts for migrant citizens whose presence they viewed as alien and temporary. But the central state's decision to retain the *hukou* system in the constructing of a new social welfare programme effectively transformed it into a tool of biopolitical control over the new migrant labour force, aimed at ensuring a pliant pool of workers for export manufacturing industries (Wang 2010). The agrarian roots of this private sector workforce should be especially emphasised, since a common trope regarding the attractiveness of China's cheap, disciplined labour force for global capital significantly overstates the extent to which it came ready-made. Rather than disciplined industrial workers marching from state factories to Foxconn assembly lines, the working class in the export sector was overwhelmingly rural and had to be made (or 'habituated') in E. P. Thompson's sense (2013; cf. Walker and Buck 2007; Henderson and Cohen 1980) in the countryside—through the urban wage differential, the manipulation of grain prices and agricultural taxes, alongside outright land dispossessions. The 1990s reforms (by calculated policy and unintended consequences) reconfigured capital, land, and labour in a form highly attractive to external capital.

4.5 The WTO and the Revival of Statist Politics

In the runup to joining the WTO in 2001, policymaking and the balance of power at the national scale—influenced by the uneven geographic development unleashed by the emergence of coastal export hubs—swung dramatically between liberal advances and conservative reaction. This highly unstable institutional environment contributed to continuing weaknesses in China's growth model. China had averaged annual increases of 10.1% in GDP from 1993 to 2000. But this was from a chronically low base, and China's industrial level remained low by world standards. Garver (2016, 357) strikingly illustrates this point:

> [China's technological backwardness] was brought home to me in the mid-1990s... on a tour of the First Automobile Works (FAW) in Changchun, Jilin... China's first large-scale automobile and truck factory, set up with Soviet assistance in the early 1950s. As it turned out, the factory we visited was still producing trucks based on designs supplied by the Soviet Union in the early 1950s. Those Soviet designs had, in turn, been based on General Motor's designs of the late 1930s. This meant that in the mid-1990s China's leading truck manufacturer was... producing obsolete vehicles in an extremely inefficient manner and foisting its inferior product on end users by government fiat and protectionism.

And as Yue (2016) observes, China's growth itself was running out of steam in the late 1990s. In 2000, capital flight measured US$48bn, and actually exceeded total FDI inflows to China by $8bn: a net loss. Growth, meanwhile, slowed substantially to 7.1% in 1999; and China's immense efforts to avoid competitive devaluations during the 1997–1998 Asian crisis by selling foreign exchange vindicated its mercantilist policy of stockpiling dollars—something that could only be achieved through greater export promotion (Panitch and Gindin 2012). Reformers had learned that exposure of (sectors of) the economy to world market forces represented a critical means of boosting competitiveness, absorbing technology and know-how, and earning foreign exchange. In this environment, accelerating the pursuit of WTO membership appeared less a choice than the logical conclusion of the growth-based social compact forged after Tiananmen. In this sense, it was not 'economic success in the 1990s that naturally led to China's deep integration, but the predicament in the country's reform and industrialization that forced China to join the WTO at the earliest possible time to keep the economy growing' (Yue 2016, 17). And joining the WTO proved undoubtedly successful in the medium term: contracted foreign direct investment quadrupled from 1999–2005 to $160bn a year (Branstetter and Lardy 2008, 642), while overall GDP growth trended sharply upwards over the following 7 years, hitting 14% in 2007–2008. The number of foreign-invested enterprises almost doubled from 2000–2008 to 434,937 (*NBS* various years), while its export volume (in current US$) exploded from US$249bn in 2000 to US$1.4tn in 2008 (*World Bank*, n.d.). On every conceivable conventional growth metric, then, joining the WTO proved a success.

If the material incentive to continue driving reform and opening was clear, politically, the reformers viewed WTO membership as a means of consolidating opening in the aftermath of Deng's death in 1997—acting as it would to lock in existing liberalisations and to commit China to a roadmap of further reform through binding international agreement. As Zhu Rongji put it in a speech in Washington in 1999, 'the competition arising [from WTO membership] will also promote a more rapid and more healthy development of China's national economy' (cited in Branstetter and Lardy 2008, 650). And the terms exacted from China were not insubstantial. Post-reverse Plaza Accord, when the United States engineered a strengthening of the dollar in part as a means of rescuing the Japanese economy, the US embrace of globalised production directed by its MNCs relied critically on the greatly strengthened institutional framework of the WTO (compared with the looseness of the GATT). The strength of the US intent to use the negotiations to prise open the Chinese economy was signified by the response to a Chinese delegation visit to the US in April 1999, where the Clinton administration outright rejected Zhu's proposals for WTO membership—despite the terms being dubbed by the lead US negotiator argued were 'broader actually than any World Trade Organization member has made' (cited in Panitch and Gindin 2012, 293). The United States was forced into a U-turn six months later in order to restore relations under threat by the blow-back from the US bombing of the Chinese embassy in Belgrade (Garver 2016, 651). But this was no real climbdown, since the agreement offered foreign investors legal protection on their investments, means of profit repatriation (limited) legal and intellectual property rights guarantees, and opened China's bond markets, telecommunications, financial services and infrastructure sectors to foreign capital.

But the victorious reformists shared far more political ground with their conservative domestic rivals than the forces of international capital. As such, if the overarching US aim was to secure market access for its firms to China, then its facilitation of China's WTO membership application came replete with unintended consequences. The flood of world manufacturing capacity into China, which dramatically captured market share against virtually every other major exporting state enabled the reformers scope to experiment with industrial policy in novel ways. Beneath the appearance of gradual convergence with global standards for investment, China began to implement a powerful, though surreptitious, process of *reregulating* industries considered of 'strategic value' to the state (Hsueh 2011). The textile sector, for instance, was largely ignored by central government industrial policy during the 2000s after state production of clothing had been mostly wound down during the 1980s and 1990s. But in the case of automobiles (to take one example), a wave of investment from foreign automakers who entered China *en masse* after 2001 aiming to take advantage of cheap semiskilled labour and improving connectivity and infrastructural provision gave policymakers considerable autonomy to experiment with industrial policy. The auto industry grew 60% year on year from 2001 to 2004—and within a decade, the PRC went from producing fewer cars than Canada to more than any other country (Panitch and Gindin 2012, 294). 'Order No. 8' passed by the new National Development and Reform Commission in 2004 stipulated a full-blown industrial policy for indigenous car production, including ensuring a 50% market share for domestic carmakers by 2010 and insisted on a minimum 40% domestic content of components for cars assembled in China. The EU, Canada and the USA filed complaints against with the WTO's Dispute Settlement Body in 2006, which two years later found in the complainants' favour (cf. Lam 2009). But Chinese regulators simply modified the legislation and established locally rather than nationally scaled subsidies for technology procurement (Hsueh 2011, 220–221), routing subsidies through provincial banks or bank subsidiaries and rendering them far harder to trace. Rather than acting as a mere instrument of US power, then, WTO procedures often acted to shield China from unilateral action by the US and other wealthy economies. The gravitational pull of cheap labour gave China the political autonomy to circumvent the spirit of WTO regulations in myriad ways, even as it gave the appearance of their observance (a trend, it should be noted, not unique to Chinese state managers). And this policy autonomy was compounded by China's 'developing country' status at the WTO which further shielded it from complaints (Strange 2011).

This new activist private sector industrial policy was one side-effect of the paradoxical strengthening of conservatism which WTO membership brought about, embodied by the Hu Jintao Wen Jiabao (Hu-Wen) leadership from 2003 and its focus on 'Scientific Development'. This was based upon a concerted central state decision to deploy the 'legacy institutions' of the plan in service of the new market economy (cf. Heilmann and Melton 2013). Another outcome was the creation of the National Development and Reform Commission (NDRC) in 2003 (a 'nodal agency' in the vein of Japan's Ministry of International Trade and Industry) tasked with identifying sectors with strategic political and economic value; and the creation of the State-Owned Assets Supervision and Administration Commission (SASAC), a holding company for large, centrally-owned state-owned enterprises aimed at 'increasing the professionalism and capacity of state efforts to govern the economy' (Pearson 2005, 320). Thus the stratospheric leap forwards in the export sector and inward investment developed in lockstep with a political strengthening of the conservative hand inside the national leadership, and an incremental shoring up of SOEs throughout the 2000s (Eaton 2015). The means by which China's Maoist party-state were deployed in the management of private capital accumulation suggests that processes of institutional 'drift' and 'conversion' identified by Hacker et al. (2015)—whereby existing and apparently anachronistic institutions find new uses—have been operative in the Chinese case.

4.6 Conclusion

On its tenth anniversary, *The Economist* (2011) celebrated China's WTO accession as a gamble from advanced economies that had paid off: it had 'blossomed into the world's greatest exporter and second-biggest importer. The marriage of foreign know-how, Chinese labour and the open, global market has succeeded beyond anyone's predictions'. Just a year later, the same publication would lead with a warning that China was not merely a free market success story but an increasingly dangerous example of 'state capitalism'—using the façade of corporate capitalism in pursuit of cronyism (*The Economist* 2012). Aspects of both pictures were accurate. The ultimate outcome of the WTO facilitated export boom of the 2000s was to mediate a political compromise between conservatives and liberals—in which a part of the proceeds of the booming export sector would be siphoned off and used to retool the significantly less profitably state sector. State enterprises were not reformed out of existence but repurposed along competitive lines. And the political control of the CCP was also consolidated, as the *nomenklatura* system of personnel management was gave each government department was shadowed by a corresponding division of the Party (McGregor 2010). In this way, China's mode of integration into the global economy shaped, but did not predetermine, the trajectory of Chinese capitalism.

The political strategy of state managers guided reform and opening from the out, which meant it was not reducible to the unfolding of an economic teleology or the outcome of an inevitable neoliberal transition. And this political strategy was itself thoroughly shaped by geopolitical motivations, since the competitive logic of territoriality drove China to pursue economic modernisation: in forms that leaned towards, but plainly did not repeat, the forms of catch-up development previously undertaken in East Asia. The analysis, then, corroborates Rosenberg's (2013, 572) claim that UCD represents a 'social theory of the international', which can 'identify aspects of social causality deriving specifically from the fact of societal multiplicity'. But applying the theory has also focused attention on why and with what effects China experienced the confluence of two very different forms of capitalist production: on the one side, the flexible accumulation of fragmented production networks, which reformers had done so much to attract to Chinese territory and were deeply implanted in coastal manufacturing cities; on the other, the remaining significance of large, vertically integrated state-owned heavy industry—subsidised by banks flush with revenues from the export sector. The next chapter further elaborates this hypothesis by mapping the contours of this accumulation system as it developed during the 2000s.

References

Anderson, Perry. 2010. Two Revolutions. *New Left Review* 61 (1): 59–96.

Andreas, Joel. 2008. Changing Colours in China. *New Left Review* 2 (54): 123–142.

Andreas, Joel. 2019. *Disenfranchised: The Rise and Fall of Industrial Citizenship in China*. Oxford: Oxford University Press.

Ang, Yuen Yuen. 2016. *How China Escaped the Poverty Trap*. New York: Cornell University Press.

Arrighi, Giovanni. 2009. *The Long Twentieth Century: Money, Power, and the Origins of Our Times*. London: Verso.

Au, Loong-Yu. (ed.). 2012. *China's Rise: Strength and Fragility*. London: Resistance.

Bernard, Mitchell, and John Ravenhill. 1995. Beyond Product Cycles and Flying Geese: Regionalization, Hierarchy, and the Industrialization of East Asia. *World Politics* 47 (2): 171–209.

Branstetter, Lee, and Nicholas Lardy. 2008. China's Embrace of Globalization. In *China's Great Economic Transformation*, ed. Loren Brandt and Thomas G. Rawski, 633–682. Cambridge: Cambridge University Press.

Brenner, Neil. 2004. *New State Spaces: Urban Governance and the Rescaling of Statehood*. Oxford: Oxford University Press.

Brenner, Robert. 2006. *The Economics of Global Turbulence*. London: Verso.

Brenner, Robert. 2009. What's Good for Goldman Sachs Is Good for America: The Origins of the Current Crisis. Preface to the Spanish edition of *The Economics of Global Turbulence*. Available online at: http://www.sscnet.ucla.edu/issr/cstch/papers/BrennerCrisisTodayOctober2009.pdf. Accessed 25 June 2017.

Brenner, Robert, and Mark Glick. 1991. The Regulation Approach: Theory and History. *New Left Review* 188: 45–119.

Breslin, Shaun. 2007. Beyond the Disciplinary Heartlands: Studying China's International Political Economy. In *China's Reforms and International Political Economy*, ed. David Zweig and Zhimin Chen, 21–41. London: Routledge.

Breslin, Shaun. 2013. *China and the Global Political Economy*. Basingstoke: Palgrave.

Buck, Daniel. 2012. *Constructing China's Capitalism Shanghai and the Nexus of Urban-Rural Industries*. New York: Palgrave.

Chang, Ha-Joon. 2002. *Kicking Away the Ladder: Development Strategy in Historical Perspective*. London: Anthem Press.

Chaohua, Wang. 2015. The Party and Its Success Story: A Response to Two Revolutions. *New Left Review* 2 (91): 5–38.

Chen, Ju-chen. 2009. Capital Dreams: Global Consumption, Urban Imagination, and Labor Migration in Late Socialist Beijing. PhD thesis, State University of New Jersey, Rutgers. Available online at: https://search.proquest.com/openview/c76adf0a7dec7bfe779d9823074da212/1?pq-origsite=gscholar&cbl=18750&diss=y. Accessed 17 May 2016.
Chibber, Vivek. 2003. *Locked in Place: State-Building and Late Industrialization in India*. Princeton, NJ: Princeton University Press.
Chin, Gregory. 2007. Between "Outside-In" and "Inside-Out": The Internationalization of the Chinese State. In *China's Reforms and International Political Economy*, ed. David Zweig and Zhimin Chen, 155–170. London: Routledge.
Cumings, Bruce. 1997. *Korea's Place in the Sun: A Modern History*. New York: W. W. Norton.
De Rambures, Dominique. 2014. *The China Development Model: Between the State and the Market*. Basingstoke: Palgrave.
Desai, Radhika. 2013. *Geopolitical Economy: After US Hegemony, Globalization and Empire*. London: Pluto.
Dickson, Bruce. 2008. *Wealth into Power: The Communist Party's Embrace of China's Private Sector*. Cambridge: Cambridge University Press.
Eaton, Sarah. 2015. *The Advance of the State in Contemporary China: State-Market Relations in the Reform Era*. Cambridge: Cambridge University Press.
Fan, Yongming. 2007. How Reform Drove China's Integration into The International Community. In *China's Reforms and International Political Economy*, ed. David Zweig and Zhimin Chen, 97–111. London: Routledge.
Fan, C.C., and Mingjie Sun. 2008. Regional Inequality in China, 1978–2006. *Eurasian Geography and Economics* 49 (1): 1–18.
Fewsmith, Joseph. 2008. *China Since Tiananmen*. Cambridge: Cambridge University Press.
Gallagher, Mary. 2005. *Contagious Capitalism: Globalization and the Politics of Labor in China*. Princeton, NJ: Princeton University Press.
Garnaut, Ross, Ligang Song, and Yang Yao. 2006. Impact and Significance of State-Owned Enterprise Restructuring in China. *China Journal* 55: 35–63.
Garver, John. 2016. *China's Quest: The History of the Foreign Relations of the People's Republic of China*. Oxford: Oxford University Press.
Gereffi, Gary. 1994. The Organization of Buyer-Driven Global Commodity Chains: How US Retailers Shape Overseas Production Networks. In *Commodity Chains and Global Capitalism*, ed. Gary Gereffi and Miguel Korzeniewicz. Westport, CT: Praeger.
Gereffi, Gary. 2014. Global Value Chains in a Post-Washington Consensus World. *Review of International Political Economy* 21 (1): 9–37.
Glassman, Jim. 2004. *Thailand at the Margins: Internationalization of the State and the Transformation of Labour*. Oxford: Oxford University Press.

Glassman, Jim. 2016. Emerging Asias: Transnational Forces, Developmental States, and "Asian Values". *The Professional Geographer* 68 (2): 322–329.

Gowan, Peter. 1999. *Global Gamble: Washington's Faustian Bid for World Dominance*. London: Verso.

Gray, Kevin. 2011. The Social and Geopolitical Origins of State Transformation: The Case of South Korea. *New Political Economy* 16 (3): 303–322.

Gray, Kevin. 2015. *Labour and Development in East Asia: Social Forces and Passive Revolution*. London: Routledge.

Hacker, Jacob, Paul Pierson, and Kathleen Thelen. 2015. Drift and Conversion: Hidden Faces of Institutional Change. In *Advances in Comparative-Historical Analysis: Strategies for Social Inquiry*, ed. James Mahoney and Kathleen Thelen, 180–208. Cambridge: Cambridge University Press.

Harris, Jerry. 2012. Outward Bound: Transnational Capitalism in China. *Race & Class* 54 (1): 13–32.

Harvey, David. 2005. *A Brief History of Neoliberalism*. Oxford: Oxford University Press.

Heartfield, James. 2005. China's Comprador Capitalism Is Coming Home. *Review of Radical Political Economics* 37 (2): 196–214.

Heilmann, Sebastian, and Oliver Melton. 2013. The Reinvention of Development Planning in China, 1993–2012. *Modern China* 39 (6): 580–628.

Henderson, Jeffrey. 1989. *The Globalisation of High Technology Production: Society, Space, and Semiconductors in the Restructuring of the Modern World*. London: Routledge.

Henderson, Jeffrey. 1999. Uneven Crises: Institutional Foundations of East Asian Economic Turmoil. *Economy and Society* 28 (3): 327–368.

Henderson, Jeffrey, and Robin Cohen. 1980. Work, Culture and the Dialectics of Proletarian Habituation. *Papers in Urban & Regional Studies* 3: 3–34.

Henderson, Jeffrey, Peter Dicken, Martin Hess, Neil Coe, and Henry Wai-Chung Yeung. 2002. Global Production Networks and the Analysis of Economic Development. *Review of International Political Economy* 9 (3): 436–464.

Hsing, You-tien. 2010. *The Great Urban Transformation: Politics of Land and Property in China*. Oxford: Oxford University Press.

Hsu, Jinn-yuh. 2009. The Spatial Encounter Between Neoliberalism and Populism in Taiwan: Regional Restructuring Under the DPP Regime in the New Millennium. *Political Geography* 28 (5): 296–308.

Hsueh, Roselyn. 2011. *China's Regulatory State: A New Strategy for Globalization*. Ithaca, NY: Cornell University Press.

Huang, Yasheng. 2008. *Capitalism with Chinese Characteristics: Entrepreneurship and the State*. Cambridge: Cambridge University Press.

Hui, Wang. 2016. *China's Twentieth Century: Revolution, Retreat and the Road to Equality*. Verso Books.

Hung, Ho-fung. 2008. Rise of China and the Global Overaccumulation Crisis. *Review of International Political Economy* 15 (2): 149–179.
Hung, Ho-fung. 2015. *The China Boom: Why China Will Not Rule the World*. Chichester: Columbia University Press.
Jessop, Bob. 2008. *State Power: A Strategic-Relational Approach*. Cambridge: Polity Press.
Jessop, Bob, and Ngai-Ling Sum. 2006. *Beyond the Regulation Approach: Putting Capitalist Economies in Their Place*. Cheltenham: Elgar.
Kaplinsky, Raphael. 2015. Technological Upgrading in Global Value Chains and Clusters and Their Contribution to Sustaining Economic Growth in Low and Middle Income Economies. UNU-MERIT Working Paper Series. Available online at: https://pdfs.semanticscholar.org/6351/e875c5fb671f4c28106c6cb674f81738becc.pdf.
Kaplinsky, Raphael, and Mike Morris. 2016. Thinning and Thickening: Productive Sector Policies in The Era of Global Value Chains. *European Journal of Development Research* 28 (4): 625–645.
Knox, Paul, John Agnew, and Linda McCarthy. 2014. *The Geography of the World Economy*. London: Routledge.
Krätke, Stefan. 2014. Cities in Contemporary Capitalism. *International Journal of Urban and Regional Research* 38 (5): 1660–1677.
Kroeber, Arthur. 2016. *China's Economy: What Everyone Needs to Know*. Oxford: Oxford University Press.
Lam, Ester. 2009. *China and the WTO: A Long March Towards the Rule of Law*. Kluwer Law International BV.
Lardy, Nicholas. 2014. *Markets over Mao: The Rise of Private Business in China*. Washington, DC: Peterson Institute.
Li, Minqi. 2016. *China and the Twenty-First Century Crisis*. London: Pluto.
Li, Linda, and Zhenjie Yang. 2014. What Causes the Local Fiscal Crisis in China: The Role of Intermediaries. *Journal of Contemporary China* 24 (94): 573–593.
Lim, Kean Fan. 2016. Emptying the Cage, Changing the Birds: State Rescaling, Path-Dependency and the Politics of Economic Restructuring in Post-Crisis Guangdong. *New Political Economy* 21 (4): 414–435.
Lim, Kean Fan. 2017. On the Shifting Spatial Logics of Socioeconomic Regulation in Post-1949 China. *Territory, Politics, Governance* 5 (1): 65–91.
Lu, Huilin, and Ngai Pun. 2010. Unfinished Proletarianization: Self, Anger and Class Action Among the Second Generation of Peasant-Workers in Present-Day China. *Modern China* 36: 5.
McNally, Christopher. 2012. Sino-Capitalism: China's Reemergence and the International Political Economy. *World Politics* 64 (4): 741–776.
National Bureau of Statistics (*NBS*). n.d. *Data*. Available online at: http://www.stats.gov.cn/english/. Accessed 11 May 2020.

Naughton, Barry. 1988. The Third Front: Defence Industrialization in the Chinese Interior. *The China Quarterly* 115: 351–386.

Naughton, Barry. 2007. *The Chinese Economy: Transition and growth*. Cambridge, MA: MIT Press.

Naughton, Barry. 2016. Inside and Outside: The Modernized Hierarchy That Runs China. *Journal of Comparative Economics* 44 (2): 404–415.

Oi, Jean. 1995. The Role of the Local State in China's Transitional Economy. *The China Quarterly* 144: 1132–1149.

Panitch, Leo, and Sam Gindin. 2012. *The Making of Global Capitalism*. London: Verso.

Pantsov, Alexander. 2015. *Deng Xiaoping: A Revolutionary Life*. Oxford: Oxford University Press.

Pearson, Margaret. 2005. The Business of Governing Business in China: Institutions and Norms of the Emerging Regulatory State. *World Politics* 57 (2): 296–322.

Pirie, Iain. 2007. *The Korean Developmental State: From Dirigisme to Neo-liberalism*. London: Routledge.

Pirie, Iain. 2013. Globalisation and the Decline of the Developmental State. In *Beyond the Developmental State: Industrial Policy into the Twenty-First Century*, ed. Ben Fine, Jyoti Saraswati, and Daniela Tavasci, 146–169. London: Pluto.

Richard, McGregor. 2010. *The Party: The Secret World of China's Communist Rulers*. New York: HarperCollins.

Riskin, Carl. 1987. *China's Political Economy: The Quest for Development Since 1949*. Oxford: Oxford University Press.

Roberts, Michael. 2016. *The Long Depression: Marxism and the Global Crisis of Capitalism*. Chicago: Haymarket.

Rosenberg, Justin. 2013. The 'Philosophical Premises' of Uneven and Combined Development. *Review of International Studies* 39 (3): 569–597.

Ruggie, John. 1982. International Regimes, Transactions, and Change: Embedded Liberalism in the Postwar Economic Order. *International Organization* 36 (2): 379–415.

Saad-Filho, Alfredo. 2014. The Rise of the South. In *Polarising Development: Alternatives to Neoliberalism and the Crisis*, ed. Lucia Pradella and Thomas Marois, 62–73. London: Pluto Press.

Saich, Tony, and Hu Biliang. 2012. *Chinese Village, Global Market: New Collectives and Rural Development*. New York: Palgrave Macmillan.

Sassen, Saskia. 2001. *The Global City*. Princeton: Princeton University Press.

Sassen, Saskia. 2006. *Territory, Authority, Rights: From Medieval to Global Assemblages*. Princeton, NJ: Princeton University Press.

Sasuga, Katsuhiro. 2004. *Microregionalism and Governance in East Asia*. London: Routledge.

Scott, Allen J. 2012. *A World in Emergence: Cities and Regions in the 21st Century*. Cheltenham: Edward Elgar.
Shaikh, Anwar. 2016. *Capitalism: Competition, Conflict, Crises*. Oxford: Oxford University Press.
Shambaugh, David L. 2008. *China's Communist Party: Atrophy and Adaptation*. Berkeley: University of California Press.
Shaoguang, Wang, and Hu Angang. 1993. *Zhongguo guojia nengli baogao* [A Report on China's State Capacity]. Shenyang: Liaoning renmin chubanshe.
Shirk, Susan. 1993. *The Political Logic of Economic Reform in China*. Berkeley: University of California Press.
So, Alvin Y. 2003. The Changing Pattern of Classes and Class Conflict in China. *Journal of Contemporary Asia* 33 (3): 363–376.
Storper, Michael. 2013. *Keys to the City: How Economics, Institutions, Social Interaction, and Politics Shape Development*. Princeton: Princeton University Press.
Strange, Gerard. 2011. China's Post-Listian Rise: Beyond Radical Globalisation Theory and the Political Economy of Neoliberal Hegemony. *New Political Economy* 16 (5): 539–559.
Stubbs, Richard. 2017. *Rethinking Asia's Economic Miracle: The Political Economy of War, Prosperity and Crisis*. Basingstoke: Palgrave.
Sturgeon, Timothy. 2002. Modular Production Networks: A New American Model of Industrial Organization. *Industrial and Corporate Change* 11 (3): 451–496.
The Economist. 2011. Shades of Grey, December 11. Available online at: http://www.economist.com/node/21541408. Accessed 9 October 2016.
The Economist. 2012. The Rise of State Capitalism, January 21. Available online at: http://www.economist.com/node/21543160. Accessed 24 April 2017.
Thompson, E.P. 2013. *The Making of the English Working Class*. London: Penguin.
Tsai, Kellee. 2005. Capitalists Without a Class: Political Diversity Among Private Entrepreneurs in China. *Comparative Political Studies* 38: 1130–1158.
Vogel, Ezra. 2011. *Deng Xiaoping and the Transformation of China*. Cambridge, MA: Belknap.
Walker, Richard, and Daniel Buck. 2007. The Chinese Road: Cities in the Transition to Capitalism. *New Left Review* 2 (46): 39–66.
Walter, Carl, and Fraser Howie. 2011. *Red Capitalism: The Fragile Financial Foundation of China's Extraordinary Rise*. Chichester: Wiley.
Wang, Fei-ling. 2010. Conflict, Resistance, and the Transformation of the *hukou* System. In *Chinese Society: Change, Conflict & Resistance*, ed. Elizabeth Perry and Mark Selden, 80–100. Oxon: Routledge.
Westad, Odd Arne. 2012. *Restless Empire: China and the World Since 1750*. London: Bodley Head.

Witt, Michael A., and Gordon Redding (eds.). 2014. *The Oxford Handbook of Asian Business Systems*. Oxford: Oxford University Press.

World Bank. 1993. *The East Asian Miracle: Economic Growth and Public Policy*. New York: Oxford University Press.

World Bank. n.d. *Indicators*. Available online at: data.worldbank.org/indicator. Accessed 12 June 2019.

Yang, Dali. 2004. *Remaking the Chinese Leviathan: Market Transition, Political Leadership, and Economic Governance in China*. Stanford: Stanford University Press.

Yeh, Anthony. 2000. Foreign Investment and Urban Development in China. In *China's Regions, Polity, and Economy: A Study of Spatial Transformation in the Post-Reform Era*, ed. Si-ming Li and Wing-shing Tang, 35–64. Hong Kong: Chinese University Press.

Yeung, Henry Wai-chung. 2014. Governing the Market in a Globalizing Era: Developmental States, Global Production Networks and Inter-Firm Dynamics in East Asia. *Review of International Political Economy* 21 (1): 70–101.

Yue, Jianyong. 2016. China, Global Capitalism and the Quest for Legitimacy. *International Politics* 53 (6): 752–774.

Zhang, Liang, Andrew J. Nathan, and Perry Link (eds.). 2001. *The Tiananmen Papers*. New York: Public Affairs.

Zhao, Suisheng. 1993. Deng Xiaoping's Southern Tour: Elite Politics in Post-Tiananmen China. *Asian Survey* 33 (8): 739–756.

Zhu, Andong, and David Kotz. 2011. The Dependence of China's Economic Growth on Exports and Investment. *Review of Radical Political Economics* 43 (1): 9–32.

Zweig, David. 1997. *Freeing China's Farmers: Rural Restructuring in the Reform Era*. London: Routledge.

CHAPTER 5

China's Boom (II): Making the 'Leap', 2001–2008

5.1 Introduction

This chapter presents a reading of the economic system which characterised China's economic 'leap', made principally in the immediate aftermath of WTO accession in 2001. I demonstrate first a bifurcation in productivity and competitiveness between sectors and geographies is important in understanding where Chinese capital became market competitive, before arguing that a symbiosis at the national scale existed between these heterogeneities. The previous chapter presented a historical account of how—emerging into the capitalist world economy after the rise of global neoliberalism, the transition from import-substitution to export-oriented industrialisation, and the deepening modularisation of manufacturing production—China evolved into such a combinatory social formation. Central state institutions retained control of the 'commanding heights' of capital goods industries and the financial sector, while subjecting small private firms in consumer goods industries to the direct discipline of the global economy. With its confluence of 'Keynesian-Fordist' vertically integrated state firms, and 'neoliberal' fragmented production networks in the light and medium manufacturing sectors, China *combined* two very different forms of capitalist production into a single, national, system of accumulation. Combined development facilitated China's developmental 'leap' (especially after 2001) primarily through implanting its coastal cities into fragmented production networks

S. Rolf, *China's Uneven and Combined Development*,
Studies in the Political Economy of Public Policy,
https://doi.org/10.1007/978-3-030-55559-7_5

and reviving its torpid state sector through corporatisation and financing from state banks, themselves flush with resources from the booming export manufacturing sector.

This chapter seeks to add flesh to the bones of this so far schematic characterisation by outlining the unique kind of capitalist development China's mode of integration into the global economy has entailed. The period of near-exponential growth in GDP during the 2000s—tracking the equally rapid growth in exports—always possessed secular limits, based upon the capacity of the world economy to absorb greater quantities of manufactures. As Chinese incomes rose, the domestic market for consumer goods also grew substantially—but never in proportion to overall growth. These limitations were laid stark in 2008, as global export markets for manufactured goods suffered a major shock (Chapters 6 and 7 explores the dynamics of the post crisis period). But the export-led boom of the 2000s sufficiently entrenched a set of political economic dynamics in China to allow for a cross-sectional analysis of the economy to illuminate some major structural features of China's form of capitalism. I develop such an analysis in three stages: first, by briefly introducing the concept of a system of accumulation (SOA) and how a semi-static political economic configuration emerges from the dynamic process of UCD. Second, by providing a broad overview of China's 'exportist' SOA as it appeared in 2008—by looking inside the export sector, China's major surplus generator, at the industrial dynamics of the clothing, electronics and machinery industries—before outlining the continuing significance of the state sector. Finally, I suggest means by which these were combined by national state institutions into an 'exportist' SOA.

I make four specific claims regarding this period of China's development: (1) China's development was principally export dependent, especially after 2001. (2) Firms operating in China's export sector (foreign and increasingly domestic) significantly upgraded their manufacturing capacity and moved out of the *lowest* value-added areas, but largely remained in comparatively *low* value-added nodes of production networks across sectors. (3) Local governments, especially in coastal industrial hubs and particularly at the sub-municipal level, became deeply intertwined with global capital; but (4) the central state was less 'internationalised' than it might otherwise have been by the globalisation of these sectors of economy, since export earnings also considerably subsidised the nationalised industries of the state sector (through the bank-facilitated redistribution of tax revenues to SOEs). This enabled China's remarkable reconstitution as a bastion of 'state capitalism', albeit one inseparable from the success of the private export-manufacturing sector.

5.2 The SOA Concept and Its Relationship with China's UCD

As argued in Chapter 3, a 'systems of accumulation' approach represents—compared with other comparative capitalisms approaches—my preferred methodology for identifying core economic sectors and their institutionally mediated relationship with the broader economy, within the wider context of uneven and combined development. With this in mind, this chapter demonstrates how China's highly variegated geographies and sectors of capitalist production become combined under the agency of the state, into an 'exportist' *system of accumulation* (SOA) comprising (temporarily) regularised patterns of capital accumulation, sets of class relations arising from these dynamics, and a distinct form of state. The argument of this chapter is that WTO membership unleashed an 'exportist system of accumulation', in which a set of core sectors in consumer goods export manufacturing underpinned national economic growth.

Use of the SOA approach suggests a solution to the puzzle of 'stalled reform' posed by Naughton (2014): exactly why, after nearly a decade of vigorous reforms (from approximately 1992 to 2001) which repeatedly undermined key constituencies of the CCP (state-owned enterprises, their workers, and the planning ministries and bureaucrats) did state managers become unable or unwilling to push reform any further towards a liberal model of capitalism? Chapter 4 discussed the *politics* of this question, but we consider here the economic aspects. While large capital goods industries evidently formed the 'core sector' of the economy under the plan, reform and opening represented a marked shift towards the creation of a new set of 'core sectors' in the export sector: first, textiles and garments, then light electronics goods and increasingly high-technology ICT components and machinery/machine tool production. However, the creation of this new set of economically dynamic and surplus-producing core sectors did not fully undermine elite social constituencies (e.g. SOE heads, planners, and state banks) tied to the old core sectors of the state economy—because the party-state, hitting upon a successful growth model, engineered the redistribution of surpluses from exports in support of less productive constituencies in its state sector in support of this conservative-liberal political compromise. As this key dynamic of the SOA took hold, these revenue streams stabilised and grew in volume, locking in the proliferation of interest groups without undermining the source of growth. Identifying China's export boom as the confluence of two 'core sectors' in the SOA approach is a fruitful extension of the UCD, which explains how China's mode of integration into the global political economy injected the national political economy with a novel growth engine, which was subsequently incorporated into the older growth model to producing an entanglement between state capitalist firms and institutions and neoliberal exportist firms and institutions. It also refutes the inevitability of any anticipated liberal transition by demonstrating how only partial reforms could become self-reinforcing (cf. Pei 2006).

5.3 China's Leap, 2001–2008: (i) The Export Sector

China's growth spurt after 2001 was overwhelmingly driven by the private sector. Lardy (2014, 158, 173; see also Holz 2018), providing a forensic analysis of China's complex system of firm registration types, concludes that even on a conservative estimate (using official Chinese data which exclude a large number of 'below-scale' small firms with annual sales revenue below 5 million RMB, which excludes more private sector firms versus SOEs), the total value of SOE output declined from around 50% in the late 1990s to just over 25% by 2008–2009. By 2011, he estimates that 253 million workers (70% of the total urban labour force of 359 million) were in urban private-sector jobs.

This shift in the economy produced a relatively neat sectoral division of ownership between state- and privately owned firms, which Lardy (2014, 331) demonstrates with reference to the value of industrial output produced by SOEs. By the end of the 2000s, SOEs predominated in the output of tobacco (99%), power generation (93%), gas and petroleum extraction (92%) and coal (54%), and maintained a strong presence in metal production (17–37%), transport equipment (44%),[1] and chemicals (18%). All three major telecommunications firms were (and remain) owned by the state, alongside the 'big five' state banks. Meanwhile,

[1] The share of state industrial production in transport equipment appears disproportionately high, since joint ventures between state firms and private foreign automakers are the predominant model of firms in this sector.

SOEs became mostly absent from key manufacturing (and primarily export-driven) sectors in electrical machinery & equipment (9%), ICT & electronics (8%), furniture (1.7%), and garments and footwear (1.4%). Observing this simple ownership distinction permits us to develop a stylised characterisation of the 'core sector' of export manufacturing as mostly private-owned and permeated by foreign investment, while heavy and extractive industry (alongside particular monopolies like tobacco and telecoms networks) remained predominately state operated and focused on domestic markets. This was in significant part an outcome of the notorious 'National Negative List' and the 'Catalogue of Encouraged Industries', which still proscribe and encourage (respectively) foreign investment in particular industrial subsectors (the use of which would later facilitate an increasingly targeted private sector industrial policy).

This private sector-dominated industrial development was also overwhelmingly export-oriented. Figure 5.1 demonstrates China's explosive GDP growth in this period, and illustrate how the social compact enforced, and the market access enabled, by WTO membership revived China's flagging growth after the late 1990s (as argued in Chapter 4).

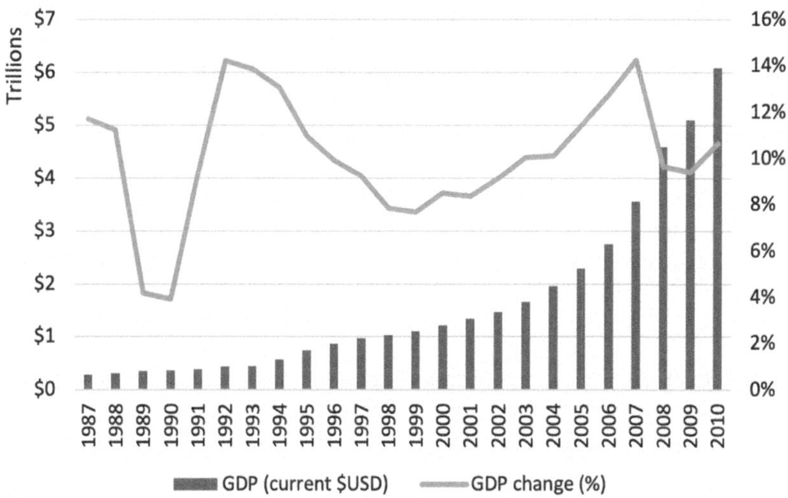

Fig. 5.1 Chinese GDP (current US$, billions, lhs) and CGDP growth rate (%, rhs), 1987–2010 (*Source* Author's calculations from World Bank indicators [n.d.])

WTO membership, the progressive commodification of China's factors of production, and the internationalisation of sectors of its economy generated a remarkable bout of GDP growth after 2001; by 2010, China was producing 19% of total world manufacturing output, almost double its share ten years prior. That this process was led by the sectors in question can be quite simply demonstrated. In 2000, the three 'core' export-manufacturing sectors identified in Table 5.1 accounted for slightly over half of China's industrial output (by value-added), while by 2007, they accounted for over two-thirds of the value-added of all industrial output (US$5.2tn). In 2000, the size of the electronics industry was roughly equivalent to that of the clothing and machinery industries (Table 5.1). But by 2007, at the height of the exportist SOA, the electronics industry came to supplant the others as China's major exporting industry, producing total output worth slightly over US$1.06tn. Almost half of total product was exported, a significant proportion considering the proliferation of small firms trading intermediaries with each other that is characteristic of the industry (see below; and Lüthje et al. 2013b). Also significant were the machine goods and transport equipment industries, responsible for a similar value (but a lower proportion) of exports to China's garment and footwear industry, though these industries remained more domestically oriented insofar as they largely served Chinese firms and consumers. This dramatic change in its export mix led Rodrik (2006) to note that China's productive structure resembled, peculiarly, an economy with a far higher per capita income.

Foreign investment and almost total dependency on the world market for manufactured consumer goods' ability to absorb this output explains Rodrik's paradox. As Baldwin and Lopez-Gonzalez (2015, 1717) put it, 'Chinese industrialisation happened by combining Chinese labour with know-how from advanced-nation firms'. Acquisition of basic startup

Table 5.1 Total value-added of major export sectors by year (billions of US$), and amount of value-added exported (billions of US$)

	2000	*Exports*	*2003*	*Exports*	*2007*	*Exports*
Electronics /ICT	220.3	*69*	358.4	*144.6*	1061.6	*488.1*
Textiles, garments & footwear	188.4	*58*	259.7	*82.5*	577.9	*195.1*
Machinery & transport equipment	203.7	*16.3*	358.5	*34.8*	912.6	*141.1*

Source Author's calculations from World Input Output Database (WIOD, n.d.) data

capital and consumer goods producing technology (virtually absent from China's industrial landscape before 1980) represented a process of 'pay-back industrialisation' for previous repression of consumer goods industries (Naughton 2007, 203), as the absence of established players meant new entrants could pick low hanging fruits in these sectors. The relative significance of foreign direct investment declined after an initial flood—given the gradually increasing significance of industrial *upgrading* of existing plant over greenfield investment in wholly new capacity, and the increasing significance of retained profits for new investments (Fig. 5.2). And many overseas firms also chose to 'domesticate' themselves rather than continue registering as foreign in order to gain access to China's still protected domestic market, becoming nominally domestic firms even when effectively operated as a branch plant. Despite a proportional decline in its significance, then, FDI remained a substantial source of investment capital in the aggregate and China has remained one of the world's largest recipients of foreign investment since the 1990s (the largest since 2015).

Measuring FDI alone is insufficient as means of characterising the significance of overseas firms to China's exportist SOA, however, because

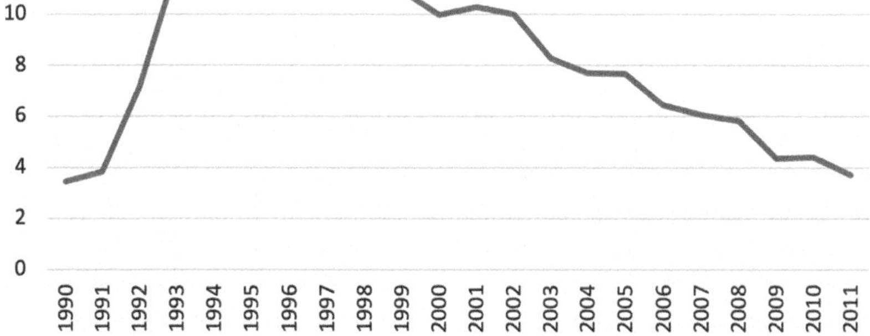

Fig. 5.2 Foreign direct investment as a percentage of gross fixed capital formation, 1990–2010 (*Source* Author, based on data from UNCTAD [2011])

the emergence of modularised GPNs across industries (see Chapter 4) problematises the character of notionally 'domestic' Chinese firms (see also Breznitz and Murphree 2011; Steinfeld 2010). Chinese exporters largely entered low value-added segments of Asian-regional or global production networks—particularly in final goods assembly—and were dependent for both technology, know-how and sales on either lead firms or 'system integrators' such as Taiwanese contract manufacturers like Foxconn in electronics. This disproportionality of exposure to competition transfers value to lead firms in less competitive nodes of the production network, insofar as these lead firms can aggressively shop around in monopsonist markets for the best deal across a large multitude of relatively homogenous Chinese suppliers (Kumar 2020). During the 2000s, this forced producers into a ferociously competitive race to the bottom (manifesting, in the advanced economies, in what outsourcers termed the 'China price': Harney 2008). This kind of trading relationship—which simply could not have existed prior to what Baldwin (2016) terms the 'great unbundling' of manufacturing processes from their design and control enabled by the ICT revolution—rendered many Chinese firms export-dependent and foreign-controlled without necessarily manifesting in direct investment relationships or showing up in FDI statistics. An Apple computer destined for export might, for example, pass through a long Chinese subcontracting network of 'domestic' firms in multiple stages of a single production process before shipping to the United States, in a process apparently sold through 'market' relations to a foreign firm with no capital of its own invested in plant. In reality this network is (to varying degrees across sectors) almost entirely controlled by and dependent upon the lead firm.

Establishing quantitative measurements of the depth of the 'dependency' of a national economy on exports and overseas capital is consequently highly complex in an age of trade in parts and components. Smith (2016, 80) shows that while US domiciled MNC imports from branch plants in China increased from $3bn to $63bn between 1992 and 2005, imports from ostensibly independent firms (but de facto 'captive' suppliers) increased to $180bn over the same period—suggesting that using FDI based measurements alone underestimate the internationalisation of China's productive capacity by roughly a measure of four. Such crude estimates are certainly indicative, but Smith (2016, 85) uses this evidence to portray China as an 'oppressed nation' trapped in an apparently fixed set of dependency relations which present no possibility of competition or upgrading by Chinese firms, and consequently of any further transformations in the global division of labour. But such estimates do not actually establish in themselves whether the exporters in question really are 'bleeding' significant quantities of value in their dependent, non-equity relations with advanced economy firms, nor do they capture any dynamism in such trends.[2] In Smith's account, China's export sector remained basically detached from the national economy and functioned as a deterritorialised manufacturing hub for MNCs, its growing GDP figures a mere 'illusion' created by the transient flows of value passing through and eluding the Chinese economy.

But it is worth exploring actual industry trends which are variable over time (Sects. 5.3.1–5.3.3). One means of doing so is through the use of newly available value-added (VA) trade data. VA data avoids problems of double counting in the production networks, where importing in order to export typically overstates the contribution of exports to domestic growth (since the value of products are counted at both the moment of import and export). This effectively eliminates Smith's objection to the GDP measure as an illusion since it identifies value captured 'within' an economy. One account comes from investment strategists at McKinsey Global Institute, who use value-added trade data to argue that China's economy succeeded by becoming significantly less internationalised or export-dependent during its economic boom precisely *because* its firms captured so little of these transient processing exports (Horn et al. 2010). These authors effectively agree with Smith's reasoning but draw opposed conclusions—for them, China's exploding GDP is no illusion and growth, therefore, must have been largely internally driven (see also He and Zhang 2010; Anderson 2007). Horn et al. (2010) calculate China's 'domestic value-added exports' (DVAE)—that is, the quantity of export values generated and retained by domestic Chinese firms which contributed to overall economic growth—to have grown between three to five times more slowly than GDP from 2002 to 2008. As such, even during the 'export boom' years, exports were contributing little and the sources of economic growth were domestic. This understanding supports McKinsey's investment strategy in sectors associated with China's domestic consumer markets, since it understands them to

[2] Smith draws heavily on the Foxconn-Apple relationship, discussed further in Chapter 6.

be substantially detached from sluggish global growth (cf. Towson and Woetzel 2015).

But there are a number of problems with this analysis. Firstly, Horn et al.'s work is an outlier: even other critics of the export-dependency thesis have (also using VA data) found a rising 'export-dependency' ratio rising from around 18% to around 23% during the boom of the 2000s (cf. He and Zhang 2010, 93). Second, both Xing (2016) and the OECD-WTO (2015) have since (and independently) developed their own value-added indicators in order to explore more precisely the foreign content of China's exports. Their measurements, though different, concur that in 2006-8 foreign value-added of Chinese exports was between 25 and 35%, and even in 2002 (when the gap between foreign and domestic firms was greater) was no higher than 40%. This recent research suggests that the DVAE measurement provided by Horn et al. (2010) of a 40–55% foreign content of exports throughout the 2001–2008 period is significantly too high.

Further, value-added estimates like Horn et al.'s (2010) do not consider the positive spillovers from taxes on and bank deposits by exporters that effectively generated subsidies for the state sector, keeping its relatively unprofitable elements afloat. Using their own VA analysis, Zhu and Kotz (2011, 22) argue that 'the estimated domestic content of exports contributed 31.7 percent' of GDP growth from 2001–2007. Deriving even stronger results from a VA analysis complemented by an examination of spillover effects, Akyüz (2011, 16) argues that 'if spillovers from exports to both consumption and investment are accounted for, it would not be an exaggeration to conclude that approximately 50 percent of Chinese growth during 2004–2007 came from exports'. Either we follow Horn et al. (2010) and conclude that exports played a mostly insignificant and highly overstated role in China's domestically driven boom; or Zhu and Kotz and Akyüz's (entirely opposed) conclusions that they contributed to such a degree that their drying up in 2008 would mark a fundamental turning point in the Chinese economy.

The evidence reviewed here and in the following chapter warrants support for this latter interpretation. China experienced a tremendous increase in the net value of its output from 2001 to 2008. In 2002, at the outset of the export-manufacturing boom proper, already 82 million Chinese worked in manufacturing (and as we have seen, the key manufacturing sectors were private-sector dominated and export-oriented). By 2009, this figure stood at 99 million (Banister 2013). While a great deal (if exaggerated by the likes of Horn et al.) of this output does represent value produced and captured elsewhere (in electronics, for instance, either by Northeast Asian component producers or US-based tech firms), this vast quantitative expansion of the manufacturing labour force served nonetheless to enrich China even though conducted on relatively unfavourable terms. (Marx [1863, ch. 20] suggests this possibility in discussing trade between differentially productive economies, where 'the richer country exploits the poorer one, even where the latter gains by the exchange').

The next section takes a closer look at the formation of China's key export sectors in clothing, electronics, and machinery. As Gereffi and Sturgeon (2013, 352) argue, under increasingly globalised manufacturing networks 'the structure and upgrading trajectories of GVCs vary significantly, and, as a result, cross-industry comparisons are essential'. The first two sectors are examples of the *transplantation* of industries from one region to another; while the third, machinery, represented the *replication* of existing technologies in the global machine tools industry, with some *exaptation* of existing competencies of engineering skills developed in the older state economy (Boschma et al. 2017).

5.3.1 Garments and Footwear

Clothing—textiles, apparel and footwear—was the first major industrial sector to be supplanted to the Pearl River Delta and other parts of China by overseas Chinese capitalists. Beginning early in the 1980s, the low cost and rudimentary nature of the fixed capital and labour processes involved allowed Hong Kong based garment firms to quickly establish manufacturing plants in SEZs in Shenzhen and other parts of the Pearl River Delta. By 1992, clothing accounted for nearly half of all Chinese manufactured exports, having played a major part in early post-Mao coastal industrialisation. Similarly, Taiwan was the world's largest exporter of footwear in the 1980s, but by the end of the decade the majority of Taiwanese-owned factories had moved to mainland China (Hsing 1998, 63). Cheap factor costs—labour and land, in China's case—made China a globally attractive site for clothing production, in an industry increasingly sensitive to small price fluctuations as the mobility of machinery and plant increased. Most investment capital initially flooded into Guangdong province, though pockets of clothing industry clusters appeared across the southern and eastern seaboards as more of the national economy was gradually liberalised (Zhang et al. 2004). By the mid-2000s, the state had basically completed its retreat from textile and clothing production, leaving 95% and 99% of these industries in private sector hands, respectively (Yeung and Mok 2004).

Despite rapid growth, the sector's advance was restrained by two factors. The first was a set of rudimentary industrial policies aimed at sectoral switching towards higher value-added capital goods and electronic components (see Sect. 5.3.2). This was broadly successful, and by 2005 the clothing sector's relative significance was, despite nominal expansion, cut in half—accounting for less than 25% of manufactured exports. Second, the multifibre arrangement (MFA) initially arranged under the GATT in 1974 upheld stringent quotas on exports of clothing, delimiting the amount of production which firms could shift to China. The MFA had a disproportionate impact upon China vis-à-vis other clothing exporters, given the national economic significance and low capital base and technological level of the industry (Brambilla et al. 2010), and its eventual expiry in 2005 provided a late boost to the Chinese clothing industry, allowing market share to significantly increase from 2006 to 2008. However, the prior impact of the MFA was not purely adverse. Moore (2002) suggests that one unintended consequence was to artificially restrict access to the bottom segments of the clothing market in advanced economies, pushing Chinese producers out of the lowest value-added tasks earlier than would otherwise have been the case. The MFA did, however, encourage the concentration of the clothing industry in cities near to Hong Kong (like Shenzhen and Guangzhou, as well as smaller cities like Dongguan and Foshan), since exporting through Hong Kong enabled China to exploit the territory's sanctioned allowance of advanced economy exports. A spurt of further post-MFA growth after 2006 has since stabilised, leaving China with an apparently fixed two-fifths of global market share in clothing markets (HKTDC 2016).

A more recent threat to the industry has been rising labour costs. Garment sector annual wages grew from an average of just 9066 yuan in 2002 to 18,711 yuan in 2008, with a dramatic spike in wage costs of 15% year-on-year in the pre-crisis years of 2006–2007 and 2007–2008 (Banister and Cook 2011). Fears that MFA expiry in 2005 would leave China in a position of total industry dominance have not, perhaps for this reason, come to pass (cf. Nordås 2004). But despite the global 'sourcing caravan'—a metaphor emphasising the clothing industry's quite unique ability to move in accordance with small changes in the wage bill—neither have other Asian countries caught up with Chinese production capacity. China's deepening domestic market, and the rise of full-package suppliers with significantly improved backward linkages and design capabilities, give it strong advantages as a supplier to lead firms compared with the industry elsewhere in Asia (Butollo 2015; Zhu and Pickles 2014), alongside the widespread uptake of CNC machinery not prevalent in comparably low-wage competitors, mean the PRC is likely to remain competitive in its mid-range niche for the foreseeable future.

Despite shrugging off these challenges, the industry has been dogged by chronically low profitability. This was reported by Zhu and Pickles (2014) to be as low as an average of 3.9% at the peak of the exportist SOA in 2008. Chronically low returns are likely related to the small scale of most private firms in the industry, the dominance of foreign intermediaries who skim off profits, the buyer-driven nature of the production network, and the acute competition between local manufacturing clusters in China. These factors inhibit the capacity of firms to absorb the kinds of wage gains noted above, even following productivity increases. This said, industrial consolidation and geographical agglomeration have together resulted in some profitability improvements for clothing industry firms. Zhu and Pickles (2014, 42) further note that while two-thirds of firms were operating on margins as low as 0.6%, the remainder earned profits of (a still low but relatively healthier) 6–10%. This accords with research by Appelbaum (2009) on economies of scale achieved by large Hong Kong firms based in China like Luen Thai, Yue Yuen and Li and Fung—which combine some in-house production capacity with surrounding 'supply chain cities' of plants surrounded by myriad small satellite suppliers, focusing their attention on their increasing capabilities in supply chain management (see also Gereffi 2008). Taiwanese footwear manufacturers (such as Yue Yuen) play a similar role as 'system integrators' (though with perhaps substantially greater in-house manufacturing capacity than clothing producers), acting as something between trading houses and factories.

Offering further support for this duality of firm types in the industry, Dallas (2014; n.d.) demonstrates the striking extent of foreign ownership in China's light consumer goods industries (especially clothing). Global lead firms looking to outsource manufacturing still primarily interact with trusted large clothing firms headquartered in advanced Asian economies (particularly Hong Kong for apparel, and Taiwan for footwear) in order to protect intellectual property and ensure quality standards. Outside of these lead firm dominated GPNs, large trading houses with few direct production facilities act as procurers of clothing goods from small scale domestic Chinese firms—inhibiting the latters' specialisation and blocking direct learning-by-doing relationships with lead firms which might otherwise lead to moves up the value chain. The negative consequences for most domestic producers are myriad, as Dallas (n.d., 48–49) finds in a research paper worth quoting at length:

> A selection of elite or entrusted suppliers (most of them foreign) are operationally interlinked with global buyers which demand... speed to market, flexibility, designs, logistics, supply sourcing and data analysis – more value-added – which reflected both in their high levels of specialization and in much higher prices... these are non-commoditized export channels in which foreign firms must retain strong managerial and operational control by directly investing in China and retaining 100% ownership stakes. By contrast, products which do not demand these heavy requirements are fully commoditized and produced for buyers through highly competitive, arms-length market ties in which [Chinese] firms face much uncertainty and instability and earn only rock-bottom prices, such that they eschew specialization by diversifying their exports through general trading.

The existence of these two distinct trade channels, both characterised by different forms of highly restricted access for domestic firms suggests that Chinese clothing manufacturers face a tough uphill battle in an increasingly less lucrative sector. This is in spite of the remarkable feat of world market share capture to 2008.

5.3.2 *Electronics and ICT*

The electronics and ICT industry is the world's largest by value of output, and total world exports of finished goods in the sector surpassed $600bn in 2008. It is highly internationalised and the most subject to global production networks (GPNs) of all industrial sectors, with the value of parts and component exports around twice that of the total output of finished goods (US$1.3tn in 2008). By output, China became the world's largest producer of electronic goods (including parts and components) during the early 2000s. But measured by value-added, China contributed 23% of total world output in the industry at the close of the decade—still second to the United States, which contributed 27% (ILO 2014).

Hong Kong investment introduced rudimentary electronics production to the PRD from the late 1980s in a range of components for consumer goods. But it was not until the increasingly globally competitive Taiwanese electronics contract manufacturers (ECMs) began to shift plants to China after the early 1990s that the country's electronics and ICT industries truly took off. A triangular relationship developed between Taiwanese firms (specialising in manufacturing services and development: 'system integration'), Silicon Valley software engineers (specialising in product development and innovation), and new domestic Chinese firms producing low value-added manufactures (with the aim of eventually upgrading their position in production networks) (Saxenian 2005). The electronics sector now accounts for the overwhelming bulk of the value-added of China's export manufactures. While China has retained significant capacity at the low end of cheap household goods and components assembly, it also acquired significant productive capacity in aspects of more complex ICT production such as semiconductors, display panels, lithium batteries, universal power supplies and memory storage during the 2001–2008 boom and beyond.

China's mode of entry into the electronics sector—accepting tasks rendered uncompetitive by relatively higher wages in Hong Kong and Taiwan—bestowed it a subordinate positionality in increasingly modularised production networks. But despite the vast increase in scale and scope of production of China's ICT and electronics firms since the early days of the industry, this pattern of foreign dominance has—at least at the surface level—not been much altered. Lüthje et al. (2013a, 139) note that over 75% of output in the sector is produced by foreign invested firms (FIEs), while for high-tech electronics, computer and consumer products this figure increases to over 90% (Steinfeld 2010, 85). China's electronics sector does not then correspond to the vertically integrated national industries that facilitated the catchup development of the postwar East Asian tigers. Instead, it broadly resembles a 'triangular' pattern of trade whereby high value-added parts and components are imported from advanced East Asian economies before being assembled in Chinese factories and exported to the advanced capitalist economies for final consumption. The emergence of this trade pattern—mostly in lockstep with the growth of the electronics sector—is statistically observable through examining China's trade deficits with South Korea, Japan and

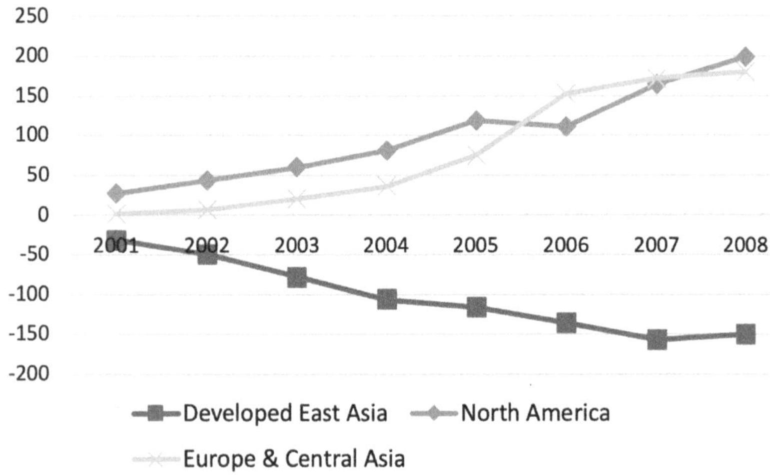

Fig. 5.3 Trade balance with major regional trading partners (billions of US$) (*Source* Author's calculations from World Bank indicators [n.d.])

Taiwan,[3] which basically mirror its attendant surpluses with the United States and (to a lesser extent) Europe (Fig. 5.3). As Athukorala (2009) shows, China has become Japan's largest market 'absorbing' 16.6% of total exports by 2005–2006, though the final destination of these exports after processing is overwhelmingly the advanced economies.

Since it is by some margin China's largest export industry, the electronics/ICT sector is key to explaining this regional transborder production structure. An investigation of the iPhone 3G provides the most well-known illustration of this unequal, non-equity production format at work. With a final retail value of $500, assembly costs in China totalled $6.80—and part of the profit generated was repatriated to Foxconn's Taiwan holding company, Hon Hai, and its shareholders (Xing and Detert

[3] Hong Kong is deliberately excluded from the 'Developed Asian Economies' category here. It ran large trade deficits with China throughout this period, a symptom of transshipment of exports—where Chinese exports are routed through Hong Kong with a markup before continuing to their final destination. As such, Hong Kong's deficit with China is mirrored in its surpluses with other advanced economies, which effectively cancel each other (with a markup remainder).

2010). The bill for (mainly Japanese and Korean) components was significantly higher at $172, while Apple took an extremely high profit share of $321 (64%). More recent industry studies broadly corroborate this relationship to date in newer iPhone models (*Supply Chain 24/7* 2017). And research on notebook computers and tablets demonstrates analogous patterns of power and control in interfirm relations, as competitive pressures are pushed down the production network—though with far less spectacular profit shares for lead firms like Dell and HP, meaning a significantly more equitable distribution of gains between advanced component producing Asian economies and US lead firms than that of the Apple–Foxconn relationship (Dedrick et al. 2010).

This disparity between output and value-added is typically explained with recourse to the dominance of the processing trade in electronics. Around half of China's exports in electronics during the 2001–2008 boom were accounted for by export processing (rising to 90% for high-tech products in 2005). The most rudimentary form of export processing ('with supplied materials') involves collecting a fee for assembling ready-made materials shipped from overseas; while 'processing with imported materials' grants firms somewhat more autonomy in making a foreign exchange transaction for parts from overseas and the firm in question takes responsibility for sourcing export markets (though this is often performed through an intermediary trading house). This form of extensively fragmented production is especially prevalent in the electronics and ICT sectors due to the low physical weight and relatively high value of the components involved (Ma and van Assche 2010). Inputs to the processing trade were valued at US$400bn in 2008—over one third of total Chinese imports in all sectors—of which, 77% were sourced from East Asian economies (principally Taiwan, Hong Kong, Japan, and Korea) (Xing 2012).

In contrast with the lowest technology industries like clothing, however, more significant domestic Chinese manufacturing capacity has developed in electronics/ICT. In this sector (likely due to the higher physical and human capital requirements for production), trade channels appear to be less distinctive and genuine spillovers and linkages encouraged substantive industrial upgrading at quite a rapid pace. In this way, the 2001–2008 boom encouraged learning by doing through GPN participation, since the processing trade brought foreign components into China which could be rapidly reverse-engineered by domestic producers, produced at lower cost, and supplied to those firms assembling for export (replacing more expensive imports). From 2000 to 2007, China experienced a 5% increase in domestic value-added of exports—largely due, as Kee and Tang (2016, 1434) find, to 'a continuous decline in the relative prices of domestic to imported input varieties'. Part of this may be accounted for by the domestic registration of foreign firms seeking access to the Chinese market, and another part is also likely accounted for by substitution of raw materials and capital goods produced in China's state sector (Sect. 5.3). But another recent IMF study (Mathai et al. 2016, 23) finds striking falls in the import intensity of electronics goods as Chinese suppliers leapt up the value chain in the computers and telecommunications subsectors, with a reduction of more than 50% in the value of imported components in these exports from 2000 to 2008. And this rise in the usage of domestic inputs in electronic goods is mirrored by a continuous decline in the relative significance of the processing trade versus more traditional forms of export manufacturing.

Export processing is typically understood as a poor means for developing workers' training and skill levels. But Amiti and Freund (2010, 41) note that while the average skill content of Chinese exports outside of the processing trade changed relatively little between 1992 and 2005, inside the processing trade some skill upgrading was statistically evident. While in 1992, the bottom quintile of 'least skill-intensive industries produced 55 percent of China's export share. By 2005, the export share that these industries produced fell to 32 percent'. China's move into exporting significantly more high-technology goods may represent *both* final stage assembly of high-value content being produced elsewhere—*and* increases in the skill content of such assembly work, compared with the rest of China's export sector.

This trend relates to the greater degree of concentration and centralisation of capital and functions that has taken place in China's electronics sector, principally in firms owned by overseas Chinese capitalists. Unlike in garments, where trading houses often dominate production networks, it is locally based (though foreign owned) manufacturers who do so in electronics/ICT assembly. Key here is the emergence of large electronics contract manufacturers (ECMs) with greater capabilities in component production, supply chain management and sourcing, and product development (Pawlicki 2016; Lüthje and Butollo 2016). Though Taiwan-owned Foxconn is the most well-known and sizeable of these firms, Table 5.2 demonstrates the foreign dominance of the sector by largescale contract manufacturers. However, while ECMs typically involve

Table 5.2 Top 10 electronics contract manufacturers with substantial operations in China, 2013

Company	*Nationality*	*2013 Revenue (Billions US$)*	*Employees worldwide (1000s)*
Foxconn	Taiwan	115	1230
Pegatron	Taiwan	31	104
Quanta	Taiwan	29	60
Flextronics	US/Singapore	25	150
Compal	Taiwan	21	43
Wistron	Taiwan	21	700
Jabil Circuit	US	18	177
Inventec	Taiwan	15	23
TPV	Hong Kong	12	32
Celestica	Canada	6	22

Source Adapted from Pawlicki (2016)

more complex operations than processing with supplied inputs, there is no direct correlation between the steady decline of processing trade exports and an increase in value-added for domestic Chinese firms. As Xing (2016, 73) observes, in 2001 (before WTO membership registered on the economy) Chinese firms captured 56% of value-added across all high-tech electronics production exports. This figure was reduced to just 28% in 2005 as foreign firms moved *en masse* into these areas, but quickly recovered to a relatively stable 45% from 2008. So foreign dominance of the sector should be qualified by noting the steep rise in domestic firms' capabilities and value-added.

The integration of China into global production networks means that transformations in modularised global industry structures had correspondingly varied impacts in China's electronics industrial districts (Yang 2007). While the Pearl River Delta formed the initial wave of overseas investment, Suzhou and the Yangtze River Delta became broadly acknowledged as the most advanced industrial region of China during the 2000s. The YRD outstripped the PRD by specialising in burgeoning notebook computer production, while the PRD had focused on PC peripheral components and assembly, which entered a slow decline into the 2000s (Sturgeon and Kawakami 2010). However, Wei et al. (2009) argue that the PRD model may be superior from the perspective of domestic firms' upgrading capacities. Large foreign enterprises moving to the YRD brought with them complete chains of subcontracted foreign enterprises, while relatively smaller foreign firms arriving in Shenzhen from Taiwan and Hong Kong during the 1990s tapped much earlier into local firm networks, pushing Chinese domestic firms towards upgrading in order to meet global requirements from the outset. Chen (2014) substantiates this by showing that domestic firms (at least in Shenzhen) spend roughly ten times more on R&D than their counterparts in the YRD—and this was further reflected in their relative level of innovation and dynamism: for instance, YRD's domestic-owned firms registered 12,560 new products in 2008, while PRD firms managed 125,412 (Chen 2014, 229).

The central Chinese state has pursued various manifestations of private sector industrial policies to improve manufacturing capacity in electronics. The 863 programme (1986) mobilised US$2bn in funding for various high-tech acquisitions over the following decade, while the 973 programme (1997) established new areas of economically relevant scientific innovation such as semiconductors and nanotechnology—though with a substantially smaller budget (Pecht 2006). Despite some successes, perhaps the fundamental issue with these industrial policies was their concentration in large, nationalised research institutes and their restriction to a handful of (mostly state-owned) beneficiaries, limiting their commercial accessibility for typical Chinese SMEs (Cao et al. 2006; Kennedy 2016). Breznitz and Murphree (2011) point more generally to the competing lines of authority between different ministries and branches of the state, deeply embedded patronage relations, and repeated, unexpected policy alterations—which together culminate in an atmosphere of 'structured uncertainty' for firms aiming to invest long-term in upgrading technologies. While Breznitz and Murphree emphasise the positive outcomes for firms emerging successfully from this tough operating environment and the possibilities for 'second-tier' innovation in the production process (as opposed to novel product innovation), these obstacles stemming from a haphazard industrial policy patently produce an environment in which it is difficult for firms to compete directly with global technological leaders.

Operating under the radar of state planners, Huawei presents the major exception to this rule for the period in question. The firm built a network of rural sales of telephone equipment during the rise of TVEs in the 1990s. It became a leading firm in the electronics sector during the 2000s through intense and long-term R&D spending and a near total lack of intervention from state agencies (though it did benefit from easy credit from state banks; cf. Nolan 2014). Lenovo (Legend), another ICT success story of the 2000s, acquired IBM's laptop production division in 2004. It does not neatly fit the category of a national champion, since it essentially acquired ready-made IBM's global R&D facilities and supply networks. As Sturgeon and Kawakami (2010, 38) point out, Lenovo's 'globalised' strategy was in no way nationally grounded: the 'structure, geography, ownership, leadership, supply base, and sources of innovation at the new Lenovo were vastly different from the national champions that emerged in Japan and later in Korea'. Heilmann et al. (2013) demonstrate how the central government's 'Torch program' (1988), a science based industrial policy, granted much greater flexibility to local governments in experimenting with high-technology development zones, innovations that proved critical for both Huawei and Lenovo in their earlier periods of growth (in Lenovo's case as an SOE bought out by management). In those areas it was most successful, this decentralised industrial policy did prove capable of integrating Chinese electronics producers into lead firm GPNs through the use of high-technology zones. But such upgrading was really the exception rather than the rule: and even to date Lenovo does not compete with the top tier global firms in the PC and notebook industry, preferring low cost, low performance market segments (Sturgeon and Kawakami 2010).

In sum, the domestic electronics/ICT industry which emerged in this boom decade displayed both elements of 'corespective' competition (in which a virtuous growth cycle restrains competition sufficiently to enable co-ordinated development through rising investment, productivity, and wages) and 'destructive' competition (a vicious cycle of falling output costs leading to downward pressure on investment and wages) (these concepts are used by Crotty 2000; drawing on Schumpeter).

5.3.3 *Machinery and Transport Equipment*

Machinery and transport equipment came to form an important and distinct part of China's exportist SOA. 'Machinery' groups relatively disparate industrial subsectors such as electrical and telecommunications machinery, with industrial tools, dies and moulds (TDM) which primarily service other industrial firms' production processes. Transport equipment is also often included in statistical data on this category, since car and vehicle production broadly share similar kinds of inputs and skill requirements—although we will show that ownership structures of machine goods and auto firms vary significantly. Agglomeration and co-location effects are generally strong because of the high value and large size and weight of the products, which renders the trade the least internationalised of the three major export sectors (cf. Canis 2012). The sector is nonetheless best understood as a part of an exportist 'ecosystem' in industrial districts, since its outputs form a critical input into consumer goods factories even when not directly produced for export—though an increasingly substantial share of China's machine tools is also sold overseas (Table 5.1). Firms selling to exporters are incentivised to cluster near to exporters to keep transport costs low and dialogue regarding customer needs open.

Early iterations of the processing trade ('with supplied inputs') in light consumer manufacturing principally involved the wholesale implantation of machinery from advanced economies to China by either lead firms or large foreign contract manufacturers, which both limited the potential for private sector machinery firms to emerge and for state firms to sell their product to exporters. But as domestic Chinese firms in sectors like electronics/ICT emerged with significant productive capacities, an intense demand for new parts, components, and machinery took root. This new demand, as well as the existence of skilled engineers from the state sector with capabilities in backwards engineering, offered space for domestic machine tool firms to enter production. By the mid-2000s, China was the world's largest market for machine tools, and this domestic market stimulated huge leaps in productive capacities of Chinese firms. In 1997, domestic Chinese firms accounted for 26.7% of market share of metal cutting machinery, while by 2000 this figure had increased to 35.9%. WTO membership allowed a rush of foreign entrants and cutthroat competition and by 2003 domestic sales fell to 24%, before recovering once again to 36.1% in 2006 as Chinese producers adapted to competition (figures from Brandt and Thun 2015, 176). As in electronics, then, while foreign enterprises still dominate the market, their entry stimulated substantial domestic productive capacity.

Chinese machinery firms are overwhelmingly small scale and produce in a semi-artisanal style based on small batch, high value orders—characteristic of the very slow modularisation of the global machine tool industry compared with electronics or clothing (Schuh et al. 2017). Commodification of parts of the machinery market (such as spring-tool manufacturing) has permitted some medium and largescale firms supplying standardised equipment to emerge (USITC 2002). Here, Taiwanese firms predominate over local producers—especially due to their close working relationships as suppliers to Taiwan-owned electronics factories. Holmes et al. (2005) find that Chinese prices in international markets were typically between 30 and 75% of average US prices, though quality and longevity were identified as major weaknesses of Chinese firms versus global export market leaders. As such, Chinese producers principally serve the lowest tiers of world export markets.

However, towards the end of the period in question, some high-technology subsectors of this field demonstrated substantive technical progress. Renewable energies technology is one such area, which presents an interesting case study of the current successes and limits facing China's high-technology machinery sector. As Nahm and Steinfeld (2014) demonstrate, the productive capacity of Chinese-owned manufacturing firms in solar panelling and wind turbine production came to far outstrip the captive supplier status at the 'bottom end' of the supply chain throughout the 2000s (Gereffi 1994). In solar power, for instance (a private-dominated industry that did not enjoy targeted industrial policy support) Chinese firms accounted for less than 1% of global solar photovoltaic production in 2001—but by 2011 accounted for more than half of global solar panelling output measured by megawattage. This remarkable 'leap' proceeded as domestic Chinese companies collaborated with foreign firms to move expensive, advanced technology from the design stage (where they initially had no capacities) towards commercialisation (where the broader manufacturing boom had produced a large class of skilled engineers).

Chinese competitive advantage in some such sectors has thus moved well beyond cheap labour per se, and towards production network niches. In these areas, China's relatively unique advantages as a vast manufacturing hub help it to translate already developed novel product innovations which are too expensive for market into commercially viable products. In particular, Chinese manufacturers' capacity for step-by-step reverse engineering and 'backward design' lures advanced economy firms to enter partnerships with Chinese producers like wind turbines; in order to draw on Chinese firms' capacities for reengineering products with cheaper components and assembly costs. However, a large part of the reason for China's capacity to 'commercialize new product better, faster, and cheaper' are the relatively low production costs facing Chinese manufacturers—mostly accounted for by the relative price of labour. And such firms face far more intense competitive pressures than their international collaborators. As Nahm and Steinfeld (2014, 298) conclude, 'the rapid expansion of manufacturing has created the risk—and reality in many cases—of overcapacity, redundant investment, and the painful sectoral shakeouts that frequently follow. Simply put, Chinese innovative manufacturers are bearing substantial risks'—and, we might add, reaping proportionately less of the rewards. Coinciding with Chinese firms' entry into the market was a collapse in world market value of crystalline silicon panels from US$5.19 in 2001 to US$1.27 in 2011.

China's modality of integration into the global auto industry exhibits a different set of obstacles to technology transfer in the machinery sector. While most automobiles produced in China are for domestic consumption (making China the biggest producer *and* consumer of cars after 2011), foreign companies continue to dominate the sector. Joint ventures (JVs) between global lead firms and Chinese car producers became the dominant mode of operation in the 1990s and 2000s and aimed to 'trade market for technology'. This led to concerns over intellectual property rights and Chinese firms' leapfrogging ahead by using the leverage of its domestic car market access to lure foreign firms into sharing their technology and know-how. But so far, JVs appear to have achieved the opposite result. Lead firms maintain 'strategic control' over production and technology, seriously limiting Chinese partners' technology and organisational upgrading opportunities (Feng 2016).

Political incapacity to rationalise the once state-dominated industry was one key source of difficulty. The central state has struggled to counter powerful and long-established provincial and municipal owned car firms to reduce the number of competing national producers, leaving over 100 firms still in production in 2012 and foreign firms dominating overall sales. JVs with global leaders, meanwhile, mean the 'Big Four state-owned automakers are effectively living off the easy earnings of their joint-venture partners. They benefit from their partners' technology and know-how, which allows them to spend less on R&D than they would need to if they had no foreign partners', writes Anderson (2012, 47). This is reflected in the fall in value-added of Chinese car firms from 2001 (from 25% in 2000 to 15% in 2005, rising to 20% since then; Timmer et al. 2015, 588). And being one of China's highest-tech sectors, autos present the contradiction contained in the confluence of high technology and China's low-wage, low-skill manufacturing economy. Zhang (2015, 166) notes that while car firms have successfully imported systems of lean production prevalent in other advanced economies, management also rely upon a 'huge-crowd' strategy of employing a mass of low-wage, unskilled workers to meet increased demand during spikes, offering firms a unique lever of flexibility but likely inhibiting further innovation in labour-saving production methods.

In sum, the machinery industry exhibits elements of contradictory tendencies also apparent in the electronics industry (of corespective and destructive competition). In the machine tool industry, experiences of 'destructive competition' may act to the benefit of the broader economy by cheapening the inputs to sectors like electronics/ICT and textiles and garments. However, in the predominantly export-oriented renewable energy and auto sectors, the state possesses a strong incentive to manage competition and rationalise industries to ensure co respective competition (though success varies widely across subsectors).

Despite the varying tendencies across the three sectors discussed here, then, all demonstrate to a greater or lesser extent the profound difficulties of pursuing catchup development in a world economy dominated by globalised production networks. On the other hand, Smith's (2016) 'dependency trap' relations with advanced economy firms do not completely capture the technological dynamism, productivity increases and capture of world market share which China's boom exhibited.

5.3.4 *The Private Sector and Cadre-Capitalism*

So far, we have observed how China's private sector drove the extraordinary expansion of the exportist SOA during the 2000s. But the extremely fast pace of change and the deepening fragmentation of global manufacturing, especially in the key electronics and ICT sectors, meant that the technological ground continued to shift beneath Chinese firms' feet—even while firms appeared to successfully upgrade their production capacity and product mixes. A purely network-oriented GPN perspective would conclude with this consideration of how global industrial characteristics shaped local conditions. The next step is to ask what kind of class relations this export boom entailed—and these class relations subsequently shaped China's industrial structure through the formation of new incentive mechanisms.

Despite increases in capital intensity across the major subsectors of the exportist SOA, the labour regime in export hubs has remained flexible, low wage, and migrant based. Wages roughly doubled across the highlighted export sectors, but this was from a very low base and by 2008

Chinese wages in international comparison remained comparable to low-wage manufacturing economies in Southeast Asia (like the Philippines) and below that of Mexico. Despite a rising labour movement, research suggests that increases in labour share of income were in fact mostly the product of an extended working day—the average of which increased persistently from the *danwei* era of 35 hour working week in the early 1990s to norm of over 50 hours per week in new private sector export factories by 2007 (Banister and Cook 2011). Private-sector membership of the All-China Federation of Trade Unions (ACFTU) was permitted and workplace branches were established in larger enterprises during this period, but the state union effectively functioned as a branch of management rather than an instrument of labour organising or wage bargaining, working to ameliorate disputes as and when they arose. The lack of a formal means of dispute resolution or labour contracts hampered workers' ability to make permanent gains from strike action, while the chronically low retention rate impeded training and encouraged further dependence on short-term, on the job learning, inhibiting skill development. Many optimistically cited Silver's (2003) thesis that where 'capital goes, [class] conflict goes', but the experience of the 2000s demonstrates that whatever the partial truth of this claim, there are also serious impediments to the emergence of a militant and successful labour movement in China (Gray 2015, 21). As Pringle (2013, 196) writes, in the 2000s:

> Collective resistance to the exploitation and abuses concomitant with rapid export-led development was largely confined to short sit-ins outside local labor offices aimed at provoking government officials into ordering capitalists to obey labor laws. However, the state's prioritizing of employment-led development, decentralized investment regimes, and often corrupt links between government officials and investors stacked the cards against these first-generation migrants whose knowledge of the factory system and the laws supposed to govern it was weak.

This reconstitution and intensified exploitation of labour necessitated a wholesale shift in the state's hegemonic project, evident in the exorcism of what Lin (2015) calls the 'language of class', which had pervaded public discourse under the plan. In the 2000s, a 'harmonious society' became the watchword of the Hu-Wen administration. In line with this, rising labour discontent in private enterprises was largely channelled through the reconstituted legal system (Gallagher 2014), which processed hundreds of thousands of employer–employee disputes by the late 2000s. The new migrant working class was encouraged to take its disputes through the legal system, but not to organise industrial action in the workplace.

What of the class of capitalists that emerged from this social process? Because domestic manufacturing capacity came so late to the game, China's exporting coastal districts became populated by overseas Chinese capitalists with investment capital to spare. Their *guanxi* relations with local states—especially at the sub-municipal level (of town and village governments)—proved key to their ability to operate in a new and sometimes hostile business environment. In fact, the depth and regularity of social interactions, and the importance of local governments as economic actors meant that at the local level, state–capital relations resemble an extreme version of urban 'growth coalitions' found elsewhere (Xu and Yeh 2009). So (2013) maps the sociological contours of this 'cadre-capitalist' class, demonstrating how it cohered at a local level around sub municipal institutions in order to secure optimal business conditions for exporters, such as minimal taxation and tax rebates, infrastructural provision, and market sourcing. Consequently, So (2013, 14) explains:

> Cadres often engage in capitalist activities in the private sector while employed by the state, thereby benefiting from their political connections and preferential access to resources, capital, technology, and licenses. On the other hand, capitalists in the private sector enjoy greater access, through their cadre patrons, to political power.

This hybrid relationship fulfilled the double mission of securing profitability for firms, and maintaining the solvency of cash-strapped governments (Oi 1995). It also left overseas Chinese with an asymmetrical form of class power over their local government counterparts, since they enjoyed an effective power of veto—the growth imperative dominated the incentive structures of local officials, and GPN participation was critical to achieving such growth. Hostility to initiatives aimed at securing workers' wages and contracts (see Chapter 6) emerged most vociferously from these interest groups and led to widespread collaboration between capital and low-level local governments in the mid-2000s.

But the disproportionate weakness of lower level institutional actors vis-à-vis overseas investors remained tempered by their political subordination to the central government. Goodman (2014) details how the *nomenklatura* system has formed a persistent organ of state control, subjecting local governments (at least down to the municipal level) to repeated personnel rotations that act to periodically upend direct (and potentially ossifying) personal relations between states and firm managers. In practice, this led to an uneasy tension between the lowest scales of government that were most responsive to the demands of investors, and those more aligned with central state imperatives, with cross-cutting lines of authority often manifesting in conflict and incoherence. Overall, though, the central state—beyond incidental successes like the (hands-off) Torch programme's influence in Lenovo's takeoff, for instance—was strikingly absent from private sector industrial policy compared with prior East Asian developers. Instead, it focused its prime attention on the state sector (see Sect. 5.4).

These interdependent relations between capital, labour regime and state capacity which emerged and solidified under the exportist SOA amount to what Song (2008) calls a 'modularity trap', the contours of which appear quite distinct compared with prior East Asian developers. Song (2008) considers only the electronics sector, where he argues that remarkable productivity increases during the 2000s did not increase profits because the modularity of production networks restricted Chinese firms' innovation—the source of profits—by encouraging the production of standardised modules for electronic goods. Consequently, substantial productivity increases, achieved through production of increasingly technologically complex components and the adoption of new assembly procedures, meant that China routed *external* international competition from other emergent manufacturers like Brazil and Mexico during the 2000s (*Economist* 2015). But for many domestic Chinese firms, the intensity of *internal* competition between suppliers, generated by the downward pressure exerted by firms in leading positions of GPNs, put such intense pressure on margins across all industrial sectors that production even of relatively complex manufactures like expensive footwear, semiconductors, integrated chips, and solar photovoltaic panels are no longer the source of high profits (or 'monopoly rents') they once were. Solar panels—which at the start of the 2000s were considered an advanced, high value-added technology—offer another revealing indication of this problem of commodification confronting successful Chinese technology acquisition and upgrading. Conversely, where centrally mandated attempts at industrial upgrading are strongest and most coherent—such as the auto industry—intra-state fragmentation of political power took on a heightened significance, where provincial governments' interests resulted in an inability to rationalise the industry and a reliance upon foreign-led innovation.

In a political economy with deep reserves of cheap labour, and a combative but fragmented labour movement, China's developing capital-intensive technological advances remain intertwined with widespread use of mass, low-skill manufacturing (cf. Butollo 2014). The concept of 'debased adaptation'—where imported technologies are modified by the fact of their incorporation into a less developed social formation—is useful to help theorise some of the distinctive problems confronting China's fast developing new industries (Trotsky 2009 4–5; Davidson 2012, 298–299). Since debased adaptations are by definition innovations implanted into a very different socio-spatial context than that where they developed, they should not be understood as the direct equivalents of these initial innovations and can have very different political economic 'meanings'. During China's 2001–2008 boom, technological upgrading adapted to the environment of low-wage, unskilled labour. The use of the 'huge-crowd' strategy identified by Zhang (2015) in China's car factories provides one excellent example of how advanced production techniques are entangled with deskilled labour processes based on China's cheap labour pool (see Sect. 5.3.3). This effect was quite general across most of the new export sectors, though with different outcomes (see also Butollo 2014, for further evidence from the electronics and clothing sectors). In the absence of a national-level 'nodal agency' with deep economic reserves and subsidies capable of rationalising the emergent industrial sectors in question through farsighted industrial policies, adaptations were destined to remain 'debased'—and China to remain a substantially less direct threat in high value-added and high-technology sectors than raw export valuations would suggest (see Fig. 5.4), instead complementing the production networks of advanced economy producers with efficient downstream assembly and basic component production.

5.4 China's Leap 2001–2008 (2): The State Sector

In contrast to the automobile sector—characterised by joint ventures between state and foreign multinationals, but de facto controlled by private foreign firms—the state maintained both operative control and dominant equity share of large SOEs. While the dynamic growth of the export sector meant state production formed an increasingly small share of total economic output during this period, state firms have continued

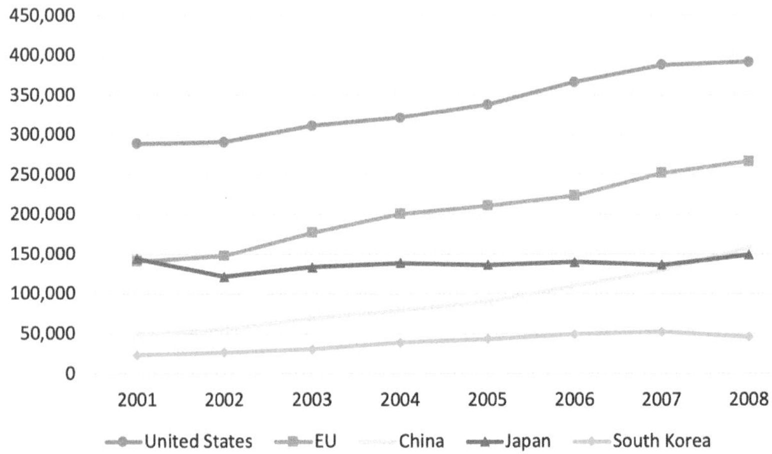

Fig. 5.4 High-tech manufacturing value added (US$, billions)—China in comparative perspective (*Source* Data from National Science Board ([2012])

to form a structural feature of China's economy by occupying key nodes of the 'commanding heights' of industry. After much optimism from liberal commentators during the early 2000s regarding China's anticipated reform towards a market economy, assessments later in the decade noticeably soured—as it became apparent that SOE reform had 'stalled' early under the new Hu-Wen administration. State managers evidently made a set of decisions around this period to preserve state control in particular areas. The 2000s were best characterised not as a transitional period but by *zhuada fangxiao* (grasp the large, let go of the small)—a policy of industrial rationalisation and scalar expansion of state firms rather than their disappearance. As Yang and Jiang (2012, 41) note, by 2007:

> [C]entral government-controlled firms accounted for 55 percent of China's total power generation, 48 percent of automobile manufacturing, 60 percent of high value-added steel production, and over 70 percent of hydro electric and thermal electric equipment production. The downsizing of the state sector as a whole has been accompanied by the simultaneous strengthening of a relatively small number of giants controlled by the central authorities.

So, while total state production fell significantly from 1994, it remained high in specific industries. SASAC (see Chapter 4) oversees 111 SOEs, which are directly owned by the central government. These conglomerates control around 23,000 smaller firms. Eaton (2015) argues that this process of 'reregulation' may have started as early as the late 1990s, when policy discussions amongst central state managers began to cohere around a project of constructing a 'national team' of world leading firms owned by the state (likely inspired by the experience of prior developmental states). The state remains careful, however, to maintain majority stakes in these national SOEs, leading some to view this process as one of only 'nominal privatisation' (Hsieh and Song 2015). National security considerations clearly play a major role in the decisions of the state over which industries to maintain dominance over, and which to allow the market to play a larger role in, with telecoms infrastructure and aviation deemed areas where the state should maintain full ownership and control (Pearson 2015, 33).

The state sector remains buttressed by the big five (formerly four) state banks: the Construction Bank of China (CBC), Bank of China (BoC), Industrial and Commercial Bank of China (ICBC), the Agricultural Bank of China (ABC) and the Bank of Communications (BoCom). Private firms—cut off as they were from bank loans—overwhelmingly financed investments through retained earnings rather than credit during the 2000s. This left the state sector to absorb a large majority of financing during this period, and by 2009 50% of outstanding loans were owed by SOEs—despite their accounting for less than 28% of industrial output in that year (Lardy 2014, 192–208). Kroeber (2016, 132) categorises China's financial system as one of 'financial repression'. Similar to that adopted by the classical East Asian developmental states, this was characterised by strict controls on interest rates, high-yielding financial products, the exchange rate, and the capital account; all with the purpose of ensuring state control of surpluses. Indeed, the strength of banking controls was such that from 2003 to 2013, the real deposit rate was negative for savers—implying that surpluses generated by the banks were fully redistributed to borrowers, rather than being returned as interest payments to lenders as in a commercial banking sector.[4]

[4]Credit has become significantly more accessible to private firms in the wake of the financial crisis of 2008–2009, through the shadow banking sector. This is explored further in Chapter 6.

Increasingly flush with surplus savings, the outcome of state institutions' strategic resolution to develop national champions has been the emergence of over 100 large scale firms, several of which have come to occupy the upper echelons of the Fortune 500 list of firms ranked by revenue and assets (*Fortune*, n.d.). These are mostly banks, petrochemicals, real estate and utility companies. Like the state-owned banks discussed previously, many SOEs beyond the financial sector similarly underwent a rigorous course of corporatisation and rationalisation during the 2000s, which left them profitable overall (though significantly less so than the private sector). China Mobile—the largest state-owned telecoms company—provides a case in point. Non-existent in the mid 1990s, a team from Goldman Sachs projected the great *potential* value of a (then non-existent) national telecommunications company, to be assembled through a merger of China's manifold local level telecoms operators. China Mobile raised \$4.5bn at IPO in New York, which provided the capital required to undertake the expensive process of rationalisation (Walter and Howie 2011, 181–182). In fact, a total of 15 SOEs were floated from 1997 to 2006, raising a combined \$73.2 billion from global investors. The 'hardening' of budget constraints—restricting the ability of SOEs to continue debt-loading and an intensified focus on profitability, rather than production quotas, as a principal strategic aim—were the primary tools of marketisation.

The implantation of foreign corporate governance techniques and the partial opening of China's major SOEs to overseas shareholding patently did not result in a convergence towards a system of private corporate governance, however. The central state was able to repurpose corporatisation towards strengthening its own power and patronage base, reinforcing one party rule and state power on the basis of powerful and competitive strategic industries. A closed capital account and tight political control over the financial sector meant China avoided the upheavals associated with much of the Asian financial sector in the 1990s—from the Japanese equity price collapse of 1991 to the regional currency crises of 1997/1998. Non-performing loans (NPLs) did surface on a significant scale in 1998, but rapid economic growth over the following decade allowed the state to recapitalise the banking sector, and for the NPLs to be repackaged and deferred into the future using four newly created asset management companies (Hung 2015). Debate continues on the success of this operation, and supporters of the Chinese model have frequently praised the capacity of the state dominated financial system to avoid the increasing volatility characteristic of deregulated capital markets. But the *Financial Times* (2016) has pointed out that the bonds on 1.4tn RMB of NPLs from 1998 remain unresolved to date since they were rolled over for another decade during the crisis of 2008–2009, scheduled to fall due in the years from 2019. Recent reports suggest difficulty in disposing of these bad loans with sufficient rapidity (*Financial Times* 2020), implying that even given the extraordinarily favourable conditions for inflating away debt (averaging 10% GDP growth for over twenty years), state-mandated lending has not been able to resolve (but merely defer) debt problems.

And despite this process of corporate rationalisation, the total number of state-owned firms remains at 110,000, despite falling from 262,000 in 1997 (Kroeber 2016, 98). The large majority of state enterprises are owned by provincial and lower tier governments, outside of central directives and barely subject to the rigorous budget constraints enforced by Beijing. Especially at the local level, as Breslin (2014, 999) notes, after bank reform, 'enterprises that had been used to receiving funding as grants through the plan simply continued to view bank loans as free money to support their activities—and so did many of the local governments that controlled them'. In 2007, at the height of the boom, Hung (2015, 65) calculates state firm profitability to be 6.8%, while private firms earned an average return of 9.5%. Subsidies remain widespread and became of especial significance as apparent corporatisation took place during the early part of the 2000s (Haley and Haley 2013).

5.5 The Intertwinement of State and Private Sector

The relatively clear equity division between state and private sector drawn so far represents a useful 'stylised fact' in organising our understanding the Chinese political economy during the 2001–2008 years. Private firms principally operated at a smaller-scale in export-oriented manufacturing in consumer goods and domestic commercial service sectors; and SOEs occupied the commanding heights of heavy and extractive industries and banking. But this model, while helpful, obscures a more complex intertwinement between these two areas of economic life. As we have just seen, SOEs remained dependent on subsidies from state banks, which primarily acquire deposits from private sector firms and households. Chinese bank deposits soared from 22% of GDP in 1994 to double that (of a far larger national product) by 2005, largely as emerging private firms deposited dollar earnings in (state) banks, rendering them flush with surplus cash with which to directly support SOEs. And beyond consumption taxes and VAT (60%) (some of which was paid in import charges by processing firms), enterprises and business taxes sourced primarily from private firms accounted for the second most important source of central government revenue in 2009 (Xu and Cui 2011).

But the state's presence in the privately owned sector is also significant. Private firms growing above a certain scale rarely escape some form of *guanxi* connections with higher scales of government. And access to capital, while mostly preserved for SOEs, is also typically open to leading private sector firms (for instance, China Development Bank financing proved critical for Huawei at an important stage of its development in the mid-2000s; Lazonick et al. 2016, 20). Beyond such exceptional examples, state actors striate the private sector in myriad other ways. Hsueh (2016) demonstrates how, while the sector is largely private-owned, critical infrastructural segments of the telecommunications industry the state owned deemed significant for geopolitical or national developmental reasons are subject to intensive central state intervention. Haier, TCL and Lenovo are global players in export manufacturing with substantial investment from state agencies (Zeng and Williamson 2007). In 2006, regulatory changes at the national scale forced private firms to accommodate party branches within their workplaces and by 2015, 52% of all private firms had established internal party cells. The presence of state and party agencies across the private sector at least calls into question the extent to which firms are driven by purely commercial decisions. While the distinction between large state firms and small private firms holds as a general categorisation, it is also the case that as the most successful private firms develop into large companies, they find themselves unable to escape political relationships and control—meaning that the (Milhaupt and Zhang 2015). On this basis, Yasheng Huang (2016, 24) argues that 'to assert confidently that Chinese economy is 65 or 75% [genuinely] private today presumes an amount of knowledge that simply does not exist'.

Second, outputs from state-owned industries formed important inputs into private sector export production under the exportist SOA. While the dominant processing trade did mean the major share of inputs being sourced from overseas, the burgeoning domestic private sector also drew—in a more limited and uneven way—on the booming output of SOEs, and helped mop up at least some of its chronic overcapacity. Table 5.3 shows the proportion of output values from state dominated

Table 5.3 Share of state-owned enterprise output value entering core export sectors (garments and footwear, electronics, and machinery & transport equipment)

Sector	*Output to export sectors, 2007 (%)*
Metal products	31
Chemicals	13
Electricity, water, gas	10

Source Author, from WIOD (n.d.)

sectors that went to the export sectors in 2007 (electronics, garments and machinery). Despite the exponential increase in the size of these export industries charted in Table 5.1, state production kept pace with their expansion to supply them with inputs. This relatively simple exercise supports the findings of a more detailed regional investigation by Meng (2016, 136), who finds that 'inland regions [producing mostly raw materials and capital goods] successfully enhanced their gain potential for value-added by increasing their participation in DVCs [domestic value chains]'—i.e. largely by supplying products to exporters.

The metal sector benefitted the most from the export boom. In 2007, US$1.4bn worth of basic and fabricated metals were sold to electronics sector firms alone, accounting for almost 15% of total output of a sector with a sales volume of $9.7bn—a greater sum than its total value of exports (less than $1bn). In the same year, the textile industry procured $320m of goods from the industrial chemicals sector—almost six times the value of chemicals imported the sector imported. And in 1995, while textile and footwear sectors accounted for 6% of the value of agricultural output, by 2007, these sectors absorbed 9% of a much larger output (all figures from the WIOD, n.d.). Such linkages between the heavy industrial SOEs and the light manufacturing export sectors were critically mediated by the political economy of state capitalism and demonstrate that, though of secondary importance, state firms did play a not insignificant role in the export boom. Further firm level research would be required to establish why private sector firms were prepared to purchase significant quantities of materials from the state sector, but (outside of utilities) the locality and regularity of supply likely factor in such decisions.

Beyond the direct input–output relations binding the state and private sectors in China is their intertwinement in currency policy. On the one hand, currency management during the 2000s served to depress the exchange value of the yuan in order to maintain export competitiveness. This was achieved through pegging the yuan to the dollar at a fixed rate of 8.28 until mid-2005, at which point a managed appreciation of the yuan was permitted. On the other, the mechanism by which the fixed exchange rate was maintained in the 2000s served to channel large foreign exchange (forex) reserves amassed by the PBoC into the state sector. Dollars earned by exporters were exchanged for renminbi with commercial banks, used to pay wage and other business outgoings. In turn, the PBoC purchased these dollars from the banks and built up a large supply of forex, with the purpose of artificially depressing the exchange rate in order to maintain cost-competitiveness in the export sector (a process known as 'sterilized intervention': see Zhang 2012). By 2008, PBoC dollar reserves had expanded to US$2tn, ten times the figure in 2001, in line with the dramatic expansion of private-sector manufacturing export earnings. This, in turn, enabled a vast expansion of the domestic money supply in the state-owned banking sector. In turn, this expanded domestic money supply could be used to finance the retooling of state-owned corporations, through subsidies and an expensive industrial policy. All this could be achieved without risking foreign capital flight or runaway inflation, bugbears of developing economies in the global south, since this money was backed by dollars earned in the highly profitable export-manufacturing sector (Shih 2019). China's broad money supply (M2) consequently expanded 244% from US$13.8tn in January 2001 to $47.5tn at the close of 2008 (for comparison, US M2 expanded 64% from $5tn to $8.2tn over the same period).

In sum, a stylised model of a private-public binary helps delineate the major contours of China's 'exportist SOA' which emerged during the decade to 2008. But this sectoral and regional economic unevenness—while real—was also combined into a unitary political economy by the Chinese state at various levels. Firstly, direct political intervention into the most successful and largest nominally private enterprises secured both their success and their political subordination to the party-state. Second, inputs from the state sector flowed into the private sector as it expanded, providing a critical market for state produce. Third, the currency management system represented a temporary alignment of interest between private-sector exporters (which benefitted from an artificially depressed currency) and SOEs, which benefitted from the vastly expanded money supply and subsidies channelled through state banks.

5.6 Conclusion

In an analysis which to some extent accords with that of this chapter, Kellogg (2015a, b) argues that China's development during the 2000s can be understood as a developmental 'leap' in the vein of Trotsky. Kellogg (2015b, 290) writes that the 'very rapid emergence of China as the world's leading center of manufacturing, as one of three key players in high-tech production, and as a rapidly emerging site for the world's top corporations, goes some way to explaining and highlighting the long-term, secular, relative decline of the United States in the world economy'. He uses four criteria in support of this argument: the growth in China's (a) per capita income (b) share of world manufacturing (c) R&D spending and (d) size of large firms. To conclude, I respond briefly to each of these arguments in order to clarify some of the particularities of my own understanding of China's UCD presented in this chapter—especially my focus on the challenges of 'debased adaptation', which serves to complicate any simple notion of the 'privilege of historical backwardness' in a global political economy where the terms of development have so radically altered.

Firstly, China's per capita income has certainly grown, though dramatic spike in inequality and the repression of labour's share of income mean that this has not consumption has fallen as a proportion of GDP since 2001 (Qi 2014). And second, while overall share of world manufacturing is significant, if we take value-added measurements China's growth appears far more complementary to the advanced economies, rather than directly competitive with them (even if this complementarity is beginning to change; Fig. 5.4). Third, Kellogg (2015b, 276) makes the dubious move of measuring R&D spending deflated by purchasing power parity (PPP), on the assumption that research is roughly equivalent on a global scale, and so– adjusting for relative weight of currencies—concludes China's spending is approaching that of the United States. By contrast, if we use real dollars on the assumption that innovation (particularly in high-technology sectors like consumer electronics) is now a global industry with a small pool of world-class researchers and relatively fixed costs, real (rather than adjusted) US$ may provide a more valid indication of relative research spending. Chinese spending in dollar terms remains below half that of the US level and the quality of innovation (as measured by 'triadic patents' registered across the USA, EU and Japanese patent offices) remained below 10% of the US level by 2010 (Kennedy 2016). Finally, the measurement of firm size by revenue should not be taken as representing the relative power of Chinese firms. China's largest firms were until very recently exclusively SOE conglomerates in protected sectors, often enjoying monopoly rents and preferential access to capital. Such firms rarely compete directly with advanced economy firms on a global scale, and thus cannot be considered an economic 'threat' on a part with, for instance, Japanese car firms during the 1970s.

These qualifications suggest that—despite significant progress in industrial upgrading—China's 2000s-era boom did not allow it to escape a modularity trap (or 'debased adaptation') across its core export sectors. China's de facto strategy for improving the terms of its integration into the world economy has been to attract, using its vast supplies of cheap labour, a large bulk of low-end global manufacturing capacity and to invest in the basic infrastructure to ensure its continuing competitiveness. Marshallian clustering made China's increasingly dense supply chains extremely competitive, while geographical supply chain consolidation on such a large scale made it difficult for other industrialising states to compete.

In 2015, the *Economist* argued (as it has regularly) for a further enlargement of China's private sector: the 'only option is to encourage more enterprise and innovation. Such dynamism will not come from stodgy state firms'. This chapter has outlined the major economic features of an exportist SOA in which regional economies in China's coastal areas were connected to global production networks, while surpluses in these areas were redistributed to state producers through the system by the institutions of the state. The 'combined development' perspective then considered how, alongside a greater fragmentation of the division of labour within particular economic sectors, firms simultaneously remain tied into a national system of accumulation reliant on and responsive to its inputs, forms of labour management, political structure and dynamics, infrastructural provision, and industrial policies. The exportist SOA thus emerged as a hybrid system, fusing a mass of low margin, labour intensive and horizontally networked exporters to a highly vertically integrated set of SOEs. The next chapter explores the crisis-tendencies of this accumulation system and attempts by the central state to contain these as they developed from 2008, when global markets for manufactured exports collapsed.

References

Akyüz, Yilmaz. 2011. Export Dependence and Sustainability of Growth in China. *China and World Economy* 19 (1): 1–23.

Amiti, Mary, and Caroline Freund. 2010. The Anatomy of China's Export Growth. In *China's Growing Role in World Trade*, ed. Robert Feenstra and Shang-Jin Wei, 35–56. Chicago: University of Chicago Press.

Anderson, Jonathan. 2007. Is China Export-Led? *UBS Investment Research: Asian Focus*. Available online at: www.allroadsleadtochina.com/reports/prc_270907.pdf. Accessed 1 December 2017.

Anderson, G.E. 2012. Auto Industry Competitiveness: Fat Profits, Fat Failures. *China Economic Quarterly* (June): 43–47.

Appelbaum, Richard. 2009. Big Suppliers in Greater China: A Growing Counter-weight to the Power of Giant Retailers. In *China and the Transformation of Global Capitalism*, ed. Ho-fung Hung. Baltimore: Johns Hopkins University Press.

Athukorala, Prema-chandra. 2009. The Rise of China and East Asian Export Performance: Is the Crowding-Out Fear Warranted? *The World Economy* 32: 234–265.

Baldwin, Richard. 2016. *The Great Convergence: Information Technology and the New Globalisation*. Cambridge, MA: Belknap.

Baldwin, Richard, and Javier Lopez-Gonzalez. 2015. Supply-Chain Trade: A Portrait of Global Patterns and Several Testable Hypotheses. *The World Economy* 38 (11): 1682–1721.

Banister, Judith. 2013. China's Manufacturing Employment and Hourly Labor Compensation, 2002–2009. *Bureau of Labor Statistics International Labor Comparisons*. Available online at: http://www.bls.gov/fls/china_method.pdf. Accessed 1 February 2017.

Banister, Judith, and George Cook. 2011. China's Employment and Compensation Costs in Manufacturing Through 2008. *Monthly Labour Review*, March: 39–52.

Boschma, Ron, Lars Coenen, Koen Frenken, and Bernhard Truffer. 2017. Towards a Theory of Regional Diversification: Combining Insights from Evolutionary Economic Geography and Transition Studies. *Regional Studies* 51 (1): 31–45.

Brambilla, Irene, Amit Khandelwal, and Peter Schott. 2010. China's Experience Under the Multi-Fiber Arrangement (MFA) and the Agreement on Textiles and Clothing (ATC). In *China's Growing Role in World Trade*, ed. Robert C. Feenstra and Shang-Jin Wei, 345–387. Chicago: University of Chicago Press.

Brandt, Loren, and Eric Thun. 2015. Competition and Upgrading in Chinese Industry. In *State Capitalism, Institutional Adaptation and the Chinese Miracle*, ed. Barry Naughton and Kellee Tsai, 154–198. Cambridge: Cambridge University Press.

Breslin, Shaun. 2014. Financial Transitions in the PRC: Banking on the State? *Third World Quarterly* 35 (6): 996–1013.

Breznitz, Dan, and Michael Murphree. 2011. *Run of the Red Queen: Government, Innovation, Globalization, and Economic Growth in China*. New Haven: Yale University Press.

Butollo, Florian. 2014. *The End of Cheap Labour? Industrial Transformation and Social Upgrading in China*. Frankfurt: Campus Verlag.

Butollo, Florian. 2015. Growing Against the Odds: Government Agency and Strategic Recoupling as Sources of Competitiveness in the Garment Industry of the Pearl River Delta. *Cambridge Journal of Regions, Economy and Society* 8: 521–536.

Canis, Robert. 2012. The Tool and Die Industry: Contribution to U.S. Manufacturing and Federal Policy Considerations. Congressional Research Report for the US Congress, CRS, Washington, DC.

Cao, Cong, Richard P. Suttmeier, and Denis Fred Simon. 2006. China's 15-Year Science and Technology Plan. *Physics Today* 59 (12): 38–43.

Chen, Ling. 2014. Varieties of Global Capital and the Paradox of Local Upgrading in China. *Politics & Society* 42 (2): 223–252.

Crotty, James. 2000. Slow Growth, Destructive Competition, and Low Road Labor Relations: A Keynes-Marx-Schumpeter Analysis of Neoliberal Globalization. Available online at: http://www.umass.edu/peri/research.html#gm. Accessed 23 March 2019.

Dallas, Mark. 2014. Manufacturing Paradoxes: Foreign Ownership, Governance, and Value Chains in China's Light Industries. *World Development* 57: 47–62.

Dallas, Mark. n.d. Between Markets and Institutions: Multinational Enterprises as Actors, and a Production Network Approach to Foreign Direct Investment. *World Politics*, forthcoming. Available online at: http://www.markpeterdallas.com/wp-content/uploads/2015/09/Mark-P.-Dallas-Between-Markets-and-Institutions_MNEs-as-Actors-and-a-Production-Network-Approach-to-FDI.pdf. Accessed 11 April 2020.

Davidson, Neil. 2012. *How Revolutionary Were the Bourgeois Revolutions?* Chicago: Haymarket.

Dedrick, Jason, Kenneth L. Kraemer, and Greg Linden. 2010. Who Profits from Innovation in Global Value Chains? A Study of the iPod and Notebook PCs. *Industrial and Corporate Change* 19 (1): 81–116.

Eaton, Sarah. 2015. *The Advance of the State in Contemporary China: State-Market Relations in the Reform Era*. Cambridge: Cambridge University Press.

Feng, Kaidong. 2016. Chinese Indigenous Innovation in the Car Sector: Being Integrated or Being the Integrator. In *China as an Innovation Nation*, ed. Yu. Zhou, William Lazonick, and Yifei Sun, 133–164. Oxford: Oxford University Press.

Financial Times. 2016. China's Debt-Shrinking Machine Loses Its Magical Power, April 25. Available online at: www.ft.com/content/4393069c-0acb-11e6-b0f1-61f222853ff3.

Financial Times. 2020. China Calls on Foreigners to Drain $1.5tn Bad-Debt Swamp, February 25. Available online at: https://www.ft.com/content/b41547b2-9971-48b2-a74f-a429402b485d. Accessed 26 February 2020.

Gallagher, Mary. 2014. China's Workers Movement and the End of the Rapid-Growth Era. *Daedalus* 143 (2): 81–95.

Gereffi, Gary. 1994. The Organization of Buyer-Driven Global Commodity Chains: How US Retailers Shape Overseas Production Networks. In *Commodity Chains and Global Capitalism*, ed. Gary Gereffi and Miguel Korzeniewicz. Westport, CT: Praeger.

Gereffi, G. 2008. Development Models and Industrial Upgrading in China and Mexico. *European Sociological Review* 25 (1): 37–51.

Gereffi, Gary, and Timothy Sturgeon. 2013. Global Value Chain-Oriented Industrial Policy: The Role of Emerging Economies. In *Global Value Chains in a Changing World*, ed. Deborah K. Elms and Patrick Low, 329–361. Geneva: WTO.

Goodman, David. 2014. *Class in Contemporary China*. Cambridge: Polity.

Gray, Kevin. 2015. *Labour and Development in East Asia: Social Forces and Passive Revolution*. London: Routledge.

Haley, Usha, and George Haley. 2013. *Subsidies to Chinese Industry: State Capitalism, Business Strategy, and Trade Policy*. Oxford: Oxford University Press.

Harney, Alexandra. 2008. *The China Price: The True Cost of Competitive Advantage*. London: Penguin.

He, Dong, and Wenlang Zhang. 2010. How Dependent Is the Chinese Economy on Exports and in What Sense Has Its Growth Been Export-Led? *Journal of Asian Economics* 21: 87–104.

Heilmann, Sebastian, Lea Shih, and Andreas Hofem. 2013. National Planning and Local Technology Zones: Experimental Governance in China's Torch Program. *The China Quarterly* 216: 896–919.

HKTDC. 2016. China: Overall Export Competitiveness Remains Intact. Available online at: http://economists-pick-research.hktdc.com/business-news/article/Research-Articles/China-Overall-Export-Competitiveness-Remains-Intact/rp/en/1/1X000000/1X0A62ZV.htm. Accessed 31 March 2017.

Holmes, John, Tod Rutherford, and Susan Fitzgibbon. 2005. Innovation in the Automotive Tool, Die and Mould Industry. In *Network Structure of an Industrial Cluster*, 119–154. Montreal: McGill-Queens University Press.

Holz, C.A. 2018. The Unfinished Business of State-Owned Enterprise Reform in the People's Republic of China. *SSRN*. Available online at: https://papers.ssrn.com/sol3/papers.cfm?abstract_id=3392986. Accessed 2 June 2019.

Horn, Jonathan, Vivien Singer, and Jonathan Woetzel. 2010. A Truer Picture of China's Export Machine: China's Growth Depends Less on Exports Than Conventional Wisdom Suggests. *McKinsey Quarterly*, September.

Hsieh, Chang-Tai, and Zheng Song. 2015. Grasp the Large, Let Go the Small: The Transformation of the State Sector in China. NBER Working Paper Series, Working Paper 21006.

Hsing, You-tien. 1998. *Making Capitalism in China: The Taiwan Connection*. Oxford: Oxford University Press.

Hsueh, Roselyn. 2016. State Capitalism, Chinese-Style: Strategic Value of Sectors, Sectoral Characteristics, and Globalization. *Governance: An International Journal of Policy, Administration, and Institutions* 29 (1): 85–102.

Huang, Yasheng. 2016. State Capitalism in China. In *The Annual Proceedings of the Wealth and Well-Being of Nations, 2015–2016*, ed. Warren Palmer, 19–51.

Hung, Ho-fung. 2015. *The China Boom: Why China Will Not Rule the World*. Chichester: Columbia University Press.

International Labour Organisation [ILO]. 2014. *Ups and Downs in the Electronics Industry: Fluctuating Production and the Use of Temporary and Other Forms of Employment*. Geneva: International Labour Office.

Kee, Hiau Looi, and Heiwai Tang. 2016. Domestic Value Added in Exports: Theory and Firm Evidence from China. *American Economic Review* 106 (6): 1402–1436.

Kellogg, Paul. 2015a. Contours of a Multipolar Century. *Rethinking Marxism* 27 (4): 558–570.

Kellogg, Paul. 2015b. Geographies of Capital Accumulation: Tracing the Emergence of Multi-Polarity, 1980–2014. In *Research in Political Economy 30: A*, 259–294. Bingley: Emerald.

Kennedy, Andrew. 2016. Slouching Tiger, Roaring Dragon: Comparing India and China as Late Innovators. *Review of International Political Economy* 23 (1): 65–92.

Kroeber, Arthur. 2016. *China's Economy: What Everyone Needs to Know*. Oxford: Oxford University Press.

Kumar, Ashok. 2020. *Monopsony Capitalism: Power and Production in the Twilight of the Sweatshop Age*. Cambridge: Cambridge University Press.

Lardy, Nicholas. 2014. *Markets over Mao: The Rise of Private Business in China*. Washington, DC: Peterson Institute.

Lazonick, William, Yu. Zhou, and Yifei Sun. 2016. Introduction: China's Transformation to an Innovation Nation. In *China as an Innovation Nation*, ed. Yu. Zhou, William Lazonick, and Yifei Sun, 1–32. Oxford: Oxford University Press.

Lin, Chun. 2015. The Language of Class in China. *Socialist Register* 51: 24–53.

Lüthje, Boy, and Florian Butollo. 2016. Why the Foxconn Model Does Not Die: Production Networks and Labour Relations in the IT Industry in South China. *Globalizations.* Published online before print (August 11).

Lüthje, Boy, Siqi Luo, and Hao Zhang. 2013a. *Beyond the Iron Rice Bowl: Regimes of Production and Industrial Relations in China.* Frankfurt: Campus Verlag.

Lüthje, Boy, Stefanie Hürtgen, Peter Pawlicki, and Martina Sproll. 2013b. *From Silicon Valley to Shenzhen: Global Production and Work in the IT Industry.* Boulder: Rowman & Littlefield.

Ma, Alyson C., and Ari Van Assche. 2010. *The Role of Trade Costs in Global Production Networks: Evidence from China's Processing Trade Regime.* The World Bank.

Marx, Karl. 1863. *Theories of Surplus Value.* Available online at: https://www.marxists.org/archive/marx/works/1863/theories-surplus-value/. Accessed 12 March 2020.

Mathai, Koshy, Geoff Gottlieb, Gee Hee Hong, Sung Eun Jung, Jochen Schmittmann, and Jiangyan Yu. 2016. *China's Changing Trade and the Implications for the CLMV Economies.* Washington, DC: IMF Departmental Paper Series (IMF).

Meng, Bo. 2016. Domestic Value Chains in the People's Republic of China and Their Linkages with the Global Economy. *Uncovering Value Added in Trade: New Approaches to Analyzing Global Value Chains*: 113–139.

Milhaupt, Curtis, and Wentong Zheng. 2015. Beyond Ownership: State Capitalism and the Chinese Firm. *Georgetown Law Journal* 103 (3): 665–722.

Moore, Thomas G. 2002. *China in the World Market: Chinese Industry and International Sources of Reform in the Post-Mao Era.* Cambridge: Cambridge University Press.

Nahm, Jonas, and Edward Steinfeld. 2014. Scale-Up Nation: China's Specialization in Innovative Manufacturing. *World Development* 54: 288–300.

National Science Board. 2012. *Science and Engineering 2012.* Washington, DC: National Science Board.

Naughton, Barry. 2007. *The Chinese Economy: Transition and Growth.* Cambridge, MA: MIT Press.

Naughton, Barry. 2014. China's Economy: Complacency, Crisis & the Challenge of Reform. *Daedalus* 143 (2): 14–25.

Nolan, Peter. 2014. Globalisation and Industrial Policy: The Case of China. *The World Economy* 37 (6): 747–764.

Nordås, Hildegunn Kyvik. 2004. The Global Textile and Clothing Industry Post the Agreement on Textiles and Clothing. WTO Discussion Paper No. 5. Available online at: https://www.econstor.eu/bitstream/10419/107040/1/wto-discussion-paper_05.pdf. Accessed 11 November 2016.

OECD-WTO. 2015. *Trade in Value Added: China*. Available online at: https://www.oecd.org/sti/ind/tiva/CN_2015_China.pdf. Accessed 25 January 2007.

Oi, Jean. 1995. The Role of the Local State in China's Transitional Economy. *The China Quarterly* 144: 1132–1149.

Pawlicki, Peter. 2016. Re-focusing and Re-shifting—The Constant Restructuring of Global Production Networks in the Electronics Industry. In *Flexible Workforces and Low Profit Margins: Electronics Assembly Between Europe and China*, ed. Jan Drahokoupil, Rutvica Andrijasevic, and Devi Sacchetto, 21–44. Brussels: ETUI.

Pearson, Margaret. 2015. State-Owned Business and Party-State Regulation in China's Modern Political Economy. In *State Capitalism, Institutional Adaptation and the Chinese Miracle*, ed. Barry Naughton and Kellee Tsai, 27–45. Cambridge: Cambridge University Press.

Pecht, Michael. 2006. *China's Electronics Industry: The Definitive Guide for Companies and Policy Makers with Interests in China*. Norwich, NY: William Andrew.

Pei, Minxin. 2006. *China's Trapped Transition: The Limits of Developmental Autocracy*. Cambridge: Harvard University Press.

Pringle, Tim. 2013. Reflections on Labor in China: From a Moment to a Movement. *The South Atlantic Quarterly* 112 (1): 191–202.

Qi, Hao. 2014. The Labor Share Question in China. *Monthly Review* 65 (8): 23–35.

Rodrik, Dani. 2006. What's So Special About China's Exports? *China and World Economy* 14 (5): 1–19.

Saxenian, AnnaLee. 2005. From Brain Drain to Brain Circulation: Transnational Communities and Regional Upgrading in India and China. *Studies in Comparative International Development* 40 (2): 35–61.

Schuh, Günther, Michael Salmen, Thomas Kuhlmann, and Jan Wiese. 2017. Highly Iterative Product Development Within the Tool and Die Making Industry. *Procedia CIRP* 61: 576–581.

Shih, Victor. 2019. China's Credit Conundrum. *New Left Review* 115: 59–74.

Silver, Beverley. 2003. *Forces of Labor: Workers' Movements and Globalization Since 1870*. Cambridge: Cambridge University Press.

Smith, John. 2016. *Imperialism in the Twenty-First Century: Globalization, Super-Exploitation, and Capitalism's Final Crisis*. New York: Monthly Review.

So, Alvin Y. 2013. *Class and Class Conflict in Post-Socialist China*. Singapore: World Scientific Publishing.

Song, Lei. 2008. The Origins, Typology of China's Modularization Trap and the Growth of Productivity. *Academic Monthly*, February. Available online at: http://en.cnki.com.cn/Article_en/CJFDTOTAL-XSYK200802016.htm. Accessed 11 February 2017.

Steinfeld, Edward. 2010. *Playing Our Game: Why China's Economic Rise Doesn't Threaten the West*. Oxford: Oxford University Press.

Sturgeon, Timothy, and Momoko Kawakami. 2010. Global Value Chains in the Eletronics Industry: Was the Crisis a Window of Opportunity for Developing Countries? Policy Research Paper, No. 5.417, September. Available online at: http://documents.worldbank.org/curated/en/438311468154773219/Global-value-chains-in-the-electronics-industry-was-the-crisis-a-window-of-opportunity-for-developing-countries. Accessed 27 April 2017.

Supply Chain 24/7. 2017. Apple's Supply Chain: The Cost of Making the iPhone 7. Available online at: http://www.supplychain247.com/article/apples_supply_chain_cost_of_making_the_iphone_7/procurement. Accessed 1 April 2017.

The Economist. 2015. The China That Works, September 10. Available online at: https://www.economist.com/news/leaders/21664143-if-economic-miracle-continue-officials-must-give-private-sector-more-freedom. Accessed 1 March 2017.

Timmer, Marcel, Erik Dietzenbacher, Bart Los, Robert Stehrer, and Gaaitzen J. de Vries. 2015. An Illustrated User Guide to the World Input-Output Database: the Case of Global Automotive Production. *Review of International Economics* 23 (3): 575–605.

Towson, Jeffrey, and Jonathan Woetzel. 2015. Why China's Consumers Will Continue to Surprise the World. *McKinsey & Company*, May. Available online at: http://www.mckinsey.com/business-functions/strategy-and-corporate-finance/our-insights/why-chinas-consumers-will-continue-to-surprise-the-world. Accessed 13 October 2016.

Trotsky, Leon. 2009 [1932]. *The History of the Russian Revolution: Volumes I, II & III*. Chicago: Haymarket.

UNCTAD. Various years. *World Investment Report*. Archive available online at: http://unctad.org/en/PublicationsLibrary/. Accessed 1 February 2017.

USITC. 2002. Tools, Dies, and Industrial Molds: Competitive Conditions in the United States and Selected Foreign Markets. USITC Investigation No. 332-435, Publication 3556, USITC, Washington DC.

Walter, Carl, and Fraser Howie. 2011. *Red Capitalism: The Fragile Financial Foundation of China's Extraordinary Rise*. Chichester: Wiley.

Wei, Dennis Y.H., Lu Yuqi, and Wen Chen. 2009. Globalizing Regional Development in Sunan, China: Does Suzhou Industrial Park fit a neo-Marshallian District Model? *Regional Studies* 43 (3): 409–428.

World Bank. n.d. *Indicators*. Available online at: data.worldbank.org/indicator. Accessed 12 June 2019.

World Input Output Database [WIOD]. n.d. Available online at: http://www.wiod.org/home. Accessed 11 December 2016.

Xing, Yuqing. 2012. Processing Trade, Exchange Rates and China's Bilateral Trade Balances. *Journal of Asian Economics* 23 (5): 540–547.

Xing, Yuqing. 2016. Estimating the Upper Limits of Value Added in the People's Republic of China's Processing Exports. In *Uncovering Value Added in Trade: New Approaches to Analysing Global Value Chains*, ed. Yuqing Xing. Singapore: World Scientific.

Xing, Yuqing, and Neal Detert. 2010. How the iPhone Widens the United States Trade Deficit with the People's Republic of China. Asian Development Bank Institute Working Paper No. 257. Available online at: http://www.adbi.org/files/2010.12.14.wp257.iphone.widens.us.trade.deficit.prc.pdf. Accessed 14 March 2017.

Xu, Hua, and Huiyu Cai. 2011. The Revenue System of China: Past, Present, and Emerging Issues. *Journal of Public Budgeting, Accounting & Financial Management* 23 (4): 544.

Xu, Jiang, and Anthony Yeh. 2009. Decoding Urban Land Governance: State Reconstruction in Contemporary Chinese Cities. *Urban Studies* 46 (3): 559–581.

Yang, Chun. 2007. Divergent Hybrid Capitalisms in China: Hong Kong and Taiwanese Electronics Clusters in Dongguan. *Economic Geography* 83 (4): 395–420.

Yang, Dali, and Junyan Jiang. 2012. Guojin Mintui: The Global Recession and Changing State–Economy Relations in China. In *The Global Recession and China's Political Economy*, ed. Dali Yang, 33–69. Basingstoke: Palgrave.

Yeung, Godfrey, and Vincent Mok. 2004. Does WTO Accession Matter for the Chinese Textile and Clothing Industry? *Cambridge Journal of Economics* 28 (6): 937–954.

Zeng, Ming, and Peter Williamson. 2007. *Dragons at Your Door: How Chinese Cost Innovation Is Disrupting Global Competition*. Boston: Harvard Business School Press.

Zhang, Lu. 2015. *Inside China's Automobile Factories: The Politics of Labor and Worker Resistance*. Cambridge: Cambridge University Press.

Zhang, Ming. 2012. Chinese Stylized Sterilization: The Cost-Sharing Mechanism and Financial Repression. *China & World Economy* 20 (2): 41–58.

Zhang, Zhiming, Chester To, and Ning Cao. 2004. How Do Industry Clusters Success: A Case Study in China's Textiles and Apparel Industries. *Journal of Textile and Apparel, Technology and Management* 4 (2): 1–10.

Zhu, Andong, and David Kotz. 2011. The Dependence of China's Economic Growth on Exports and Investment. *Review of Radical Political Economics* 43 (1): 9–32.

Zhu, Shengjun, and John Pickles. 2014. Bring In, Go Up, Go West, Go Out: Upgrading, Regionalisation and Delocalisation in China's Apparel Production Networks. *Journal of Contemporary Asia* 44 (1): 36–63.

CHAPTER 6

The 'Rebalancing' Fallacy: 2008 and Its Aftermath

6.1 Introduction

Many neoclassically oriented economists credit China's entry into global manufacturing networks with producing the country's astonishing growth spurt—implicitly taking such labour practices as unfortunate collateral in the broader march towards economic development globalisation is bringing. More critical political economists have tended to instead view manufacturing production networks as a new iteration of dependency relations based on internationally exploitative unequal exchange of manufactured goods (Lo 2016; Smith 2016). But this poses a puzzle: if China's economy is so deeply integrated with those of the global north, how come it demonstrated such remarkable resilience to the otherwise 'global' economic crisis of 2008 which wreaked various forms of havoc across virtually all other economies? Could this unique buoyancy in fact signify China's rise as an autonomous centre of capital accumulation in the world economy?

This chapter interrogates the views of those optimists who expect China, having reaped the benefits (or suffered the consequences) of an open economy, to now 'rebalance' away from dependence on the export sector and towards serving increasingly wealthy domestic markets. Such rebalancing is unlikely, I argue, because such accounts mistake long-run trends in the data which demonstrate, on the contrary, that China's economy remains profoundly imbricated with the global economy.

S. Rolf, *China's Uneven and Combined Development*,
Studies in the Political Economy of Public Policy,
https://doi.org/10.1007/978-3-030-55559-7_6

Surpluses accumulated through export-led growth and captured by the state, alongside its distinctive form of control over the financial sector, have together allowed the Chinese government to insulate itself from global headwinds for a long period. As these surpluses have dwindled, state managers have turned to fictitious capital—debt—creation as a means of sustaining growth and social stability. As such, the exportist SOA outlined in the previous chapter underwent a critical transformation after 2008. But it is only through a return to the profitability of investments across its core export sectors can China hope to sustain its dynamic growth rates into the future.

It is consequently misleading to point to China's post-crisis performance as evidence of its potential emergence as an autonomous region of growth. Its 'core sectors'—which generate the large surpluses upon which China relies to sustain its sky-high investment rate—as yet remain deeply embedded in global production networks in which Chinese firms remain by and large subordinates, rather than competitors, to advanced economy firms.

6.2 The Effects of the Crisis of 2008 in China

China's GDP statistics do not much reflect the global economic crisis of 2008. Despite the turmoil in markets unfolding across much of the world economy, in 2008 and 2009, Chinese GDP grew by 9.6 and 9.1%, respectively (Fig. 6.1). Though down from the spectacular 14.2% growth rate posted in 2007, this was not substantially less than the average of 11.2% between 2002 and 2007. The global economic crisis looked like a normal 'bad' year. As Hsing (2012) points out, this apparent stability led to the widespread argument that China had 'delinked' from dependence on the US and European markets, and was now functioning as a largely autonomous pole of growth in the world economy (cf. Dollar 2008). In this perspective, China's domestic market has developed so substantially that the falloff in exports had little impact on its real drivers of growth: domestic consumption and investment. And, despite a lull in 2008–2009, export performance nevertheless rebounded from a nadir in 2009 in line with the recovery in the world economy after 2010. China improved its overall share of world manufactures output from 9% at the outbreak of the crisis to 13% by the close of 2014, a level around which it has fluctuated since. The deepening of supply chains and a decline of imports in parts and components for final-stage assembly operations both fueled this

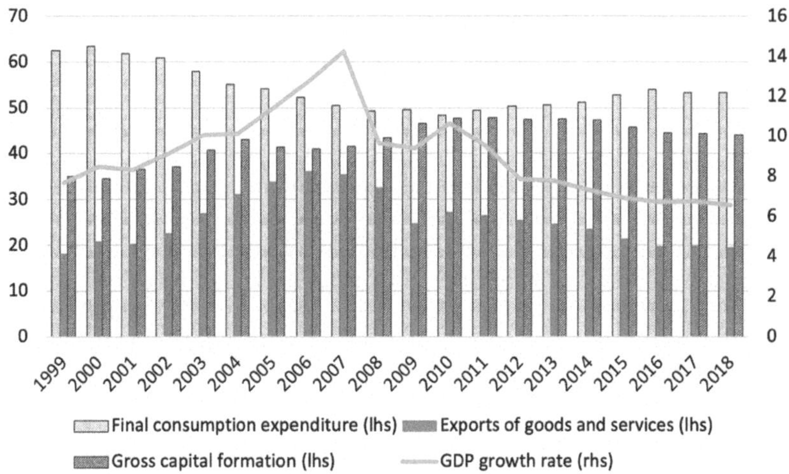

Fig. 6.1 GDP components in China (%, lhs) and GDP growth rate (%, rhs), 1999–2018 (*Source* World Bank indicators [n.d.])

growth, as China further developed its domestic capacity as a components supplier to global production networks (GPNs) beyond a mere final-stage assembler of parts produced elsewhere (Mathai et al. 2016)—though equivalent increases in exports of raw materials (like steel) were just as significant as industrial upgrading in fueling the recovery of China's export earnings.

While the global economic crisis presented an opportunity for China to consolidate its role as world factory in the medium term, the short-term consequences were severe. China's balance of trade, which had improved by an average of 70% year-on-year from 2002 to 2007, improved by just 17% in 2008 and deteriorated substantially—for the first time in over a decade—by 32% in 2009 (figures from Hsing 2012, 252). The fall in exports accounted for a net loss of 1.9 GDP percentage points in 2009 (Akyüz 2011, 14), while from 2007 to 2013, China's annual trade surplus fell from 10% of total GDP to just 2%. This overnight falloff in export demand and earnings had an immediate social impact. The best research demonstrates that anywhere between 20 and 36 million workers were left unemployed as small and medium-sized manufacturers across China's export heartlands suffered a deep shakeout, resulting mostly from the collapse in demand for final consumer goods in the crisis-ridden advanced economies (Giles et al. 2012). While (unreliable) official statistics register just a 0.1% drop in employment nationwide, even these report layoffs being heavily concentrated in the coastal exporting areas, with a 3.8% fall in industrial employment in Guangdong and a 3.3% fall in Zhejiang province. Employment mostly revived after 2010 along with exports, but this recovery was now insufficient to drive economic growth on a national scale as it had done during the 2000s. As such, while exports proved vital for the economy during the 2000s, they have contributed relatively little to China's economic growth since 2009 (Fig. 6.1); and the overall rate of growth slowed in line with this decline (to 6.8% in 2017).[1] 2008 represents the end of the exportist 'system of accumulation' (SOA), though *not* the end of Chinese exports.

6.3 China's 'Rebalancing': Contrasting Theories

If exports stopped contributing to China's GDP growth after 2008, where has its subsequent economic growth come from? From a formal macroeconomic accounting perspective, it follows that investment and consumption drove growth from 2009 onwards, as confirmed in Fig. 6.1. This was a celebratory cause for some, who understand this as a form of 'delinking' from dependency on world markets, and based upon sound fundamentals built up during the previous decade. If accurate, then sustainable domestic investment and consumption demand should continue to sustainably drive catch-up growth (albeit at a lower overall rate) into the medium term.

Box 6.1 The 'middle-income trap'

David Shambaugh (2016, 42) describes the 'middle-income trap' as 'a concept used by developmental economists to describe a newly industrialising economy that reaches a mean income threshold—usually about $11,000 (China is currently at $9771, or $18,236

[1] Figure 6.1 shows net exports not adjusted for import intensity of exports, consequently minimising the contribution of exports during the 2000s and overstating losses from 2008. For an explanation, see Akyüz (2011, 6–12).

PPP equivalent, as of the end of 2018, according to the World Bank)—which begins to compromise the economy's competitive advantages in low-wage manufacturing'. The implication is that China's period of rapid growth is likely to end in the near future, and history suggests that growth will thereafter contract quite sharply (before reaching the level of the advanced economies) (Eichengreen et al. 2013). In a complementary argument, Pritchett and Summers (2014) identify a long-run trend of 'regression to the mean' in GDP growth. But the trap/regression is simply an (inductive) projection of past trends, and conflates economic growth across the time and space of different national states as though they represent comparable units and processes. The timing and circumstance of China's industrialisation in relation to the global political economy are radically different to virtually all previous experiences of catch-up growth. Global trends like the rise in economic inequality within national economies (Piketty 2014) and the shift from national vertically integrated industries to GPNs, seem to complicate any simple notion of 'national development' by which an economy converges with advanced capitalist countries in per capita income. While the middle-income trap may be far too general a concept for comparisons between experiences to be meaningful, it does suggest that we should not *assume* convergence is the inevitable outcome of China's high-growth period.

But looking below headline growth figures also potentially warrants an alternate view: that 2008 represented a real crisis and a major turning point for China's political economy towards debt-fueled state intervention as a form of counter-cyclical crisis deferral. This, I argue, was only possible because of the *combined development* China had experienced up until this point, where the state's economic role remained undiminished across the commanding heights of the raw materials, capital goods and financial sectors. Fiscal stimulus could consequently act as an effective shock absorber to the decline of the export industry by ramping up investment across these sectors *regardless of demand conditions*—in contrast to most advanced economy firms which relied principally on monetary instruments (or fiscal support to the banking sector alone). However, with the crucial link between surplus dollar earnings from competitive exports and the growing domestic money supply now broken (see Sects. 5.4–5.5), most of the credit created has necessarily appeared as a liability on the balance sheets of Chinese banks, and much of the investment has flooded into unproductive speculation (cf. Magnus 2018). Here, I spell out in more detail different versions of the former hypothesis (that China *is rebalancing*, or *could rebalance* given the right policy mixture, in order to maintain sustainable catchup growth).

The export-manufacturing sector (mainly consisting of small, private firms) revealed (despite its competitiveness) a fundamental vulnerability of intertwinement with the global credit wave built up in the advanced economies (Chesnais 2016). But despite its near-collapse, this sector remained mostly beyond the reach of targeted state support due to the small size of exporters, their very limited access to bank finance, and lack of personal relationships with higher levels of government. Central government fiscal stimulus and credit provision to sustain national economic growth were instead directed towards *state* firms: vertically integrated, nationally owned and centrally (or provincially) coordinated. Tax rebates for exporters and a lowering of the VAT rate likely helped, but these were relatively minor interventions compared to the assistance received by SOEs. A stimulus package of RMB 4 trillion (US$600bn) was announced in November 2008 by the central government (of which RMB 1.2 trillion was directly funded by Beijing). And repeated rounds of smaller cash injections and bank loans have continued since, most recently in early 2016. As Eaton (2015) notes, this led to the popularisation of the phrase 'the advance of the state, retreat of the private sector' (*guojin mintui*) by state managers and the Chinese media.

Many have registered retrospective criticisms of this rescue package. Hung (2015, 160) is representative of received opinion when he declares it a 'missed opportunity' for Chinese state managers to break away from dependence on an unequal growth model predicated upon low-wage exports:

> To the disappointment of those who advocated the use of the stimulus to rebalance the Chinese economy, the stimulus package in the end carried no more than 20 percent of social spending, and the majority of the spending went into the same old investments in fixed-capital assets, such as high-speed rail, and the expansion of sectors already plagued by overcapacity, such as steel and cement… [Thus,] it was not able to generate much

increase in the share of disposable income, employment, and domestic consumption in the economy.

Hung is far from alone. The notion of an economic 'rebalancing' of the Chinese economy towards the domestic market has found currency across the political economic spectrum (and goes beyond the immediate question of the content of the economic stimulus program itself). From neoclassical perspectives which view a crony state capitalism as repressing household income in favour of SOEs (Huang 2008), to China's 'New Left' who view the CCP as dominated by a misguided form of neoliberal policymaking designed to hold down wages (Wang 2009), a need to 'rebalance' the economy is probably the consensus view among economists and commentators to date. Fundamental across different such accounts is the argument that the investment component of GDP growth is much too high, and the consumption component too low. The experience of previous East Asian developmental states has cohered into a form of (Rostowian) orthodoxy regarding the anticipated stages of China's catch-up growth: first, an intensive export-led manufacturing boom, then, a rise in consumer spending and the growth of the service sector, and an attendant switch to a headquarter economy as lower-value-added sections of the value chain move elsewhere (or, potentially in the Chinese case, inland). And—since at least 2005—Chinese state managers have also been open to the perceived limitations of the exportist system of accumulation have proposed strategies and policies aimed at 'rebalancing' Chinese growth. Most notably, Premier Wen Jiabao's candid comments in 2007 deemed Chinese growth 'unsteady, unbalanced, uncoordinated, and unsustainable':

> Unsteady development means overheated investment as well as excessive credit supply and liquidity and surplus in foreign trade and international payments. Unbalanced development means uneven development between urban and rural areas, between different regions and between economic and social development. Uncoordinated development means that there is lack of proper balance between the primary, secondary and tertiary sectors and between investment and consumption. Economic growth is mainly driven by investment and export. Unsustainable development means that we have not done well in saving energy and resources and protecting the environment. (cited in Pettis 2013, 71–72)

Perhaps one reason the rebalancing hypothesis has proven popular outside of China is because it offers an apparent solution to (and partial excuse for) the weak, debt-reliant US growth model which blew up in 2008. 'Rebalancing' here is understood as principally a question of international macroeconomics, in which national economies are expected to develop according to an equilibrium which curbs permanent surpluses and deficits (Shaikh and Weber 2018). Roach (2014), for instance, argues that restrictions on the growth of consumption in China lay behind its rise an export powerhouse, while cheap Chinese exports permitted a mirror-image 'overconsumption' of goods in the US. In spite of its large current account deficit, growing US consumption was in part facilitated by the credit bubble enabled by Chinese deposits of surpluses in US Treasury bonds (Setser 2007). Correcting this imbalance by restricting US consumption and debt deleveraging is the proposed solution, while pressuring China to raise its rate of consumption (by ending Chinese citizens' supposed 'cultural' propensity to save) (Obstfeld and Rogoff 2009). But it is not clear that weaknesses in the US economy should be attributed to Chinese trade imbalances—not least since the US's trade deficit with China is reduced by between 25 and 50% once the location of value-added in GPNs is accounted for (Xing 2016, 63–64). While according to official figures China's consumption share is very low at around 36% of GDP (compared with an average of 50–70% for most large economies), Gatley (2013) argues that the true figure (after accounting for big ticket consumer spending and financial services) is around 40%—while Liu et al. (2016) argue that it should be revised upwards even further. So, although it is commonplace to link US economic difficulties to the global 'imbalances' associated with the rise of China, the evidential basis is at least weaker than it first appears.

Inside China, what kind of economic restructuring is recommended to resolve these putative global imbalances? Responses to this question might be broadly divided into three camps: Keynesian, liberal and radical. Pettis (2013) provides the clearest statement of the Keynesian case. He argues that unsustainable overinvestment has occurred as China has exported the surplus product which Chinese consumers are unable to absorb, because of the artificial repression of wages and a virtual absence of social security. But, despite the inevitable growth slowdown changing this model necessitates, it need not *necessarily* entail a crisis:

> One can easily posit a case in which China's GDP grows by 3 percent annually, Chinese household income grows at 5 percent, and consumption at 5 or 6 percent. In that case Chinese households will continue to feel better off and to have improving economic prospects. But by definition if household income grows faster that GDP, there must implicitly be a transfer of resources from the state to the household sector. For much of the past three decade [sic] we have seen the opposite, so the household share of the rapidly growing pie has contracted. (Pettis 2013, 93)

So while transfers from workers to firms through low wages and high productivity gains helped finance the boom, a sustainable future growth model would rely on reverse transfers from the state and firms to workers and consumers (directly via wage increases and indirectly through financing social security measures).

A version of the liberal argument is given in Lardy and Borst (2013), who—while granting that financing a social safety net might boost consumption—place more weight on an opening of the financial and service sectors to foreign investment. This, argue Lardy and Borst (2013, 3), should act to raise interest rates and speed up the privatisation of SOEs (as their soft-financing by state banks is restricted by the competition introduced into the banking sector). In turn, capital might be lured away from a saturated manufacturing and into the undercapitalised service sector, dampening manufacturing capacity and offering Chinese savers a better return on their capital. These policies, they contend, helped Japan's economy rebalance towards a high-consumption economy during the 1980s (though they neglect to consider Japan's 1980s manufacturing profitability decline, nor the eventual collapse in property and equity values).

There are difficulties with both of these positions. The neoliberal emphasis on opening the service sector—which now accounts for over half of China's GDP—might provide a lucrative new set of markets for Chinese savers (as well as Western financial services firms and retailers), but it seems unlikely to provide the income growth required to significantly improve the consumption share of GDP. Qu and Li (2016, 4) find that productivity growth in service sector firms continually lags that of manufacturing by roughly half, while in 2015, 'each worker in the manufacturing sector generated RMB 45,000 more output than their counterpart in the three biggest services sectors'. Manufacturing is widely understood to result in outsized productivity gains proportionate to the rest of the economy (Rodrik 2013), while the service sector would likely prove unable to offer the kind of wage growth manufacturing workers have experienced over the past decade. Financial sector liberalisation, a rise in interest rates and cutting off the supply of easy credit to SOEs and other less profitable investments, would likely improve the return on assets for banks. But any spate of SOE bankruptcies thus induced would also generate unemployment and increase the pool of unutilised labour: heightening the lack of consumption at least in the short term and possibly depressing overall wages. Overall, this zero-sum picture of private and state firms obscures the more complex symbiosis at work in China's hybrid political economy outlined in Chapter 5.

What for the Keynesian solution? A longstanding political economy tradition has posited either restricted workers' consumption, or (in a fundamentally similar explanation) a disproportion between production and consumption, as the cause of crises (Baran and Sweezy 1966; Aglietta 2010). Most recently, post-Keynesian analyses have been popularised as an alternative to the dominant neoclassical explanations of the recession of 2008/2009. Piketty (2014) locates the root of the crisis in rising wealth inequality in the US, while Stockhammer (2013) argues that declines in the wage share of income led to debt being used to finance consumption, thus producing a bubble to defer a crisis which eventually manifested in subprime mortgage markets. For Vermeiren (2013), like Pettis (2013), the restricted share of labour in Chinese national income accounts for China's need to 'export' surplus capacity, overproduced relative to domestic consumption needs. This is a peculiar characterisation, since China's consumer goods manufacturing industries developed in processing zones to a great extent detached (economically and, in the case of places like Shenzhen, physically by barbed-wire fencing) from the wider national economy (Cartier 2001). China did not merely export already existing excess capacity onto world markets (cf. Breslin 2011), but developed—largely at the behest of overseas multinationals—new sectors and plant capacity specifically targeted at the world economy.

For Marx, a disproportionality between production and consumption ('underconsumptionism') was a permanent feature of capitalism and no barrier to growth in and of itself—since capital, by definition, aims to extract surpluses through expanding the divergence between the cost of labour and labour-power. Underconsumption is a permanent feature of a capitalist economy and thus a necessary, but insufficient, explanation for any particular crisis:

> It is a pure tautology to say that crises are provoked by a lack of effective demand or effective consumption… If the attempt is made to give this tautology the semblance of greater profundity, by the statement that the working class receives too small a portion of its own product, and that the evil would be remedied if it received a bigger share, i.e. if its wages rose, we need only note that crises are always prepared by a period in which wages generally rise, and the working class actually does receive a greater share in the annual product destined for consumption. From the standpoint of these advocates of sound and 'simple' (!) common sense, such periods should rather avert the crisis. It thus appears that capitalist production involves certain conditions independent of people's good or bad intentions. (Marx 1992, 486–487)

Consequently, while the national income share of Chinese workers is not an irrelevance, Marxist political economy instead forefronts the profitability of investment as the prime determinant of growth in a capitalist economy, since this determines the viability of future investments. In turn, wages earned through participation in profitable enterprise are the major determinant of the income growth of the working class, and these are tied to economic cycles which move rather independently of wages—so it is not given that a simple redistribution of national income share towards labour would provide a panacea for stable economic growth. As Ross (2012) points out, in the Chinese case, reducing investment in order to increase the consumption *share* of China's GDP would in fact only serve to reduce the overall *magnitude* of economic growth and reduce consumption in real (though not relative) terms. Martin Wolf (2017)—an supporter of Keynesian rebalancing policies—candidly admits the difficulties involved: 'household disposable income is only a little above 60 per cent of GDP, while private consumption is about 40 per cent of GDP… If one wanted consumption to grow faster than now, the share of household incomes in GDP or of household wealth in total wealth needs to soar. The former would squeeze profits and investment. The latter would mean transferring public assets to households. Neither looks technically and politically workable'.

What the Keynesian argument fails to adequately address is how tight and declining profit margins for Chinese manufacturers might be improved through a redistribution of income *away* from capital. And there is increasing evidence (across a variety of measurements—e.g., McKinsey 2016; Pauls 2016; Roberts 2016, 200; Li 2016, 79) that not only is profitability below advanced economies in high-tech manufacturing, but that returns have been falling persistently across private and state sectors alike since around 2004. McKinsey (2016, 32) calculate annual, economy-wide returns on invested capital (based on a 3-year rolling average, taking data from 3000 publicly traded firms)to average 7.4% in 2014, well below the profitability of investments in the US, which generated a return of 10.2% on the same measure. An increase in wages, under such circumstances, could only further restrict access to capital for use in productivity-enhancing investments.

The traditional Keynesian, demand-side argument for rebalancing is given a radical edge in the work of Lüthje and his associated collaborators (2016; Butollo 2015; ten Brink 2013; McNally et al. 2013), who develop an idiosyncratic version of the rebalancing hypothesis rooted in the conceptual apparatus of the Parisienne Regulation School (Aglietta 2010; Boyer 1990). They posit a distinction between 'extensive' and 'intensive' accumulation regimes: the first based on adding more workers, extending working hours, or intensifying the pace of work (what Marx called absolute surplus value production), the second based on productivity gains achieved through labour saving investments in plant and machinery (*relative* surplus value production). In this view, rebalancing the economy away from the exportist system of accumulation and towards one based mainly on consumption requires more than just state-mediated income transfers, but institutions of collective bargaining capable of securing wage gains in line with productivity improvements. Consequently, for these authors, 'rebalancing' is more a question of class power and institutional form, rather than state-directed redistributive politics.[2] This version of the rebalancing hypothesis is plainly attractive insofar as it offers a potential source of complementarity between the (central) state, labour and capital and explicitly links improvements in wages and working conditions with technological progress and shifts up the value chain. Eli Friedman (2014, 1014) views a 'class compromise' as key to achieving this: 'rebalancing the economy requires overcoming forces in society that are tied to the current

[2] Lüthje (2014) raises the important distinction between *sectorally specific* regimes of accumulation, which views the auto industry and electronics as more conducive to 'intensive' forms of accumulation than lower technology sectors (like textiles)—but also points out how high-tech industries are often plagued by the allure of cheap labour in China which inhibits investment in industrial upgrading (see also Lüthje et al. 2013; Butollo 2014).

model of growth, and this cannot be accomplished through purely technocratic (depoliticized) means. A labour movement that has mobilised its rank and file in fighting for and winning new rights will likely have an interest and some capacity in fighting for the enforcement of those rights'. On this view, with an increase in the bargaining power of workers, an 'intensive' regime of production might emerge—initiating a virtuous spiral of economic growth based on a rising labour share of GDP.

But, insofar as this radical account cleaves to the Keynesian redistributive argument, it fails to address the question of profitability. As Brenner and Glick (1991) have compellingly demonstrated, sustained wage gains for broad sectors of the population have historically followed from long-run profitable investment cycles in the manufacturing sector (which tighten the supply of labour and achieve dramatic productivity gains relative to investment in physical capital)—rather than from the institutionalisation of collective bargaining, or the formal linking of wages to productivity growth through wage accords (both of which are typically side or after-effects of a boom: Harman 2010, 165). In fact, even the paradigmatic intensive accumulation regime—the Fordist class accord in the postwar US economy—does not live up to the ideal Regulationist typology, since 'the ratio of the wage index to the labour productivity index for the private nonfarm economy *falls* fairly steadily for the entire period from 1948 to 1970' (Brenner and Glick 1991, 93), during precisely the period when wage gains were greatest and the US 'consumer economy' is understood to have developed.

And if the Regulation School's historical case is weak, it also demonstrates conceptual difficulties—most fundamental of which is to neglect to treat investment as one form of consumption. While orthodox macroeconomic theory separates the two, in the Marxist schema, there is no fundamental difference as to whether output is consumed by the public or is utilised as capital for reinvestment. As Harvey (2010, 110) puts it, the 'effective demand for yesterday's surplus product depends upon… [workers'] consumption plus the new demand generated out of tomorrow's further expansion of production'. So even if workers' consumption is restricted, 'capital generates its own internal effective demand' through investment-led growth. And this capital-led demand is contingent upon the anticipation of profit. The radical explanation does not show, or seek to show, that greater workers' compensation would in and of itself lead to more sustainable growth than a high rate of (profitable) investment, and thus offers no *economic* justification for its rebalancing prescription.

And, a final difficulty by which the neoliberal, Keynesian, and radical versions of the rebalancing hypothesis alike are bound is an underlying methodological nationalism. All such accounts are predicated upon the acceptance of 'global imbalances' outlined above, which understands *nationally bounded* matrices of production and consumption to form a series of natural equilibria. As Pradella (2015, 21–35) elaborates in a discussion of Smith and Ricardo, this methodological nationalism evolved from classical political economy's reluctance to identify the exploitation of labour as the source of surplus value—and its consequent assumption that states, as self-enclosed economic units, could always resolve crises within their borders. By contrast, Marx (1990, 256–258) explicitly rejected Say's law and held that the money-form permits a separation between production and consumption and enables crisis formation. The rebalancing assumption (that all states should strike a production-consumption balance at the national scale) seems especially anomalous under contemporary globalised capitalism—which has separated in space and time the production and consumption of virtually all the necessities of daily life.

6.4 Rebalancing Policies

Having questioned versions of the rebalancing consensus that view the consumption share of GDP as critical indicator of economic health, what are the prospects of China pursuing a sustainable medium-term growth path and avoiding the so-called 'middle income trap' (see Box 6.1)? The current consensus is that China's economy is suffering from slower growth because of artificially restricted consumption, so rebalancing from exports and investment towards the domestic consumer market ought to be a fairly simple question of overcoming vested interests in order to raise domestic incomes and generate a virtuous cycle of growth. I have developed a critique of such positions on the premise that the problem is instead one of a decline in the profitability of investments due to a prolonged downturn in the global industrial cycle—making state attempts to sustain high-growth rates and increase consumption into the future significantly more onerous. If this hypothesis is correct, then would might anticipate policy initiatives based upon the rebalancing hypothesis to fail in their attempts to sustain economic growth. This section explores some of the practical difficulties being encountered by state attempts to transform the system of accumulation, before considering how cheap labour and weak firms have reinforced each other to inhibit a wide-ranging economic transformation.

6.4.1 Hukou Reform

In March of 2014, the Party's 'new-type urbanisation plan, 2014-20' (NUP) committed to a comprehensive reform of the *hukou* system, giving an extra 100m migrant workers urban citizenship by 2020 while hinting at a future abolition of the system (Chan 2014). Dollar (2014) argues that 'reforming the *hukou* system would affect rebalancing in several ways. An important source of productivity growth is the movement of labour from small-scale farming to higher-paying jobs in manufacturing and services. Relaxing restrictions on mobility should lead to higher productivity growth, higher incomes for those currently registered as rural residents, and greater government expenditure on social services'. But implementing this policy has proven immensely difficult, as local governments lack funding and incentives to integrate migrant workers into urban life. A chronic lack of social housing is one issue—Zhang et al. (2017) find that 89% of urban housing was privately owned in 2010, while much (perhaps most) new real estate development is of luxury housing for investment purposes rather than provision for low-income groups (see below). And since the central state is concerned to avoid further population growth in its megacity regions, it has doubled down on *hukou* restrictions in cities like Beijing and Shanghai while directing migrants to smaller, second- and third-tier cities least able to bear the cost of extending the benefits of urban citizenship (restrictions on *hukou* transfer to cities of between one and three million were completely lifted in early 2019). Powerful local growth coalitions in megacities, meanwhile, remain politically opposed to *hukou* liberalisation (Zhang and Li 2016).

Despite such difficulties, the latest data from the National Bureau of Statistics suggests that permanent urban residents (i.e., those with urban rather than rural *hukou* registration) had increased from 56.1 to 60.6% of the total population between 2015 and 2019 (from 771.16 million to 848.43 million) suggesting the government was broadly on course to hit the 100m target outlined in the NUP (*NBS* 2020). A principle local-level driver of *hukou* conversion is the lure of tax revenues local governments can earn from rural land conversions, driven in turn by the increasing penetration of large-scale agribusiness into the smallholder-dominated Chinese countryside (Zhan 2017).

6.4.2 *Welfare Provision*

A lengthy process of constructing a social security net has been undertaken since the widespread SOE layoffs of the late 1990s, legislated for most significantly in 2011 by the introduction of the Social Insurance Law introducing minimal pensions, unemployment and medical insurance. China has since achieved some form of health insurance coverage for 95% of the population, and minimum state-subsidised pensions. But although it has surpassed the poorest East and South East Asian economies, public social spending remains chronically low in China at slightly over 8% of GDP (up from 5% in 2005), versus an average of 21.1% of GDP in OECD countries and 23% in Japan, the regional leader (OECD 2017). The bulk of the obligation for social insurance payments remains with employers, rather than government, and this responsibility is typically bartered down (or completely away) by local governments when negotiating the terms of overseas investments (*CLB* 2017). But while some argue that addressing the welfare question more systematically would drive a boost in consumer spending, others are sceptical. Welfare provision is rarely a consumption-boosting policy in itself, since contributions are usually levied on workers' wages. As such, it simply represents a different form of saving rather than increasing its overall magnitude—while the system as a whole is likely to take decades to bear fruit in the consumption share of GDP data. As Kroeber (2016, 192) points out that 'creating a social safety net is likely to have a modest impact at best on consumer behavior, especially during the period when households are putting more into the welfare system through tax payments than they are receiving in benefits'.

Since the *hukou* system (see above) is thought to reinforce weaknesses in China's social security provision by restricting access to urban social services for China's 290 million migrant workers and their families, many argue that even gradual reform of *hukou* constraints should result in substantially increased welfare provision and thus consumer spending. My query of the assumed link between welfare coverage and consumption notwithstanding, reform of the *hukou* system—even if successful on its own terms—is highly unlikely to boost consumption for two key reasons. First is that most welfare benefits have been delinked from *hukou* registration in favour of personal contribution systems which eliminate the benefit of registration for many 'floating' migrants. At the same time the benefits still associated with urban *hukou* (including access to minimal levels of healthcare) are increasingly, though unevenly, available to migrants as semi-portable benefits through their (unconverted) rural *hukou*, through schemes such as the New Rural Cooperative Medical System (Müller 2016). Second (and more significantly), many migrants are simply unwilling to give up rural *hukou* even given the opportunity—because the rural land-use rights associated with it can form a far more durable social safety net than the minimal benefits associated with urban *hukou* (Andreas and Zhan 2016), in a situation where at least the bottom fifth of urban dwellers are worse off than the average rural dweller. Finally, the state is unlikely to be willing to go too far or fast with this process since migrant's rural landholdings offer a powerful stabiliser against the emergence of a permanent urban underclass, an unregulated informal sector and slum conditions associated with urbanisation in most of the global south (Chan 2014), while rural land dispossessions threaten China's (still largely intact) food sovereignty.

6.4.3 Pro-labour Policies

2008s New Labour Contract Law mandates contractual legal protection for private sector workers, an end to the use of repeated fixed-term contracts, and stipulates social insurance payments that employers and workers must make. Minimum wage legislation at various state scales has also been introduced since the mid-2000s (Chan and Zhai 2013). Friedman and Kuruvilla (2015, 183), among others, associate such pro-labour legislation with economic rebalancing—arguing that as 'rising wages and increased domestic consumption is in line with the central government's wishes to "rebalance" the economy, so they may provide tacit support' for industrial action aimed at upholding legislated rights. Zhuang and Ngok (2014), however, cite a great deal of research demonstrating how such legislation goes largely unimplemented on the shop floor (for instance, less than half of Chinese workers were covered by a contract of any kind in 2013). Weak enforcement is a problem of both disempowered state agencies, and a lack of grassroots union strength—primarily because of how the All-China Federation of Trade Unions (ACFTU), the only legal trade union in China (representing 280 million members), is heavily imbricated in party-state networks. The ACFTU typically represents the interests of the state and capital in the event of industrial disputes, rather than those of workers, though there is increasing evidence of workers 'using' the official union structure to achieve not insignificant gains at a plant level (Zhang and Yang 2019).

While weak enforcement agencies and unions are one part of the problem, (sector specific) workarounds pursued by firms are also to blame. Zhu and Pickles (2014, 48) cite research into the impact of the law on hiring practices, where the 'indirect effect in many factories has been the adoption of a more cautious hiring policy and the consolidation of work contracts around key technical personnel, with a parallel increase in short-term and temporary work contracts' for remaining workers. Similarly, research by Chan and Hui (2014) demonstrates how local governments in exporting regions have collaborated with international chambers of commerce in order to water down the stipulations of the law so that they did not become prohibitively expensive for capital.[3] More generally, the costs of such provisions must be borne by employers who are in highly cost-sensitive market areas (see Chapter 5), and as such any increase risks driving industrial relocation (increasingly widespread in previously industrialised coastal areas) with low-wage migrants following in tow, rather than boosting the labour share of income.

6.4.4 *Geographic Reorientation of End Markets*

Another rebalancing strategy being explored is to encourage export-oriented firms to shift production towards China's booming domestic market. Total national income was recently estimated to be around US$5tn, while Chinese consumer spending more than doubled from $650 billion to $1.4 trillion from 2000 to 2010 (Towson and Woetzel 2015). So, runs this argument, exploiting higher domestic incomes and shifting to domestic consumers as a source of demand might point to the future for Chinese export firms. Yang (2014) points to the technical and political economic difficulties in managing such a transition from global to national production networks, since the majority of China's processing firms and municipal governments are mutually interdependent on the export regime. However, as Butollo (2015) argues (drawing on the experience of township governments representing garment clusters in Guangdong), local governments seem just as likely to actively engineer such a transition through various industrial policies if it appears

[3]This experience is indicative of the means by which business associations have allowed capital to constitute itself as a political force in an authoritarian regime, while local governments function as institutional vehicles for the advancement of such pro-capitalist politics within the state hierarchy.

to present a viable growth strategy. However, many of the downsides raised by sceptics of the benefits of 'South-South' trade (that is, trade between developing countries—see Horner 2016) are evident in attempts to engineer a domestic market transition in China: low domestic incomes, a greater intensity of competition and fewer prospects for industrial upgrading due to the generally low technological level, productivity and profit margins. Many firms are understandably reticent about shifting from previously high-income economies to new markets where cost rather than quality is the prime factor shaping markets.

Moreover, in line with the general slowdown in Chinese economic growth, the Chinese domestic market for consumer goods itself shows signs of slowing. Growth of China's domestic clothing sector is slowing rapidly, increasing by less than 5% year-on-year (Fung Business Institute 2016). Demand for consumer electronics in China has also been shrinking since 2016, with an average fall in sales volume of 4% year-on-year from 2017 to 2019. While consumer electronics sales values rose by 17.3% from 2014 to 2019 in current prices—a minimal level of growth after accounting for steady consumer price inflation. This is fully in line with trends we would expect to see following a significant drop in households' income growth associated with the structural slowdown of the export sector since 2008. Besides the question of cooling domestic Chinese consumer demand, it is unclear why consumer spending should be considered preferable to a high rate of saving, since switching from the latter to the former mostly serves to redirect capital from the financial sector (where they are typically redeployed towards investments by state banks) to retailers in the service sector—a sector we have already noted (see Sect. 6.2) is less productive and pays lower wages than manufacturing and construction.

6.5 Rebalancing and the 'Middle-Income Trap'

In sum, these state policy goals suffer from the weaknesses of the 'rebalancing' hypotheses insofar as they misattribute economic performance of capital to the consumer spending ratio—rather than the profitability of investments. If generally weak profitability and sluggish global export markets render a positive-sum expansion of effective demand difficult, what about a zero-sum improvement in China's global competitive standing vis-à-vis the advanced economies—that is, a genuine convergence in competitiveness? While China currently poses little competitive threat to the core industries of the advanced economies, I want to return to the redistributive question posed by Keynesians and radicals with a hypothetical: that an increased labour share of income might be of service to Chinese capital insofar as it represents a forced investment in the capacities of what Marx terms the 'collective worker'—or, an increase in what others have since termed the 'social wage' (concepts of which I can only include a too brief discussion here; cf. Harman 2010, 132–139; Shaikh 2003). In his chapter on struggles over the length of the working day, Marx (1990) identified a tendency for the ferocity of competition between capitalists to damage the basis of workers' social reproduction, their productivity, and thus to weaken capital itself (cf. Barker 2013; Cammack 2015). State regulation of working times could both improve productivity and increase profits—since an overly long working day means the 'sum of the expenses for the reproduction of labour-power will be greater; just as in a machine the part of its value to be reproduced every day is greater the more rapidly the machine is worn out' (Marx 1990, 377). Might a recomposition of labour-capital relations in favour of workers concurrently benefit Chinese capital in general, insofar as it manifests in improved profitability and competitiveness of Chinese enterprises due to productivity gains (an argument made by McKinsey 2016)?

For migrant workers (the overwhelming majority of those in manufacturing), the 'incomplete proletarianisation' established by the *hukou* system, the weakness of workers' shop floor organisation and the absence of formalised collective bargaining structures, weak minimum wage enforcement, and the lack of social security do likely act to inhibit firm-level investment in human capital. This is because they collectively render workers highly mobile and unlikely to stay in one job for very long. Average annual job turnover fluctuates around 20% across the Chinese economy, but anecdotal evidence from manufacturing firms gathered during fieldwork visits in China's factory visits suggested that it was not uncommon for a firm to replace 20% of its assembly line staff on a *monthly* basis in south China's factory districts (interview data). Here, the radical account of rebalancing is on firmer ground, since it accounts for Chinese firms' weak structural position in production networks by appeal to these constraints facing the labour productivity improvements. Despite the dramatic upsurge in labour protests, strikes and pro-worker legislation (especially after the crisis of 2008–2009: *CLB* 2014), the economy's competitive advantage in low-wage manufacturing has not been substantially eroded and the structural characteristics of the labour regime remain in place. Chinese firms remain largely 'exempt from wage and employment "rigidities", which under capital intensive regimes of accumulation usually would trigger restructuring of production technologies, work organization, and production regimes' (Lüthje 2014, 18). And China's low-wages permit 'outdated' fixed capital (like obsolete sewing machinery in garment factories) to remain in use, disincentivising further productivity improvements such as production line automation or the adoption of industrial robotics. This ensures that many forms of technological advancement remain 'debased adaptations', hampered by their sitedness in generally low-productivity workshops, as discussed in Chapter 5.

Consequently, advanced economy firms have continued to deepen their niches in high-value-added activities while using Chinese producers as bases for outsourced manufacturing. A recent report for the European Commission confirms this picture: the 'EU and China have highly complementary production structures with the EU specialising in high and medium skill value added and China increasingly orienting its GVC participation towards low-skill and capital value added. These complementarities allow firms to exploit the benefits of specialisation and obtain important cost advantages in production' (Gasiorek and Lopez-Gonzalez 2013, 86). This is striking, because unit labour costs (real wages over productivity gains)

have increased dramatically in China since 2005. One widely circulated study registers a trebling of manufacturing wages from 2005 to 2016, from $1.20 to $3.60 per hour (*Euromonitor* 2017), and while this might overstate the case, it does broadly accord with the trend mapped by the IMF of a persistent and steep increase in unit labour costs (Fig. 6.2). A further recent crossnational comparison confirmed that since 1978, while real incomes for the bottom 50% of earners in the US have fallen by 1%, in France they have increased by 39%, while those of China's bottom half have increased over 400% (Alvaredo et al. 2017). Any such sustained increase of wages above productivity should logically indicate the emergence of an 'intensive' accumulation regime hypothesised by the 'radical rebalancing' theorists discussed above. But the labour share in GDP has not substantially increased, and still stands below its level in 2001—though a persistent decline throughout the 2000s has been somewhat ameliorated since 2010 (Qi 2014). And in international comparison, wages remain very low (roughly 10–15% those of the US and other advanced economies in 2016, though somewhat higher in large cities), meaning that even while Chinese exports increase in price, the aggregate

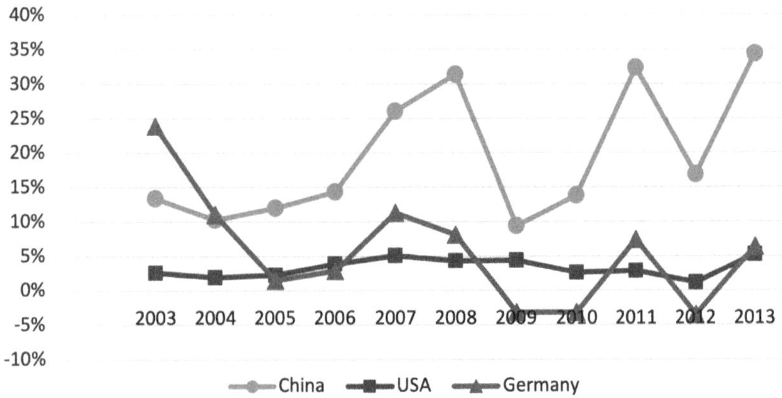

Fig. 6.2 Changes in unit labour costs, various countries (percent) (*Source* The Conference Board [n.d.])

effect of advanced economy outsourcing to China utilising GPNs should continue to be a reduced cost of imports—so long as volume growth of outsourcing outpaces increases in Chinese workers' wage share (a process the European Central Bank [2011] positively refers to as the 'share effect'). Moreover, a slowdown in the sustained wage growth evident in the exportist SOA is increasingly evident since the mid-2010s. In sum, the effect of the 'China price' enjoyed by producers thanks to low wages and moderately high productivity has not yet dissipated (cf. Harney 2008).

Previous East Asian developers transitioned away from low value-added manufacturing through outsourcing by their lead firms in response to wage rises, retaining and deepening 'core competencies' in branding and research. Crucially, Gray (2015) notes the key role played by organised labour in this regional industrial transition, one often repressed in orthodox accounts of the developmental state (Johnson 1982; Amsden 1989; Wade 1990). Despite their idiosyncratic developmental trajectories, Japan, Korea and Taiwan experienced successive 'Lewis turning points' as a growth spurt dried up the supply of cheap labour, which enabled workers to win substantial wage gains and encouraged industrial upgrading:

> Taiwan reached its Lewisian turning point in the late 1960s and Korea in the mid-1970s... whereby the transition from the 'unlimited labour

> supply' to limited labour supply led to increased structural power… of workers. These transitions ultimately underpinned the rise of labour movements in the 1980s and led to wage increases that ultimately undermined the authoritarian labour regime. (Gray 2015, 73)

Gray anticipates China's following in this regional lineage, pointing to recent labour unrest as a sign that labour markets are likely to similarly tighten. And the data presented above suggest this is a distinct possibility. But there exist three noteworthy factors which appear to compromise this possibility. First, recessions of 1973 and 1997–1998 aside, the global economy and export demand remained strong throughout much of this earlier period, while momentum was firmly in the direction of globalisation with successive rounds of tariff and trade barrier removals culminating in the move from the GATT to the WTO. This gave Korea and Taiwan the impetus needed to sustain export booms until the late 1990s, in tandem with repeated rounds of upgrading and industrial restructuring, to become increasingly autocentric economies with per capita incomes rising towards those of the global north. By contrast, contemporary China confronts conditions of long-term global economic stagnation, a slowdown in trade, and export markets that appear less amenable to economies supplying cheap labour. Even absenting from weak global demand conditions, China's export volumes would have to become unimaginably larger than today's if they were to match the significance of exports for an economy like Taiwan's, for instance, on a per capita basis.

Second (and despite much speculation about the tightening of labour markets), the supply of labour in China is very much contingent upon the labour regime imposed by GPN-integrated manufacturing. *Hukou* inhibits the movement of many underemployed rural workers to the cities, particularly in the older age categories. And this immobility dovetails with the age and gender demands of the labour regime in globalised industries. As Kam-Wing Chan (2010, 523) argues, in clothing and electronics assembly work—the biggest export-manufacturing employers—demand for assembly line workers primarily targets young (often female) labour aged from 16 to 30, ostensibly possessing 'youthful eyesight and high manual dexterity'. By the age of about 30, these characteristics are perceived by employers to have been exhausted and migrants often struggle to find work, often returning to the countryside to raise children. Employer complaints of a 'labour shortage' should thus be qualified:

> While there is a "famine" in the young ages, a vast ocean of unemployed or underemployed rural labor, mostly ages 35 and above, remains, the size of which is estimated at close to 100 million... the depletion of young surplus rural labor is far from being the exhaustion of all surplus labor in the countryside. The situation is still very different from the full-employment scenario postulated in the Lewis model when the "turning point" is reached. The co-existence of migrant labor shortages and large surpluses in the rural sector may be quite unique to China's industrialization and urbanization experience, because of the prolonged and continuing rural and urban social segmentation. (Chan 2010, 523)

To what extent this age and gender segregation might become undone as labour shortages bite remains unclear, and many factories I have recently visited complained that they had lately been 'forced' to hire older, male workers for assembly line roles typically performed by young women (interview data). But, to the extent that it does hold a significant portion of the un(der)employed portion of the labour force in the countryside, far from only repressing workers' consumption share, the *hukou* system and the age bracketing of the workforce contributes to labour shortages in the cities and rising manufacturing wages. Weighed against this is, of course, the division imposed upon the labour force between resident and non-resident workers, and the inaccessibility of social security for most migrants—factors which significantly reduce the 'social wage'. It suggests that adjudicating China's Lewis turning point is a complex procedure, entangled with cultural political economies of age and gender as well as post-Maoist legacies of citizenship and mobility rights.

Third, Gray's account does not register how the predominance of GPNs in China's core manufacturing sectors further complicates the picture, through its adverse effects on Chinese corporate power. Kincaid (2003, 163), in a critique of underconsumption theory, notes that—even without nominal wage increases—productivity gains can have the effect of 'reducing the prices of commodities, and raising real wages'. So, one important mechanism by which workers would typically gain (in income terms) from productivity improvements is by the cheapening of wage goods. And this mechanism does seem to have been at work in previous East Asian developers as they came to resemble advanced economies with large household consumption demand forming a market for domestically produced goods. However, to the extent that Chinese firms are subordinate players in GPNs, this tendency (rising productivity increasing real wages by cheapening consumer goods) is diverted, since windfall productivity gains tend to ricochet *up* the production network to lead firms based in competitor economies—as these firms act then to reorganise production networks through generalising innovations and sourcing new, cheaper, suppliers. Milberg and Winkler (2013, 123–124) argue it is this 'asymmetry of market structures in GVCs, and the ability of lead firms to generate and maintain the asymmetry, that is at the core of the [advanced economy] oligopoly firms' cost-cutting strategy that has helped them maintain their cost markups'. And since China's core manufacturing sectors mostly function as an export hub for advanced economy consumer markets, advanced economy lead firms typically capture the gains that might otherwise have accrued to workers. A $50 reduction in the sale price of an iPhone is of little value to China's factory workers so long as the asking price remains far beyond their reach.

So while weak labour organising is one part of this story, another is that China's entry into GPNs has produced very few globally competitive firms in the vein of Japanese and Korean car producers, or even midscale Taiwanese fabless chip firms—and those large, vertically integrated Chinese firms that have emerged remain overwhelmingly in the heavily protected state sector (Nolan 2014; Rugman et al. 2016). Kaplinsky and Morris (2016) describe China's mode of integration into the world economy as 'thinning in' to very particular areas of the production network, using small firms to perform the least desirable tasks in long supply chains while gradually aiming to upgrade their capacities (rather than 'thickening in', by constructing vertically integrated export firms). Implicit in widespread concerns regarding wage increases is the acceptance that China remains mostly in competition with other low-wage economies, rather than encroaching on advanced economy firms. This leaves open a broader question: if Chinese wages continue to increase significantly, is incremental 'second-tier' innovation—the small improvements in manufacturing process (rather than novel product development) at which Chinese firms are increasingly adept—a secure enough niche to sustain producer price inflation at the expense of overseas lead firms?

While recent value chain analysis has hypothesised a possible shift in the balance of power as large first-tier suppliers begin to emerge (Appelbaum 2009), the case of Foxconn is sobering. In the aftermath of worker suicides at its Shenzhen plant in 2010 wages and operating conditions were marginally improved. Apple responded to higher costs and negative publicity by diversifying its supplier base to Pegatron and other large

ECMs based in the Pearl River Delta (Chan et al. 2013). Foxconn, in turn, shifted some production inland, tapping the rural underemployed in new plants (its Chengdu facility opened in 2010) as a source of lower wages. At least in this instance, intense pressure to improve conditions at a single plant (Foxconn's coastal Longhua facility) came up short against the pressures from lead firms and the capacity of large contract manufacturers to reorganise production networks. And, this was in spite of substantial firm-level progress in second-tier innovation. Foxconn now produces touch screens for electronic cars, lithium batteries, industrial robots, displays for smartphones, tablets and medical equipment. But despite acquiring a great deal of technical knowledge through learning-by-doing for lead firms, it has resisted moving directly into mobile phone manufacturing and other forms of novel product innovation, since the firm is extremely hesitant to be seen as competing with its major customers (Apple continues to represent around half of total orders). In spite of ballooning revenues of over US$132bn, Foxconn's operating margin remains just over 2% (van Liemt 2016).

Beyond this individual case, the mixture of relatively high-technology with low margins remains pervasive across China's electronics sector, even as firms have moved far beyond performing rudimentary assembly work in the last decade. Lüthje and Butollo (2016, 8) observe that despite the 'substantial upgrading of the ECM [electronics contract manufacturing] industry… [and] rapid growth of Chinese telecommunications equipment makers headquartered in the PRD [Pearl River Delta], such as Huawei and ZTE', a 'restructuring and diversification of production… is occurring under the auspices of ongoing low profit margins and cut-throat competition in ECM'. Even in the case of wholly domestic-owned firms now emerging in the smartphone sector (Oppo, Vivo, ZTE, Huawei), competing with global leaders by replicating their complex interaction between branding, research and dense supply chain networks appears a near impossibility: while these firms have taken a significant amount of domestic market share and increasingly branched out into global sales, they operated on razor thin profit margins. While each turned over US$200m in profit in the third quarter of 2016, Apple entrenched its dominant share of global earnings share (taking 91% of profits—$6.7bn) (Sui 2016; Grimes and Yang 2017). Manufacturers suffered from 60 consecutive months of producer price deflation from mid 2012, while in 2015, the value of China's manufacturing exports stagnated for the first time since the crisis of 2008 (UN Comtrade 2015). This suggests that after rebounding from the crisis, China is at last finding the secular limits of its current place in the global division of labour as its export engines encounter severe pressures.

This reciprocal interaction between weak firms and weak labour bears a strong resemblance to phenomena Silver (2003)—in a discussion of the globalised car industry —terms the 'contradictions of semiperipheral success' facing catch-up economies:

> Windfall profits that accrued to U.S. automakers helped them underwrite a stable labor-capital accord and mass consumption social contract that lasted for more than four decades after the CIO struggles of the 1930s. In contrast, the lower profit levels associated with the intense competitive pressures towards the end of the life cycle (and the relative national poverty of the favored new sites of production) make such social contracts increasingly difficult to sustain economically. In other words, late-developers of mass production automobile industries have experienced the social contradictions of, capitalist development (including strong working classes) without the benefits that might allow them to deal with those social contradictions successfully.

Whatever the prime direction of causality, it is clear that this is having an adverse affect on China's capacity to move further up the value chain and to compete directly with the advanced economies in lucrative market segments. As Ghemawat and Hout (2016) write, 'China is not transitioning from low-end, first-generation exports to high-end, second-generation exports as quickly as Japan or South Korea did. When those countries' GDPs per capita were at China's current level, capital goods made up more than 25 percent of their exports, and their performance on capital goods exports continued to improve, rather than leveling off as China's has'.

Data from China Customs (n.d.) confirms this picture, with 'processing trade' exports still responsible for around a quarter to a third of China's total exports by 2019 (Fig. 6.3). Such exports are by definition GPN-linked, and thus vulnerable to the monopsony power of global lead firms described in the previous chapter. Of these processing exports, the vast majority are actually carried out by foreign-invested or foreign-owned enterprises (>80% in 2019). Foreign firms were responsible for over 40% of China's total export value in 2018, both processing and ordinary (China Customs, n.d.). A recent analysis demonstrates the predominance of US multinationals across leading market sectors in China

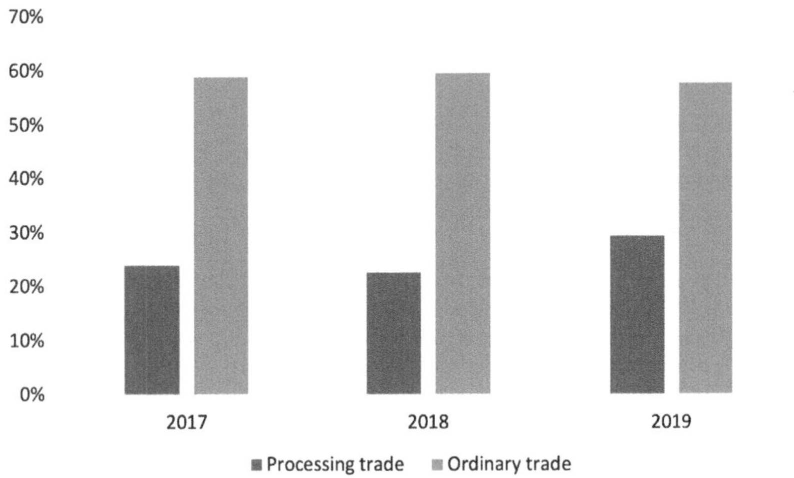

Fig. 6.3 Processing exports versus ordinary exports (% of all exports), 2017–2019 (*Source* General Administration of Customs, PRC [n.d.])

(Starrs 2018, 192–193), while net IP receipts for Chinese firms (payments for foreign technology licenses minus income from licenses) amounted to nearly US$25bn per annum by 2017, from virtually zero at the turn of the millennium—further evidence of the predominance of advanced economies in proprietary technology (Baldwin and Okubo 2019).

6.6 Summary

By the end of the second decade of the twentieth century, China had become the world leading exporter of manufactured goods, almost doubling its global share from 2008 to 2015 (peaking at nearly 17% at the close of 2015 before falling back to around 15% since). Moreover, its indigenous manufacturing capabilities across almost all industrial sectors far outstripped those of comparator countries (Brazil, India, Mexico, Vietnam) as participation in GPNs stimulated technology transfer and learning-by-doing. However, the contradictions of late development hampered Chinese efforts to develop world-beating corporate champions of its own outside of a few exceptions which received state subsidies and protections (Haier and Huawei, for instance). This was due to both structural and agential factors: the collapse and subsequent slowdown of the export sector in the aftermath of the 2008 global economic crisis severely weakened growth prospects of manufacturers by capping global demand for their output, while the absence of sufficiently well-developed industrial policy mechanisms between SMEs and government inhibited the ability for the state to rationalise and pick winners (a result of China's model of combined development which tied central state managers to large SOEs and banks, while local governments were stripped of funds).

This growth slowdown thus did not provide an opportunity for economic 'rebalancing' of China's 'export dependency', as both Keynesians and liberal economists alike have argued. Instead, it significantly weakened China's surplus-producing private sector (and with the major source of income growth for Chinese workers) and reduced the rapid income growth which allowed huge pricate sector investment to 2008. It further drove the state banking sector into debt-financing of (already overproducing) SOEs, leading to sometimes chronic overcapacity and a persistent trend towards producer price deflation. These state firms thus weighed heavily on global prices of everything they produced (from steel to solar panels) during the 2010s, eliminating both competitors' and Chinese profit margins in such product lines. This occurred at the same time as the positive inflow of dollars from export earnings was effectively put on halt as China reached a stable share of lethargic export markets. As such, ramping up of production through debt-finance posed a threat to the value of the renminbi and serious concerns about capital flight, since increases in the money supply were no longer backed by increasing forex earnings. The next chapter explores why, for the time being, this threat was not realised: the effects of asset price inflation in the real estate sector which has increasingly kept the economy afloat and sustained bank balance sheets and consumer spending in the face of a slowdown.

References

Aglietta, Michel. 2010. *A Theory of Capitalist Regulation: The US Experience*. London: Verso.

Akyüz, Yilmaz. 2011. Export Dependence and Sustainability of Growth in China. *China and World Economy* 19 (1): 1–23.

Alvaredo, Facundo, Lucas Chancel, Thomas Piketty, Emmanuel Saez, and Gabriel Zucman. 2017. Global Inequality Dynamics: New Findings from WID.world. National Bureau of Economic Research Working Paper No. 23119.

Amsden, Alice. 1989. *Asia's Next Giant*. Oxford: Oxford University Press.

Andreas, Joel, and Shaohua Zhan. 2016. Hukou and Land: Market Reform and Rural Displacement in China. *The Journal of Peasant Studies* 43 (4): 798–827.

Appelbaum, Richard. 2009. Big Suppliers in Greater China: A Growing Counterweight to the Power of Giant Retailers. In *China and the Transformation of Global Capitalism*, ed. Ho-fung Hung. Baltimore: Johns Hopkins University Press.

Baldwin, Richard, and Toshihiro Okubo. 2019. GVC Journeys: Industrialisation and Deindustrialisation in the Age of the Second Unbundling. *Journal of the Japanese and International Economies* 52: 53–56.

Baran, Paul, and Paul Sweezy. 1966. *Monopoly Capital: An Essay on the American Economic and Social Order*. New York: Monthly Review.

Barker, Colin. 2013. Marx on the Factory Acts. Notes for a Talk Given at the Historical Materialism Conference, London. Available online at: https://drive.google.com/file/d/0Bz3wUg3e6r_4cE9HRGZhbjdWNXc/edit?usp=sharing. Accessed 3 May 2016.

Boyer, Robert. 1990. *The Regulation School: A Critical Introduction*. New York: Columbia University Press.

Brenner, Robert, and Mark Glick. 1991. The Regulation Approach: Theory and History. *New Left Review* 188: 45–119.

Breslin, Shaun. 2011. China and the Crisis: Global Power, Domestic Caution and Local Initiative. *Contemporary Politics* 17 (2): 185–200.

Butollo, Florian. 2014. *The End of Cheap Labour? Industrial Transformation and Social Upgrading in China*. Frankfurt: Campus Verlag.

Butollo, Florian. 2015. Growing Against the Odds: Government Agency and Strategic Recoupling as Sources of Competitiveness in the Garment Industry of the Pearl River Delta. *Cambridge Journal of Regions, Economy and Society* 8: 521–536.

Cammack, Paul. 2015. Production and Social Reproduction in the Contemporary World Market: The Social Reproduction Complex. Paper Presented at the 9th Pan-European Conference on International Relations, Giardini Naxos, Sicily, 23–26 September. Available online at: https://www.academia.edu/15926705/Production_and_social_reproduction_in_the_contemporary_world_market_the_social_production_complex. Accessed 10 November 2016.

Cartier, Carolyn. 2001. *Globalizing South China*. London: Blackwell.

Chan, Kam Wing. 2010. A China Paradox: Migrant Labor Shortage Amidst Rural Labor Supply Abundance. *Eurasian Geography and Economics* 51 (4): 513–530.

Chan, Kam Wing. 2014. China's Urbanization 2020: A New Blueprint and Direction. *Eurasian Geography and Economics* 55 (1): 1–9.

Chan, Chris King-Chi, and Elaine Sio-ieng Hui. 2014. The Development of Collective Bargaining in China: From 'Collective Bargaining by Riot' to 'Party State-led Wage Bargaining'. *China Quarterly* 217: 221–242.

Chan, Chris King-Chi, and Yujian Zhai. 2013. Active Labour Market Policies in China—Towards Improved Labour Protection? *Journal of Asian Public Policy* 6 (1): 10–25.

Chan, Jenny, Ngai Pun, and Mark Selden. 2013. The Politics of Global Production: Apple, Foxconn and China's New Working Class. *New Technology, Work and Employment* 28 (2): 100–115.

Chesnais, Francois. 2016. *Finance Capital Today: Corporations and Banks in the Lasting Global Slump*. Leiden: Brill.

China Labour Bulletin [*CLB*]. 2014. *Searching for the Union: The Workers' movement in China 2011–13*. February.

China Labour Bulletin [*CLB*]. 2017. *China's Social Security System*. Available online at: http://www.clb.org.hk/content/china%E2%80%99s-social-security-system. Accessed 1 May 2017.

China Labour Bulletin [*CLB*]. n.d. Strike Map. Available online at: http://maps.clb.org.hk/strikes/en. Accessed 26 July 2017.

Dollar, David. 2008. Is China Delinking from the US Economy? Available online at: http://blogs.worldbank.org/eastasiapacific/node/2804. Accessed 1 August 2016.

Dollar, David. 2014. Sino Shift. *Finance and Development*, June 2014. Available online at: http://kleykampintaiwan.com/files/Global_Economy/IMFonChina_June_2014.pdf. Accessed 16 January 2017.

Eaton, Sarah. 2015. *The Advance of the State in Contemporary China: State-Market Relations in the Reform Era*. Cambridge: Cambridge University Press.

Eichengreen, Barry, Donghyun Park, and Kwanho Shin. 2013. Growth Slowdowns Redux: New Evidence on the Middle-Income Trap. National Bureau of Economic Research, Working Paper Series No. 18673.

Euromonitor. 2017. China Still Lucrative for Business Despite the Rising Wage Rates. Available online at: http://blog.euromonitor.com/2017/03/china-still-lucrative-businesses-despite-rising-wage-rates.html. Accessed 21 March 2017.

European Central Bank [*ECB*]. 2011. *Monthly Bulletin: July 2011*. Available online at: https://www.ecb.europa.eu/pub/pdf/mobu/mb201107en.pdf. Accessed 12 December 2016.

Friedman, Eli. 2014. Alienated Politics: Labour Insurgency and the Paternalistic State in China. *Development and Change* 45 (5): 1001–1018.

Friedman, Eli, and Sarosh Kuruvilla. 2015. Experimentation and Decentralization in China's Labor Relations. *Human Relations* 68 (2): 181–195.

Fung Business Intelligence. 2016. *In Depth—China's Apparel Market*. Available online at https://www.fbicgroup.com/sites/default/files/MarketOverview_p1.pdf. Accessed 11 January 2017.

Gasiorek, Michael, and Javier Lopez-Gonzalez. 2013. China-EU Global Value Chains: Who Creates Value, How and Where? Growing Linkages and Opportunities. Available online at: http://trade.ec.europa.eu/doclib/docs/2014/january/tradoc_152123.pdf. Accessed 1 March 2017.

Gatley, Thomas. 2013. China's Missing Consumption. *Gavekal Dragonomics* research note (June). Available online at: https://chinaeconomybookdotcom.files.wordpress.com/2016/01/dg_130703_chartbook-chinasmissingconsumption_gatley.pdf. Accessed 9 October 2016.

General Administration of Customs, PRC. n.d. Available online at: http://43.248.49.97/indexEn. Accessed 1 February 2020.

Ghemawat, Pankaj, and Thomas Hout. 2016. Can China's Companies Conquer the World: The Overlooked Importance of Corporate Power. *Foreign Affairs* 95: 86.

Giles, John, Albert Park, Fang Cai, and Yang Du. 2012. Weathering a Storm: Survey-Based Perspectives on Employment in China in the Aftermath of the Global Financial Crisis. World Bank, Policy Research Working Paper No. 5984.

Gray, Kevin. 2015. *Labour and Development in East Asia: Social Forces and Passive Revolution*. London: Routledge.

Grimes, Seamus, and Chun Yang. 2017. From Foreign Technology Dependence Towards Greater Innovation Autonomy: China's Integration into the Information and Communications Technology (ICT) Global Value Chain (GVC). *Area Development and Policy*. Published online before print.

Harman, Chris. 2010. *Zombie Capitalism: Global Crisis and the Relevance of Marx*. London: Verso.

Harney, Alexandra. 2008. *The China Price: The True Cost of Competitive Advantage*. London: Penguin.

Harvey, David. 2010. *The Enigma of Capital and the Crises of Capitalism*. Oxford: Oxford University Press.

Horner, Rory. 2016. A New Economic Geography of Trade and Development? Governing South-South Trade, Value Chains and Production Networks. *Territory, Politics, Governance* 4 (4): 400–420.

Hsing, You-tien. 2012. No Crisis in China? The Rise of China's Social Crisis. In *Aftermath: The Cultures of the Economic Crisis*, ed. Manuel Castells, Joao Caraca, and Gustavo Cardoso, 251–277. Oxford: Oxford University Press.

Huang, Yasheng. 2008. *Capitalism with Chinese Characteristics: Entrepreneurship and the State*. Cambridge: Cambridge University Press.

Hung, Ho-fung. 2015. *The China Boom: Why China Will Not Rule the World*. Chichester: Columbia University Press.

Johnson, Chalmers. 1982. *MITI and the Japanese Miracle: The Growth of Japanese Industrial Policy, 1925–1975*. Stanford: Stanford University Press.

Kaplinsky, Raphael, and Mike Morris. 2016. Thinning and Thickening: Productive Sector Policies in The Era of Global Value Chains. *European Journal of Development Research* 28 (4): 625–645.

Kincaid, Jim. 2003. Underconsumption Versus the Rate of Profit: A Reply to Burkett and Hart-Landsberg. *Historical Materialism* 11 (1): 161–177.

Kroeber, Arthur. 2016. *China's Economy: What Everyone Needs to Know*. Oxford: Oxford University Press.

Lardy, Nicholas, and Nicholas Borst. 2013. A Blueprint for Rebalancing the Chinese Economy. Peterson Institute for International Economics Policy Brief No. PB13-02, February, Washington, DC, Peterson Institute.

Li, Minqi. 2016. *China and the Twenty-First Century Crisis*. London: Pluto.

Liu, Fang, Jun Zhang, and Tian Zhu. 2016. How Much Can We Trust China's Investment Statistics? *Journal of Chinese Economic and Business Studies* 14 (3): 215–228.

Lo, Dic. 2016. China Confronts the Great Recession: 'Rebalancing' neoliberalism, or Else? In *Emerging Economies During and After the Great Recession*, ed. Philip Arestis and Malcolm Sawyer, 232–269. London: Palgrave Macmillan.

Lüthje, Boy. 2014. Why No Fordism in China? Regimes of Accumulation and Regimes of Production in Chinese Manufacturing Industries. IFS Working Paper No. 3.

Lüthje, Boy, and Florian Butollo. 2016. Why the Foxconn Model Does Not Die: Production Networks and Labour Relations in the IT Industry in South China. *Globalizations*. Published online before print (August 11).

Lüthje, Boy, Siqi Luo, and Hao Zhang. 2013. *Beyond the Iron Rice Bowl: Regimes of Production and Industrial Relations in China*. Frankfurt: Campus Verlag.

Magnus, George. 2018. *Red Flags: Why Xi's China Is in Peril*. New Haven: Yale University Press.

Marx, Karl. 1990. *Capital*, vol. I. London: Penguin.

Marx, Karl. 1992. *Capital*, vol. II. London: Penguin.

Mathai, Koshy, Geoff Gottlieb, Gee Hee Hong, Sung Eun Jung, Jochen Schmittmann, and Jiangyan Yu. 2016. China's Changing Trade and the Implications for the CLMV Economies. IMF Departmental Paper Series. IMF: Washington, DC.

McKinsey Global Institute. 2016. China's Choice: Capturing the $5 Trillion Productivity Opportunity, June. Available online at: http://www.mckinsey.com/global-themes/employment-and-growth/capturing-chinas-5-trillion-productivity-opportunity. Accessed 28 April 2017.

McNally, Christopher, Boy Lüthje, and Tobias ten Brink. 2013. Rebalancing China's Emergent Capitalism: State Power, Economic Liberalization and Social Upgrading. *Journal of Current Chinese Affairs* 42 (4): 3–16.

Milberg, William, and Deborah Winkler. 2013. *Outsourcing Economics: Global Value Chains in Capitalist Development*. Cambridge: Cambridge University Press.

Müller, A. 2016. Hukou and Health Insurance Coverage for Migrant Workers. *Journal of Current Chinese Affairs* 45 (2): 53–82.

National Bureau of Statistics. 2020. *Statistical Communiqué of the People's Republic of China on the 2019 National Economic and Social Development*. Available online at: www.stats.gov.cn/english/PressRelease/202002/t20200228_1728917.html. Accessed 21 February 2020.

Nolan, Peter. 2014. Globalisation and Industrial Policy: The Case of China. *The World Economy* 37 (6): 747–764.

Obstfeld, Maurice, and Kenneth Rogoff. 2009. Global Imbalances and the Financial Crisis: Products of Common Causes. Centre for Economic Policy, Research Discussion Paper Series No. 7606. Available online at: http://eml.berkeley.edu/~obstfeld/santabarbara.pdf. Accessed 1 March 2017.

OECD. 2017. *A Decade of Social Protection Development in Selected Asian Countries*. Paris: OECD Publishing.

Pauls, Robert. 2016. Capitalist Development, Contradictions and Crises in China, 1993–2011. Dissertation, Ruhr-Universität Bochum. Available online at: http://hss-opus.ub.ruhr-uni-bochum.de/opus4/frontdoor/index/index/docId/5015. Accessed 6 March 2017.

Pettis, Michael. 2013. *The Great Rebalancing: Trade, Conflict, and the Perilous Road Ahead for the World Economy*. Princeton: Princeton University Press.

Piketty, Thomas. 2014. *Capital in the Twenty-First Century*. Cambridge: Harvard University Press.

Pradella, Lucia. 2015. *Globalisation and the Critique of Political Economy: New Insights from Marx's Writings*. London: Routledge.

Pritchett, Lant, and Lawrence H. Summers. 2014. Asiaphoria Meets Regression to the Mean. National Bureau of Economic Research. Available online at: https://www.nber.org/papers/w20573. Accessed 2 March 2020.

Qi, Hao. 2014. The Labor Share Question in China. *Monthly Review* 65 (8): 23–35.

Qu, Hongbin, and Jing Li. 2016. China's New Challenge: Faster Services Expansion, Slower Productivity Growth. HSBC Global Research Report, July 21. Available online at: https://www.research.hsbc.com. Accessed 11 January 2017.

Roach, Stephen. 2014. *Unbalanced: The Codependency of America and China*. New Haven: Yale University Press.

Roberts, Michael. 2016. *The Long Depression: Marxism and the Global Crisis of Capitalism*. Chicago: Haymarket.

Rodrik, Dani. 2013. Unconditional Convergence in Manufacturing. *The Quarterly Journal of Economics* 128 (1): 165–204.

Ross, John. 2012. Investment Will Boost China's Economy. *China Daily*. Available online at: http://www.chinadaily.com.cn/opinion/2012-09/28/content_15790139.htm. Accessed 11 July 2017.

Rugman, Alan, Quyen Nguyen, and Ziyi Wei. 2016. Rethinking the Literature on the Performance of Chinese Multinational Enterprises. *Management and Organization Review* 12 (2): 269–302.

Setser, Brad. 2007. The One Thing the US Exports to China. CFR blog. Available online at: https://www.cfr.org/blog/one-thing-us-really-exports-china. Accessed 6 August 2018.

Shaikh, Anwar. 2003. 'Who Pays for the 'Welfare' in the Welfare State? A Multi-Country Study. *Social Research* 70 (2): 531–550.

Shaikh, Anwar, and Isabella Weber. 2018. The US-China Trade Balance and the Theory of Free Trade: Debunking the Currency Manipulation Argument. The New School for Social Research, Working Paper 05/2018.

Shambaugh, David. 2016. *China's Future*. Cambridge: Polity Press.

Silver, Beverley. 2003. *Forces of Labor: Workers' Movements and Globalization Since 1870*. Cambridge: Cambridge University Press.

Smith, John. 2016. *Imperialism in the Twenty-First Century: Globalization, Super-Exploitation, and Capitalism's Final Crisis*. New York: Monthly Review.

Starrs, Sean Kenji. 2018. Can China Unmake the American Making of Global Capitalism? *Socialist Register 2019* 55: 173–200.

Stockhammer, Englebert. 2013. Rising Inequality as a Cause of the Present Crisis. *Cambridge Journal of Economics* 39 (3): 935–958.

Sui, Linda. 2016. Apple Captures 91% Share of Global Smartphone Profits in Q3 2016. *Strategy Analytics*. Available online at: https://www.strategyanalytics.com/strategy-analytics/news/strategy-analytics-press-releases/strategy-analytics-press-release/2016/11/22/strategy-analytics-apple-captures-record-91-percent-share-of-global-smartphone-profits-in-q3-2016. Accessed 18 April 2017.

ten Brink, Tobias. 2013. Paradoxes of Prosperity in China's New Capitalism. *Journal of Current Chinese Affairs* 42 (4): 17–44.

The Conference Board. n.d. *The Conference Board International Labour Comparisons*. Available online at: https://www.conference-board.org/ilcprogram/. Accessed 11 January 2020.

Towson, Jeffrey, and Jonathan Woetzel. 2015. Why China's Consumers Will Continue to Surprise the World. *McKinsey & Company*, May. Available online at: http://www.mckinsey.com/business-functions/strategy-and-corporate-finance/our-insights/why-chinas-consumers-will-continue-to-surprise-the-world. Accessed 13 October 2016.

UN Comtrade. 2015. Various Aatasets. Available online at: http://comtrade.un.org. Accessed 23 May 2017.

van Liemt, Gijsbert. 2016. Hon Hai/ Foxconn: Which Way Forward? In *Flexible Workforces and Low Profit Margins: Electronics Assembly Between Europe and China*, ed. Jan Drahokoupil, Rutvica Andrijasevic, and Devi Sacchetto. Brussels: European Trade Union Institute (ETUI).

Vermeiren, Matthias. 2013. Foreign Exchange Accumulation and the Entrapment of Chinese Monetary Power: Towards a Balanced Growth Regime? *New Political Economy* 18 (5): 680–714.

Wade, Robert. 1990. *Governing the Market*. Princeton: Princeton University Press.

Wang, Hui. 2009. *The End of the Revolution: China and the Limits of Modernity*. London: Verso.

Wolf, Martin. 2017. China Faces a Tough Fight to Escape Its Debt Trap. *Financial Times*, April 11. Available online at: https://www.ft.com/content/1c096f7e-1ddc-11e7-b7d3-163f5a7f229c. Accessed 12 April 2017.

World Bank. n.d. *Indicators*. Available online at: data.worldbank.org/indicator. Accessed 12 June 2019.

Xing, Yuqing. 2016. Estimating the Upper Limits of Value Added in the People's Republic of China's Processing Exports. In *Uncovering Value Added in Trade: New Approaches to Analysing Global Value Chains*, ed. Yuqing Xing. Singapore: World Scientific.

Yang, Chun. 2014. Market Rebalancing of Global Production Networks in the Post-Washington Consensus Globalizing Era: Transformation of Export-Oriented Development in China. *Review of International Political Economy* 21 (1): 130–156.

Zhan, Shaohua. 2017. Hukou Reform and Land Politics in China: Rise of a Tripartite Alliance. *The China Journal* 78: 25–49.

Zhang, Li, and Meng Li. 2016. Local Fiscal Capability and Liberalization of Urban Hukou. *Journal of Contemporary China* 25 (102): 893–907.

Zhang, Lu, and Tao Yang. 2019. Worker Activism and Enterprise Union Reform in China: A Case Study of Grassroots Union Agency in the Auto Parts Industry. *Development and Change*. Available online at: https://onlinelibrary.wiley.com/doi/abs/10.1111/dech.12551?casa_token=9ea4HKDAPo0AAAAA:zJIKcKfxv3I3gb7HZD0yGe_9jsgC1awhackUl24Bd9u-xJpB9OTpRBmEhv73hLuephWkYlFy-adxvQ.

Zhang, Zhao, Niamh Moore-Cherry, and Declan Redmond. 2017. A Crisis of Crisis Management? Evaluating Post-2010 Housing Restructuring in Nanjing, China. *Housing Policy Debate*.

Zhu, Shengjun, and John Pickles. 2014. Bring In, Go Up, Go West, Go Out: Upgrading, Regionalisation and Delocalisation in China's Apparel Production Networks. *Journal of Contemporary Asia* 44 (1): 36–63.

Zhuang, Wenjia, and Kinglun Ngok. 2014. Labour Inspection in Contemporary China: Like the Anglo-Saxon Model, but Different. *International Labour Review* 153 (4): 561–585.

CHAPTER 7

The State Resurgent

7.1 Introduction

The previous chapter outlined China's continuing interdependence with the global economy. I argued that the profitability crisis and growth slowdown caused by the 2008 global crisis render 'economic rebalancing' unlikely, since the structural decline of the export sector interrupted the principal source of domestic earnings growth. Reviving growth under these circumstances thus entailed a switch to debt-financed and state-led investment. This Keynesian-Fordist investment surge underpinned consumption and wage growth throughout the 2010s, while delivering mixed results in reviving the productive (principally private-owned) manufacturing sector. As such, while the exportist system of accumulation (SOA) degenerated during 2008–2009 and its aftermath, what has come to replace it is far more ambiguous: a system of accumulation on the one hand still dependent on export earnings (sizeable, but no longer growing in line with GDP), and on the other, predicated upon huge debt-financed capital injections from state banks and enterprises for growth. The sheer scale of intervention from state agencies has, in this perspective, led to a nascent 'state capitalist' SOA.

This chapter outlines the contours of this emergent state capitalist SOA and probes its growth dynamics and crisis-tendencies. I begin by examining in more detail the kinds of state-led investment and the evolution of China's combined development in an era of the resurgence of the

S. Rolf, *China's Uneven and Combined Development*,
Studies in the Political Economy of Public Policy,
https://doi.org/10.1007/978-3-030-55559-7_7

Keynesian-Fordist state sector. I examine the recent history of the corporate sector to demonstrate how the state has encroached upon the private economy for both political and economic reasons. This encroachment, I argue, both represents China's first serious attempt at infant industry-style industrial policy along the lines of prior East Asian developers, and simultaneously a risky Keynesian attempt at ramping up investment, independent of demand, to stimulate growth and productivity. I then go on to explain why so much of the bout of state-financed stimulus in infrastructure after 2008 found its way, alongside the overproduction of heavy goods, into real estate investment. Real estate has increasingly come to form a new 'growth engine' for China's economy in the post-crisis period, while playing an important role in stimulating the consumer component of GDP growth. This has driven much economic growth during the latter part of the decade to 2020. However, this risks what Harvey (2016) refers to as a 'switching crisis': whereby investments flow from the productive manufacturing sector into unproductive speculation on the built environment, deferring—but ultimately heightening—the crisis which has built up in the real economy over preceding years. Without the recovery of productive sectors (able to generate surpluses without state support), China remains seriously vulnerable to a sharp slowdown in growth and the destructive possibilities of a financial crisis.

7.2 The State Resurgent

China's exportist system of accumulation (SOA) experienced the effects of faltering profitability of capital, rather than a failed strategy of rebalancing, in the aftermath of the global economic crisis of 2008–2009. A collapse in demand 2008, followed by a levelling off of exports, through the 2010s, gradually fed into a slowdown in profits, wage growth and (with a lagging effect) consumer demand. Paradoxically, given the evident weakening of the main profit-earning centre of the Chinese economy, China's investment rate has increased markedly since the global crisis of 2008. Despite accounting for an already high 40% of GDP in 2008, fixed asset investment peaked at 48% in 2011 and has since remained slightly below 45% (for comparison, the US investment to GDP ratio has fluctuated around 20% over the same period). There are two principal reasons for this exorbitantly high investment rate, which has become the prime driver of China's economic growth since 2008. First is the central state's programme of forced investment in state-owned enterprises (industries often already suffering overcapacity), primarily to fuel infrastructure expansion. Second is a continued increase of (private and public) investment and a shift of savings into in housing and real estate, where profits remain healthy, and which is increasingly coming to substitute for private sector manufacturing investment.

After regaining ground since 2008–2009, private sector investment in China trended sharply downward from 2014, bottoming out as it approached total collapse in the summer of 2016 (panicking policymakers) before staging a weak recovery to 2018. But SOE investment in fixed capital compensated for the loss of export earnings and decline in private investment, meaning that (in the language of 'rebalancing') a 'narrower external imbalance has come at the cost of growing internal imbalances' (Zhang 2016, 8). But, since low-return SOE investment has historically been financed by export generated surpluses, any increase in the investment rate of SOEs—especially if accompanied by a fall in export earnings—could only be funded by an expansion of credit and the money supply. And credit creation did indeed spike dramatically from 2008. China's debt load increased to over 250% of GDP in 2019 (other estimates put the figure higher), from 150% (of a then much smaller) national product in 2005. This US$28.2tn in debt has been overwhelmingly run up by corporations (rather than households, banks, or local governments), which owe two-thirds of this money. The majority of this corporate debt is owed by state firms.[1] Many central banks pursued quantitative easing to rescue financial institutions, but the increase in China's supply of broad money since 2007 amounts to US$16tn—greater than increases in rest of the world combined, and dwarfing that of the US (c. $5tn) and the Eurozone ($1tn) (Mandeng 2016). As of 2018, M2 was estimated at over 180 trillion RMB (two times the size of GDP).

Just how sustainable is China's debt-financed, state-led investment? Kroeber (2016, 212) describes China's earlier development as a process of 'capital widening', where simply increasing the (chronically low) ratio of capital to total GDP permitted windfall gains in productivity. But today,

[1] Though the flood of lending surging through the economy has also resulted in the emergence of a shadow banking sector which increasingly targets small, private firms with high interest rate loans (Tsai 2015). This explosion of underground lending is no surprise given the quantity of renminbi printed since 2008, and despite a regulatory crackdown in 2018 was estimated at over US$8tn in 2019.

the value of China's total capital stock is quickly approaching 3 times the value of GDP—double its ratio in 1994—a level of capital saturation only reached by Japan in the early 1980s and Korea in the year 2000, after they were considered advanced economies. The upshot is that as China's capital stock accumulates, so do pressures to extract returns commensurate to the scale of the sunk capital investment. Boosting productivity by adding new machinery becomes relatively more expensive, increasing pressure to utilise existing investments more productively. Figure 7.1 demonstrates how the rapid investment rate of the past decade has accumulated into a vast capital stock (split more or less evenly between private and state sectors) with a value of around US$63tn in 2017. In this scenario, China's strategy of directing further investment into the state sector has precisely the opposite effect, especially since it suffered from both relatively low returns and industrial overcapacity even before 2008. An OECD (2015, 125) report cites official government statistics showing 'up to USD [$] 6.8 trillion of ineffective investment had been undertaken since 2009, a very large share of which consisted of local governments' industrial and infrastructure projects'.

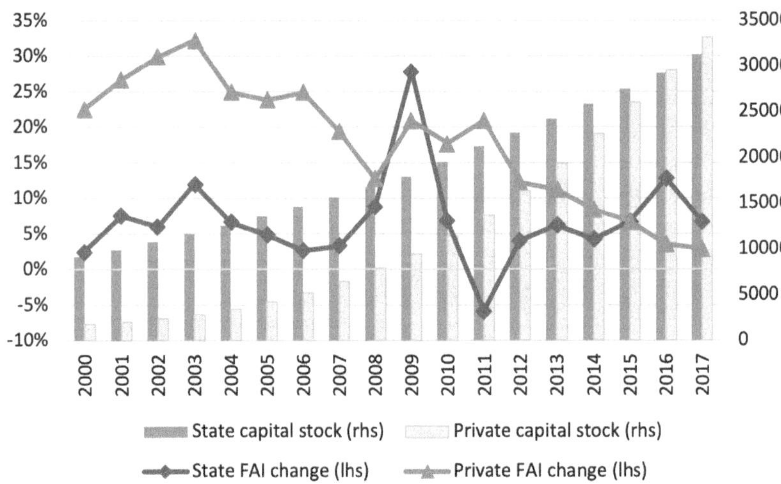

Fig. 7.1 State and private fixed asset investment in China (% change, lhs; total stock in billions of 2011 US$, rhs) (*Source* Author's calculations from *NBS* [various years], *IMF* [n.d.])

There is evidence of both poor and sound investment choices being made by the bureaucracy. Consider, in the formert category, the crisis of overcapacity in the steel industry generated by China's ramping up of investment since 2010. Total global demand for steel amounted to 1.5bn metric tons (MT) in 2015, while total world capacity stood at 2300bn MT. This 800bn MT in overcapacity was overwhelmingly due to China's addition of an extra 552 MT of capacity since 2008, independent of market demand. Indeed, China produced more steel in 2015 (803.3bn MT) than the next 30 producers *combined* (for comparison, Japan, the second largest producer, produced 105 MT), while repeated central state efforts to run-down unnecessary steel mills have so far proved ineffectual (Brun 2016). And rather than winding down output, China was projected to produce over 1tn MT of steel in 2019. This story of runaway capacity could be repeated across a range of heavy goods industries like coal, ship-building, chemicals and oil refining. An important study into the returns on a large sample of Chinese infrastructure projects found two-thirds to be loss-making, operating at 40% below their projected usage, a decade or more after completion and thus acting as a major net drag on economic activity (Ansar et al. 2016).

A more qualified picture is needed when we examine high-tech areas where the state has a significant stake. In aerospace engineering, a flood of government investment has achieved remarkable results in leapfrogging to the technological frontier. China's first domestic constructed passenger aircraft, (state-owned) Comac's C919, conducted a successful test flight in May 2017. However, such definitive achievements do not necessarily represent the desired 'indigenous innovation' called for in documents like CM2025. Although this did represent a major milestone in some regards, the *Financial Times* (2017) reported 'the wings and the tail are made in China, but many of the most important and most technologically advanced parts are purchased from foreign companies, such as GE and Safran, which provided the engine, and Honeywell, which supplied the wheels and brakes and communication and navigation systems… the C919 is still 10–15 years out of date, compared to the latest versions of the A320 and Boeing 737, meaning it will probably cost more to run.' In biotechnology, impressive examples of innovation are taking place in cell and gene therapies for cancer treatment, for example. But such biotech developments are highly reliant on basic research funding from state agencies (*Financial Times* 2019).

These examples are, in different ways, representative of the key characteristic of the state capitalist SOA: a transformation of corporate governance in the Chinese economy, with the emergence of large national champions in frontier industries which straddle the state-private divide. Such firms are usually nominally privately owned, but enjoy dense interconnections with the state—both in terms of ownership and effective control. Alternatively, they may be nominally state-owned, but with significant private equity ownership, and possessing dense interconnections with private sector suppliers and customers. While the exportist SOA represented a confluence of spatially and sectorally separate 'neoliberal' and 'Keynesian-Fordist' ideal typical economies in the private and state sectors, respectively—albeit combined by central state institutions and the surplus-recycling mechanism outlined above—the state capitalist SOA is increasingly blurring this boundary. In Comac's case, this is evident in both its web suppliers—a mixture of foreign companies and over two hundred domestic private sector firms, as well as giant state partners like AVIC—and its funding model: retained profits and state bank loans, alongside over US$2bn raised from private Chinese capital injections in 2017 alone (*China Daily* 2017). Such examples of direct business-state interactions are now the defining feature of the 'state-embedded private sector', the core sector of the new state capitalist SOA. The firms in these new core sectors come from firms which matured in the traditional state and private sector backgrounds (as in Comac and Huawei, respectively), as well as new privately owned (and publicly listed) firms in sectors like financial and digital services (Alibaba Group and Tencent) and real estate (Vanke, Poly). Figure 7.2 represents the emergence of this new core sector of the economy, with firms drifting from 'purely' state-owned or private-owned to join this state-embedded private sector.

Unlike traditional manufacturing SMEs in the exportist SOA, such giant firms enjoy close interconnections with the national state, national-level ministries and access to state financing (through banks and new venture capital firms). Part of the reason for the emergence of these firms straddling the public-private boundary is the distinct path-dependency of China's industrial policy: from 2003, the first serious and sustained attempts at infant industry industrial policies began to emerge, with a distinct focus on mega-projects aimed at basic science and research (Chen and Naughton 2016). This was most evident in 2010s Strategic Emerging Industries plan which identified a range of frontier industries (e.g., new energy vehicles, biotechnology) that China aimed to develop corporate

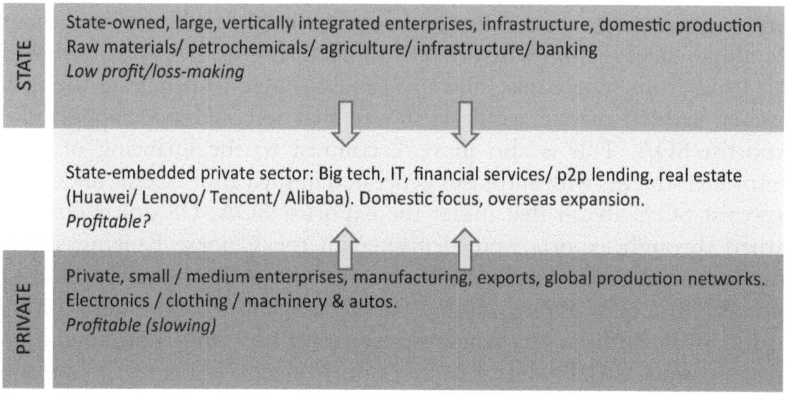

Fig. 7.2 The state and private sectors, and the state-embedded private sector (*Source* Author)

champions in by 2020. The Made in China 2025 plan announced in 2015 effectively builds on this legacy of state technology investment by aiming to develop German-style industry 4.0. As such, the overwhelming focus has been entering entirely new production lines rather than achieving industrial upgrading within the existing export sector. Finally, the very distinction between the manufacturing and service sector is increasingly porous in industries like tech (see the Conclusion to this volume). All such emergent industries rely upon the intermingling of private and state capital, while many are subject to de facto barriers to entry (in the case of software companies the Great Firewall, while bank licences have hampered payments firms like Visa entering China until 2020). A law requiring all firms of over 50 employees to host a CCP cell with some managerial input has become more strictly enforced, while members of leading private sector firms increasingly sit on the National People's Congress. Furthermore, state venture capital firms have taken sizeable minority stakes and board positions across many private sector firms of size. Those firms which emerged from the exportist SOA and rose to national and global prominence as genuinely private companies (e.g., Lenovo and Huawei in electronics) have inexorably found themselves embedded in this 'state-embedded private sector'.

Ascertaining the competitiveness of firms operating in this sphere of the economy is far more difficult than for those in the self-evidently surplus generating export sector of the early 2000s. Much new investment spending—be it in infrastructure or manufacturing—is debt-financed with soft loans from state banks, and this capital is able to penetrate the new state-embedded private sector in a way that it could not support the exportist SOA. This is also in stark contrast to the financing of state sector investments with surpluses generated in the export sector under the exportist SOA. Recall that under the exportist SOA, US dollar reserves earned through exports were deposited in the Chinese banking sector and exchanged with state banks for yuan. This enabled an expansion of both the domestic money supply (backed by dollars) and loans to low-return SOEs without sparking runaway inflation. Dollar earnings have dried up since 2010, while repeated efforts since 2015 to maintain the value of the yuan (facing the headwinds of capital flight and economic slowdown) have meant a sharp outflow of dollars as the PBoC burned though a quarter of its supply to purchase renminbi. Even this could not halt an inexorable slide past 8 RMB to the US$ in 2019, down from 6:1 at the start of the decade. Figure 7.3 provides a graphic visualisation of the uptick in both money creation and the total debt burden in the

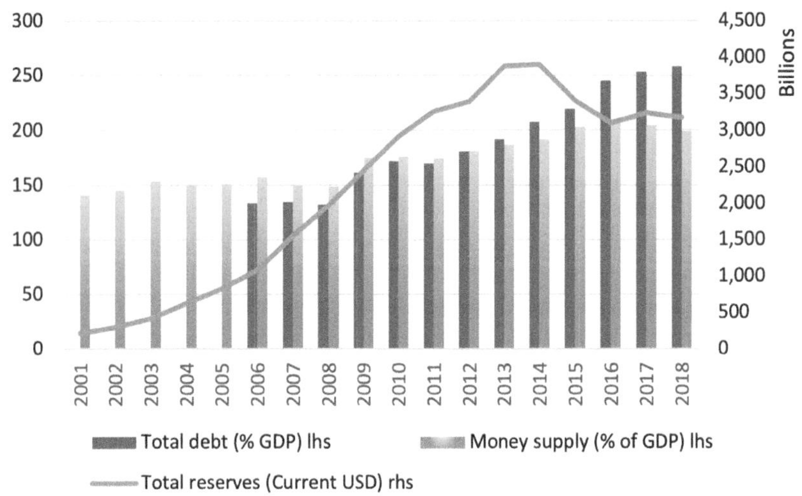

Fig. 7.3 Total debt and money supply (% of GDP, lhs) and total forex/gold reserves (billions of US$, rhs) (*Source* World Bank indicators [n.d.] and IMF [n.d.])

economy, which basically coincide with the decline of dollar reserve accumulation. In sum, China has switched from a surplus generating economy to a debt-reliant economy fighting capital flight on multiple fronts. As such, the viability of the new state capitalist SOA remains to be seriously tested by the competitive pressures of the world economy.

7.3 The Real Estate Boom

This increasing debt burden demonstrates the limits of China's Keynesian industrial strategy of forced investment—one which risks eroding profitability through the bulk of output produced, which risks effectively writing off the principal. But one area where 'overinvestment' is commonly understood to make sense is urbanisation, which is viewed as a means of promoting economic and productivity growth for China in the medium- to long-term (Green 2010; Roach 2014). According to the World Bank (2014), because urban services are more productive than farming and more labour-intensive (and thus capable of absorbing more workers) than manufacturing, simply urbanising a greater portion of the rural population should lead to further growth and productivity gains in and of itself. At the outset of reform, fewer than 20% of Chinese lived in cities; while the 50% urbanisation threshold was passed in 2012. But although nowhere has such a great quantity of people become urbanised in such a short space of time, proportionately, the growth of the urban population remains below that of previous East Asian developers at equivalent points in their development trajectories. So in principle, urbanisation has room to continue. But assuming investment in urban infrastructure can unproblematically boost growth runs into a number of problems. First is that urbanisation is not a guarantee of employment generation in itself, even in the urban service sector. As Miller (2012, 162) argues, 'if the economy does not create enough jobs, China could easily find itself succumbing to the same bleak predicament as many Western societies: handing over welfare payments to a disenfranchised urban underclass living in run-down public housing estates.' As such, this theory is vulnerable to the criticisms made of 'rebalancing' approaches in the previous chapter. And second, undermining the *hukou* system also represents a threat to the regime of social reproduction, insofar as cheap migrant labour has been largely produced by concentrating the social costs of childcare, ill health, and retirement in the countryside.

These questions aside, I want to examine whether China's contemporary *form* of urbanisation—especially its highly speculative and profit-driven nature—might be fruitfully represented by what David Harvey (2016) conceptualises as a 'switching crisis'. In an article titled 'The urban process under capitalism' originally published in 1978, Harvey develops a simplified model of capitalist investment comprising primary, secondary and tertiary sectors. The primary circuit of capital, manufacturing and productive services, is where value is created—but tends to experience overaccumulation since productivity is improved by reducing the quantity of labour versus capital utilised. The secondary circuit of capital comprises infrastructure, real estate and the built environment, and tends to suffer from underinvestment (since 'investments tend to be large-scale and long-lasting, often difficult to price in the ordinary way, and in many cases open to collective use by all individual capitalists'; Harvey 2016, 128). The tertiary circuit is made up of investments in R&D and welfare expenditures, which again tend to experience underinvestment in typical conditions but which are liable to be changed by class struggles over the social wage. For our purposes, we set this tertiary circuit to one side to focus on the interplay between manufacturing, finance and real estate.[2]

Harvey's theory models the dynamics of crisis-formation, by tracing how low profitability due to overaccumulation in manufacturing can be resolved, temporarily, by redirecting investment into the (underdeveloped) secondary circuit—housing, infrastructure and the built environment. This redirection of capital usually requires the formation of liquid capital markets alongside a 'state willing to finance and guarantee long-term, large-scale projects' by issuing fictitious capital (like bonds and central bank loans) which provide investors a degree of confidence (Harvey 2016, 132). Such urban fixed capital investments typically pay off in the short run, insofar as they compensate for historic underinvestment during a prior manufacturing boom and so serve to 'level out' the balance between circuits. The speculative nature of the capital flow also rewards early entrants to a building boom, who see prices often rise spectacularly from their base during a frenzied bidding competition for land. But

[2] Interestingly, Harvey (2012, 60) has been among the more perceptive Western geographers to have considered the China's contemporary urbanisation drive, though he does not mobilise his own concept of a switching crisis to do so. He does observe that the 'speculative scale of the Chinese development seems to be of an entirely different order than anything before in human history'.

since it is virtually impossible to guarantee the productivity of long-term, large-scale investments (especially when they are precipitated by a flood of capital escaping the crisis-ridden primary sector) or to correlate these with the needs of renewed manufacturing profitability, sectoral switching typically represents a strategy of (temporal) *crisis-deferment* rather than resolution. Harvey (2016, 136) notes that 'manifestations of crisis thus appear in both the secondary and the tertiary circuits of capital. But there is a substantial time-lag because of the long turnover time of such investments'. Eventually 'the crisis takes the form of a crisis in the valuation of assets',—that is, falling real estate prices.[3]

This theory of a switching crisis bears at least some relevance for the contemporary Chinese case, where the recent scale of investment in real estate and urban construction has been enormous. A booming urban property market emerged during the 2000s following the 'Decision on the deepening reform of urban housing system', which privatised the bulk of state-owned enterprise housing in 1998, alongside very low initial land valuations and an ageing housing stock. By 2008, nearly 10% of GDP growth was generated by investment in real estate—70% of which was residential construction.[4]

[3] Christophers (2011, 1352), in perhaps the most scrupulous deployment of Harvey's theory to date (see also King 1989; Beauregard 1994) warns that looking for definitive empirical verification of the theory may be too demanding, because of the complexity of accurate empirical measurement of intersectoral value transfers and fictitious capital formation. He suggests two empirical strategies which should at least be strongly indicative that the process is at work: First, an empirical measurement of the relative significance of investment in the built environment compared with investment in productive activities (data which I consider sufficiently available in the Chinese case), and second, the propensity of institutional investors to switch their portfolios from manufacturing investment to real estate investment. Since systematic evidence of this latter type is not readily available in the Chinese case, we must rely largely on the first, supplemented by more general observations which we would expect to accord with a disproportionate flow of investment into the built environment where returns seem increasingly unlikely to materialise in the long-run.

[4] Land remains state owned, but land-use rights were separated from ownership in 1988, and the dynamic of financially struggling local governments turning over rural land for urban usage was entrenched thereafter as early as 1994 with shifts in the taxation regime. Initially, land development was mostly for industrial usage, since the system of dormitory migrant labour (where factories provide accommodation) required minimal residential construction. It was only during the late 1990s that an urban property market was established—by transferring ownership of the bulk of all housing from the state to previous tenants.

Property, then, became economically significant for China's national economy before the crisis of 2008, and to this extent was coterminous with development of the 'real' economy (cf. Hsing 2010). Property prices peaked once in 2011 following a post-crisis boom, when China registered its first small decline in housing values, before recovering later in the year (a pattern repeated in 2014–2015). However, in parallel with the ramping up of state spending on infrastructure, the overall pattern of the post-2008 period has been marked by a dramatic spike in the upward trend of investment in property. Figure 7.4 demonstrates a rate of fixed asset investment in real estate consistent with that of total FAI, though it survived the recent downturn in 2018–2019 brought about (in part) by the Sino-US trade war. Figure 7.5, meanwhile, demonstrates the significant and sustained growth in real house prices China has experienced since 2008.

Real estate almost doubled in significance to generate close to 20% of GDP growth in 2017 = 9 and attracted over US$1.5tn of fixed asset investment annually through 2014–2017. Property in 40 cities increased in price by 60% from 2008 to 2014, while average prices stood at

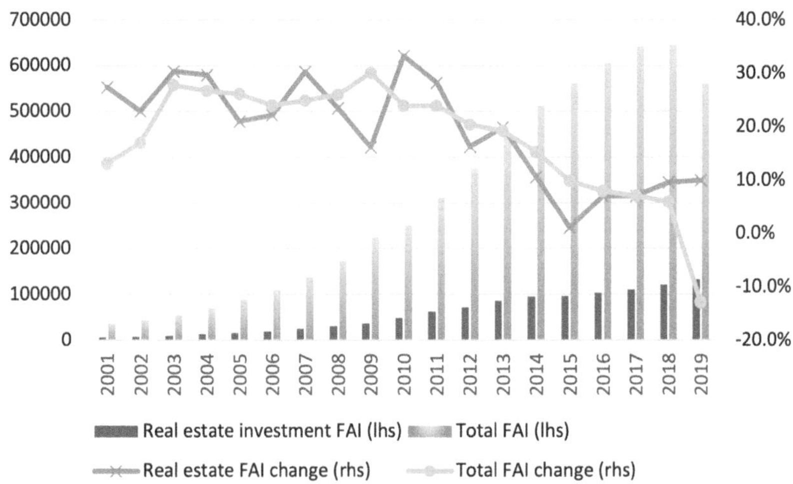

Fig. 7.4 Fixed asset investment (FAI) in real estate and total FAI (100 m yuan, lhs) and rate of change of real estate and total FAI (%, rhs) (*Source NBS* [various dates])

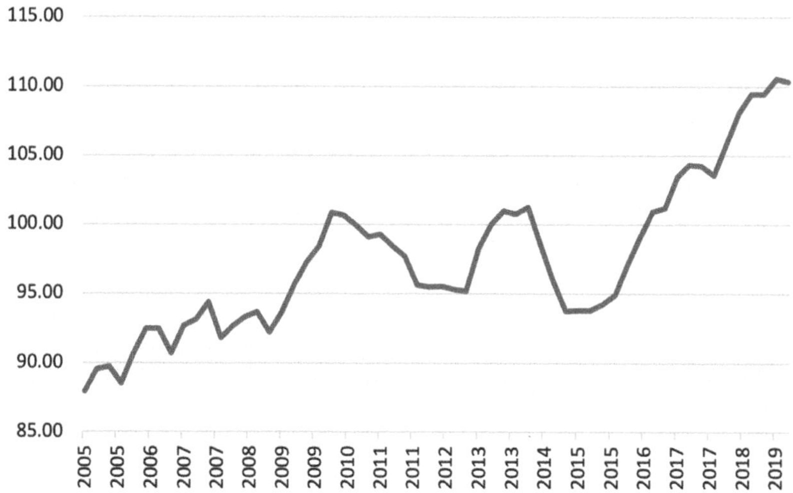

Fig. 7.5 Real house price index for China (2010 = 100) (*Source US Federal Reserve Bank of St Louis* [n.d.])

494% of total household disposable income in 2016 (second only to Australian ratio) (McKinsey 2015, and see Fig. 7.5). China poured more concrete between 2011–2013 than did the US during the twentieth century (MacCarthy 2014), the country accounts for more than half of the world's skyscrapers (Wood 2014), and available real estate floorspace increased by over 50% in major and 200% in smaller cities between 2009 and 2014 (Woodworth and Wallace 2017, 5–6). Investors who purchased property in the early days of private housing sales have benefitted from soaring prices. One recent estimate puts Chinese real estate as an asset class at 3–4% of total global GDP (Powell 2018). Consequently, the decline of exports and attendant increase in state spending have led to real estate playing a far more significant (arguably key) role in the post-2008 system of accumulation—the one sector where private investors feel confident of earning a return, and one upon which officials increasingly depend to generate revenue. This is evidenced by the sheer volume of activity in the market for housing. 90% of all Chinese own a property, while over a third of the population owns at least two.

Real estate has become an increasingly critical locus of economic activity. With a closed capital account and US$30tn of savings deposited in state banks, a giant cash surplus struggles to find a productive outlet within the national economy. Moreover, an important recent study by Wu (2019) demonstrates the two-way process between money creation and land financing at work in the Chinese case after 2008. While post-2008 central bank stimulus and subsequent rounds of money creation was one means by which land and property values came to be rapidly inflated, the surge in the M2 (broad money) supply was also an *effect* of the creation of fictitious capital through local governments' land development schemes. As rural or unutilised land was brought online through its conversion into real estate, local governments could mortgage it and turn it into a speculative asset, with the sales proceeds conjuring 'fictitious capital' which could circulate through the financial system in advance of the real revenue streams it may (or may not) generate in future.[5]

Research by *Deutsche Bank* finds that in 2015, local governments sourced 43% of their tax revenues from property and construction (vs. 10% from manufacturing activities)—while off-budgetary revenue earned from land-use sales was equivalent to half again of all aboveboard revenue (*ValueWalk* 2017). And an enormous quantity of debt has also been mobilised in service of this construction binge. Nearly three quarters of the 4 trillion RMB stimulus package of 2008–2009 was funded by local (rather than central) government, funnelled from state banks to local urban development projects through local government financing vehicles (LGFVs). Nominally independent (but de facto state operated) LGFVs serve as investment houses for local governments unable to borrow directly from state banks. While relatively insignificant before 2008, these had proliferated to over 10,000 by 2014 (Breslin 2014). Beyond the fictitious capital funding local government expenditures, many regular bank loans are collateralized against housing values and returns on infrastructure projects. McKinsey (2015) highlights that half of China's total debt of US$28.2tn is linked, directly or indirectly, to real estate markets. The housing boom is also intimately tied to improving consumptive capacities of Chinese, since rapid price rises are compensating for slowing incomes, generating a 'wealth effect'. In 2016 alone, it is estimated that price rises in major (first-tier) cities increased the wealth of homeowners by 24 trillion RMB. This is one major reason why consumption could continue

[5] That money is largely created by private banks (or in this case, local government financing vehicles) and not only central banks is increasingly understood. See McLeay et al. (2014) and Skidelsky (2018).

to grow so rapidly through the decade from 2010 even as (particularly toward the latter part of the decade) wage growth began to slow markedly.

One highly visible manifestation of this increasingly entrenched urbanisation dynamic is the now notorious phenomenon of 'ghost cities' (Shepard 2015). This first came to public attention following reportage on the case of Kangbashi in Inner Mongolia—then an entirely uninhabited urban development constructed thirty minutes drive from the established city of Dongsheng in the Gobi Desert. Completed in 2010, Kangbashi is capable of housing 300,000 citizens, though was home to just 28,000 in 2011 (Sorace and Hurst 2016). Since then, a flood of reports on apparently deserted urban developments (more often new city districts than entire cities) have appeared, while images of uninhabited skyscrapers and carless city streets add to the dramatic sensibilities of such journalism. For some, this speculative urban construction makes eminent sense considering the likely scale of China's future urbanisation. Miller (2012, 123), for instance, argues that China 'can digest a few white elephants', because 'every year, China's cities must absorb more than 20 million new inhabitants'. For Sorace and Hurst (2016, 30), however, ghost cities lay bare the performative aspect of urbanisation—that cities must be constructed before they can be inhabited, but that this significant temporal gap between their production and realisation opens up a significant space for crises. As such, speculative urbanisation is underlain by a mistaken 'assumption that the *construction of urban landscapes* will eventually result in *urbanization* by attracting financial investment and residents', which may not be the case.

Do these trends amount to a potential housing bubble? Optimistic accounts of China's speculative urbanism hinge around two important contentions. First, it is argued that a bubble is unlikely in Chinese real estate markets because mortgages require very high downpayments (often around 30%), making repayment crises less likely than elsewhere. Second, because capital markets are shallow and essentially detached from the real economy, they cannot well facilitate switching of private investment from manufacturing and into house price speculation. This second point ignores the extent to which, in the absence of developed capital markets, China's state has played a highly significant role in directing assets into real estate—by using its control over bank finance to redirect savings towards urban development. And despite the security offered by large mortgage downpayments, a fall in house prices due to oversupply (or even a crisis of debt repayments elsewhere in the economy which depresses the value of housing)—would have some impact on the banking sector: since housing represents 60% of total personal wealth, and against which a majority of bank deposits are collateralised. While state control of banking might avoid a full-blown financial crisis, in Japan, this could not halt a permanent slide in corporate and land prices during the 1990 s and a 'zombie decade' of stagnant growth (Mikuni and Murphy 2003).

Finally, while further urbanisation is a likely an economic and social requirement of China's future development, the dynamics of the urban process evidently function as a barrier to the only possible means by which the outputs of the real estate sector could be sustainably valorised—to offer housing to rural migrants partially locked out of cities' socio-economic life by their non-resident status. China's urbanisation is consonant with the increasingly global pattern of what geographers refer to as 'neoliberal urbanism'. As He and Wu (2009, 284) explain, 'the local state and enterprises have jointly endeavored to promote rapid urban (re)development, which is strongly based on real estate development… The elements of neoliberalization, e.g. privatization and commodification, drastic inter and intra-urban competition and radical urban socio-spatial transformation, are emerging in China'. One concrete impact of these broader socio-spatial trends is the result that a great bulk of housing—constructed as a site for investment—is at the top end of the market, in luxury, secure condominiums. These are far beyond the reach of the bulk of migrant workers (and to some extent appear purposefully designed to exclude them and their attendant social security bills), while their high price commands a strong return for investors (cf. Gaulard 2013). Unsurprisingly, given this market mismatch, inventories of unsold housing are piling up, and 5 billion square metres of floorspace were on the market in mid-2016 (up from 3 billion in 2012). But even were prices to fall substantially, it seems unlikely that such high-end housing would be adapted for and sold to cities' lowest-income residents.

Attempts to rationalise the urbanisation process have proven inadequate. The Twelfth Five-Year Plan mandated the construction of 36 million units of social housing from 2011–2016, but nearly half of this stock was in university dormitories and other public constructions with only tenuous claim to the label 'social housing'—while local governments frequently build highly unsuitable social housing constructions cheaply, far away from amenities and transport links, in order to fulfil obligations to the plan. Analysis of panel data suggests that ferocious competition over land and the heavy reliance of local government finances on taxes earned from sales following the land conversion (Jin and Choi 2019). Miller (2016) reports that mortgage uptake among first-generation migrants has increased substantially in the past year, as new housing developments in interior provinces aimed at low-income returning first generation migrants come online. But the number of migrants with mortgages remains at just 1.3%—a figure that does not appear likely to change significantly in the near future. Local governments (in the final instance responsible for nearly all real estate development) are driven overwhelmingly to pursue economic growth, while property buyers are primarily chasing a return on their invested assets rather than residency (Sorace and Hurst 2016). China's housing market appears to function more as a sinkhole for investment, than to meet the housing needs of the polity. This capital switching might not conform exactly to Harvey's patterning, but its broad-strokes approximation should concern those those invested (both economically and socially) in China's accumulation system.

7.4 Conclusion

The danger signs facing the Chinese state-capitalist SOA are increasingly evident—not least in the continuing (gradual) slowdown in growth, two dramatic stock market crashes which spooked investors in July 2015 and January 2016, and the large scale capital flight which prompted China's spending of US$1tn in foreign currency reserves to prop up the yuan during 2016.[6] However, despite the multiple and complex crisis-tendencies which this chapter has aimed to identify, I do not definitively side with those pessimists who regularly predict the imminent demise of the Chinese economy. As argued in the previous chapter, we should be cautious about extrapolating from the experience of past catch-up developers, since today's geopolitical economy is radically different from that encountered by previous catch-up developers. The next, concluding,

[6] It is possible that China is nearing the end of its liquid forex reserves (which amounted to a total of US$4tn in 2015), since it is believed that many bank loans are capitalized against the remainder, making it impossible—or at least highly dangerous—to deploy them in service of the yuan in the face of further capital flight. If this is the case then any further capital flight would be hard to stem, since controls cannot be made watertight, and it would be impossible to continue purchasing renminbi with dollars to maintain the value of the yuan.

chapter, identifies areas of optimism in the state-embedded core sectors with a focus on the digital economy.

This said, the evidence surveyed here does appear to suggest that a clearing out of unproductive and increasingly indebted firms is likely necessary before a renewed round of accumulation could plausibly restore China's growth to the high rates experienced previously. It further attests to the intrinsic irrationality of globalised system of capitalist production of which China remains a major constituent part, and to the limits imposed upon any Keynesian-Fordist attempt to defer or mitigate the systematic tendencies towards overaccumulation of capital embedded in its dynamic. China's compressed urbanisation process has drawn together central government, for whom urbanisation is increasingly a national accumulation strategy, local governments, who rely on the revenues from turning over land for developments, and investors (including an upper strata of the non-migrant working class), who have so far secured healthy returns by purchasing property. This switch of investment flows may have deferred the depth of economic crisis in the short term, but its future consequences remain to be seen. To the extent that growing consumer spending (via the wealth effect) is tied to the overinflated real estate sector, any slowdown in real estate investment will also significantly harm consumption. China's growth pattern is increasingly marked by the effects of the collapse of its export sector in 2008 and the manifold attempts of the state to maintain growth in the face of the long depression weighing on the global economy. Despite the remarkable attempts by the state to mediate the dynamics and defer the impact of this crisis, it has not escaped unscathed.

References

Ansar, Antif, Bent Flyvbjerg, Alexander Budzier, and Daniel Lunn. 2016. Does Infrastructure Investment Lead to Economic Growth or Economic Fragility? Evidence from China. *Oxford Review of Economic Policy* 32 (3): 360–390.

Beauregard, Robert. 1994. Capital Switching and the Built Environment: United States, 1970–89. *Environment and Planning A* 26: 715–732.

Breslin, Shaun. 2014. Financial Transitions in the PRC: Banking on the State? *Third World Quarterly* 35 (6): 996–1013.

Brun, Lukas. 2016. *Overcapacity in Steel: China's Role in a Global Problem.* Durham: Duke University Press.

Chen, Ling, and Barry Naughton. 2016. An Institutionalized Policy-Making Mechanism: China's Return to Techno-Industrial Policy. *Research Policy* 45 (10): 2138–2152.

China Daily. 2017. COMAC Sets Up Major Investments for Future. Available online at https://www.chinadaily.com.cn/business/2017-08/22/content_30940595.htm. Accessed 1 September 2017.

Christophers, Brett. 2011. Revisiting the Urbanization of Capital. *Annals of the Association of American Geographers* 101 (6): 1347–1364.

Financial Times. 2017. China's Aviation Finally Takes Off with Help from the West, May 17.

Financial Times. 2019. Chinese Biotech: From Copycat to Innovator, October 10.

Gaulard, Mylène. 2013. Changes in the Chinese Property Market: An Indicator of the Difficulties Faced by Local Authorities. *China Perspectives* 2: 3–14.

Green, Stephen. 2010. China Can Urbanize Its Way to Prosperity. *The Wall Street Journal Asia*, June 25.

Harvey, David. 2012. The Urban Roots of Financial Crises. In *Socialist Register 2012: The Crisis and the Left*, ed. Leo Panitch, Greg Albo, and Vivek Chibber. Merlin: Pontypool.

Harvey, David. 2016. *The Ways of the World*. Profile: London.

He, Shenjing, and Wu Fulong. 2009. China's Emerging Neoliberal Urbanism: Perspectives from Urban Redevelopment. *Antipode* 41 (2): 282–304.

Hsing, You-tien. 2010. *The Great Urban Transformation: Politics of Land and Property in China*. Oxford: Oxford University Press.

IMF. n.d. *Global Debt* Database. Available online at https://www.imf.org/external/datamapper/datasets/GDD. Accessed 10 January 2010.

Jin, Chengua, and Mack Joong Choi. 2019. The Causal Structure of Land Finance, Commercial Housing, and Social Housing in China. *International Journal of Urban Sciences* 23 (2): 286–299.

King, Ross. 1989. Capital Switching and the Role of Ground Rent: 2 Switching Between Circuits and Switching Between Submarkets. *Environment and Planning a* 21: 711–738.

Kroeber, Arthur. 2016. *China's Economy: What Everyone Needs to Know*. Oxford: Oxford University Press.

MacCarthy, Niall. 2014. China Used More Concrete in 3 Years Than the U.S. Used in the Entire 20th Century. *Forbes*, December 5. Available online at https://www.forbes.com/sites/adp/2017/05/23/why-its-best-to-forget-trendy-benefits-and-concentrate-on-core-offerings/#6ffad4ee6ffa. Accessed 1 November 2016.

Mandeng, Ousmene. 2016. The Chinese Money Wall (update). Available online at http://www.ousmenemandeng.com/comments/16-10-6-Chinese-money-wall-updated.html. Accessed 1 December 2016.

McKinsey Global Institute. 2015. Debt and (not Much) Deleveraging. Available online at http://www.mckinsey.com/global-themes/employment-and-growth/debt-and-not-much-deleveraging. Accessed 29 April 2017.
McLeay, Michael, Amar Radia, and Ryland Thomas. 2014. Money Creation in the Modern Economy. *Bank of England Quarterly Bulletin* Q1: 14–27.
Mikuni, Akio, and R. Taggart Murphy. 2003. *Japan's Policy Trap: Dollars, Deflation, and the Crisis of Japanese Finance*. Washington, DC: Brookings Institution Press.
Miller, Tom. 2012. *China's Urban Billion: The Story Behind the Biggest Migration in Human History*. London: Zed Books.
Miller, Tom. 2016. The Migrant Housing Solution. *Gavekal Dragonomics* research note, May 24.
National Bureau of Statistics (*NBS*). n.d. *Data*. Available at http://www.stats.gov.cn/english/. Accessed 11 May 2020.
OECD. 2015. *OECD Urban Policy Reviews: China 2015*. Paris: OECD Publishing.
Powell, Jamie. 2018. Chinese Real Estate, Charted. *Financial Times*, July 19.
Roach, Stephen. 2014. *Unbalanced: The Codependency of America and China*. New Haven: Yale University Press.
Shepard, Wade. 2015. *Ghost Cities of China: The Story of Cities Without People in the World's Most Populated Country*. London: Zed Books.
Skidelsky, Robert. 2018. *Money and Government: The Past and Future of Economics*. New Haven: Yale University Press.
Sorace, Christian, and William Hurst. 2016. China's Phantom Urbanisation and the Pathology of Ghost Cities. *Journal of Contemporary Asia* 46 (2): 304–322.
Tsai, Kellee. 2015. The Rise of Shadow Banking in China: The Political Economy of Modern Chinese State Capitalism. *HKUST Thought Leadership Brief*, August: No. 10.
US Federal Reserve Bank of St Louis. n.d. Real Residential Property Prices for China. Available at https://fred.stlouisfed.org/series/QCNR628BIS. Accessed 9 November 2019.
ValueWalk. 2017. Deutsche Bank Warns: Chinese Property Bubble Is Getting Bigger. Available online at http://www.valuewalk.com/2017/03/chinese-property-bubble-soar/. Accessed 20 June 2017.
Wood, Anthony. 2014. *Best Tall Buildings: An Overview of 2013 Skyscrapers*. London: Routledge.
Woodworth, Max, and Jeremy L. Wallace. 2017. Seeing Ghosts: Parsing China's "Ghost City" Controversy. *Urban Geography* (Published online before print).
World Bank. n.d. *Indicators*. Available online at data.worldbank.org/indicator. Accessed 12 June 2019.

World Bank. 2014. *Urban China: Toward Efficient, Inclusive, and Sustainable Urbanization*. Washington, DC: World Bank.

Wu, Fulong. 2019. Land Financialisation and the Financing of Urban Development in China. *Land Use Policy* (Published online before print). Available at https://doi.org/10.1016/j.landusepol.2019.104412. Accessed 17 December 2019.

Zhang, Longmei. 2016. Rebalancing in China: Progress & Prospects. *IMF Working Paper*. Asia & Pacific.

CHAPTER 8

Conclusion: China Cracks the Whip: The Geopolitical Economy of Chinese Externalisation

8.1 Introduction

On the morning of January 17, 2017, President Xi Jinping proclaimed, before the delegates gathered at the World Economic Forum in Davos, China's commitment to the globalisation project. He promised that China would play a significant role in upholding global economic openness into the twenty-first century, and avoid the collapse into rival economic blocs which precipitated the second world war. He committed China to 'developing global free trade and investment, promote trade and investment liberalization and facilitation through opening-up and say[ing] no to protectionism'. Addressing delegates at China's National People's Congress in Beijing nine months later, Xi's tone was markedly different. Then, in a three-and-a-half-hour address, Xi promised that China would become 'a global leader in terms of composite national strength and international influence' (*Xinhua* 2017), able to defend its sovereignty and project global economic and military power. Neither statement was anomalous. Instead, each is broadly representative of contradictory but deep-rooted discourses and practices in China's foreign policy orientation. On the one hand, China continues to play its (increasingly formidable) military and diplomatic cards with notable caution, and is doing little to actively undermine the basic functioning of the multilateral trading order

S. Rolf, *China's Uneven and Combined Development*, Studies in the Political Economy of Public Policy, https://doi.org/10.1007/978-3-030-55559-7_8

which has underpinned its economic success. Indeed, Chinese state institutions are among the most active participants in and financial backers of all the major institutions of global governance (cf. Xu 2017). But the shift from Deng's motto of 'hide your strength, bide your time' (*tao guang yang hui*) to 'striving for achievement' (*fen fa you wei*) in the international arena under Xi's leadership has undoubtedly transformed both the practices and perceptions of Chinese power and influence, particularly in the sphere of geoeconomics. It is no longer difficult to compile an extensive list of examples of China's increasingly 'threatening' behaviour represented by—for example—the expansion of its naval activities in the Asia Pacific, its use of 'debt-trap diplomacy' to ensnare states in relations of economic subordination, or even its threat to the entire US-led world order through initiatives like the Belt and Road which bypass existing multilateral organisations.

These contradictory foreign policy commitments have provided fertile ground for the construction and maintenance of traditional Realist and Liberal foreign policy perspectives within US policy and scholarly circles. Warnings abound about the inevitable transformation of China's economic prowess into a hegemonic threat to the United States' world order (Mearsheimer 2014). In its strongest version, concern about Chinese expansionism is pressed into the perspective of a 'Thucydides trap': a tragically inevitable great power conflict (Allison 2017) rooted in classical realism. Trump's administration appears favourable to this view (USESRC 2019), while economic nationalists have come to occupy critical positions in great offices of state or as key presidential advisors (Robert Lighthizer, Peter Navarro and—until 2019—John Bolton). The principle concern among US hawks is both specific opposition to the Chinese state capitalist model, alongside broader trepidation regarding the emergence of a potential challenger with geopolitically autonomous institutions outside of the US security architecture in the Asia Pacific. On the other hand, liberal voices continue to call for continued economic engagement in spite of increasing geopolitical tension, with the expectation that US maintenance of the liberal international order should ultimately derail any state capitalist attempt at supremacy (Nye Jr. 2020; Ikenberry 2018; Farrell and Newman 2020). A similarly polarised debate is evident in the Chinese academy and think tanks, where a predominant realism is subject to the scrutiny of liberals favouring the maintenance of economic interdependence and geopolitical compliance with the US-led order (Zeng et al. 2015; Shih 2018).[1]

Constructivist attempts to emphasise the role of perceptions and ideological representations at work in these mounting tensions posit a more complex relationship between economic growth and its realisation in geopolitical strength (cf. Chung 2019; Wu 2020). Such accounts correctly observe that an objective increase in geoeconomic or geopolitical strength does not in itself equate to an expansionist strategy. However, important to note here are the heterogenous state-society complexes at play in the emergent US-China rivalry (cf. de Graaff and Apeldoorn 2018). The nature of the U.S. as a hegemon whose firms rely upon open borders for capital and its global military operations in support of its globalist economic interests renders it structurally predisposed to feel threatened by a militarily independent and techno-nationalist rival such as China, whatever 'grand strategy' orientation the latter espouses or actually possesses.

In this chapter, I outline a provisional conclusion to the historical pattern charted in this book. I do so by drawing on both UCD as a general framework for the global political economy which examines the reciprocal interactivity between sociological and geopolitical forces, alongside the turbulent systemic impact caused by China's specific experience of UCD. In this interpretation, the contradiction between Chinese efforts on the one hand to continue to foster global economic integration through the existing US-led international system, while, on the other, toward pursuing a significant geopolitical economic expansion of national 'reach' into the Asia Pacific region and beyond, is partially explicable by reference to China's status as a combinatory social formation,—with very different forms of capitalism operating within its territory. These (as outlined through Chapters 4–7) comprise a 'neoliberal' form comprising the plethora of globally connected export-manufacturing SMEs which form the major surplus generating sectors of China's economy in export manufacturing; a 'Keynesian-Fordist' sector, represented by the giant but largely uncompetitive SOEs in heavy goods and extractive industries, cushioned by soft loans, subsidies, and dense interconnections with both

[1] In the Chinese case, 'Western' IR thought contends with the 'Chinese School Movement' of international relations: for a critical account which emphasises the fundamental similarities of the Chinese School and dominant Western theoretical traditions in international relations, see Lu (2019).

the state-owned financial sector and the central and provincial Chinese governments (with growing overseas interests in Belt and Road activities); and the state-embedded private sector, where new corporate giants in frontier industries like biotechnology, the digital economy and new energy vehicles straddle the state-private boundary and display elements of both global competitiveness and potential weakness.

China's government is, then, caught upon the horns of a material dilemma in terms of its future orientation towards the international system. The economy remains export-dependent and so reliant on the open economic environment which the United States has overseen and upheld since the end of the Second World War. But global market saturation, a prolonged depression, and limited successes in further improving its competitive edge and usurping market share from higher-grade manufacturers (initiatives like *Made in China 2025* notwithstanding), have rendered this surplus generating part of the economy weak for over a decade. The Chinese state is also, however, unable for structural reasons to fully open its own economy (and thus definitively unable to concede to the demands of the United States in its trade war—see below), since this would likely entail the dismantling of many SOEs, ruinous capital flight, and a consequent weakening—if not disintegration—of the party-state in its current form. It is also far from clear that such a course would indeed do much to boost economic growth anyway. For this reason, it has opted for an infant industry strategy of picking winners in frontier industries and doubling down on leapfrogging through foreign technology acquisition.

This strategy has increasingly antagonised successive US administrations eager for China to continue with economic liberalisations. The economic dilemma confronting China is also then an 'external' one to the Chinese political economy. As the Xi Jinping administration has to pursue profound increases in a variety of state economic interventions, while looking for viable external outlets for surpluses generated through investment-led growth in the state sector, these strategic US decisions are being reciprocally validated and reinforced by the mounting geopolitical tensions they brought by China's geoeconomic reorientation (*Economist* 2020). The US has consequently become increasingly concerned about the costs of economic interdependency within its deteriorating relations with China, and to view the mass of critical global manufacturing capabilities located on Chinese sovereign soil as a profound threat to US economic dominance and military security. As such, China's 'domestic' political economy dynamics are vectored through the geopolitical economic dynamics of power competition in the international states system, and geoeconomic and geopolitical competition are becoming inseparable in a race for technological, economic, diplomatic and military supremacy (Schneider-Petsinger et al. 2019; Gourevitch 1978).

To examine the dramatic evolution of this process in more detail, first, I examine the most dangerous potential flashpoints of China's newly assertive foreign policy: the South and East China Seas, where China is contending with the U.S. and its allies to assert a more significant role in the regional security order. The discussion moves on to examine the linkages between this geopolitical rivalry and the most profound contest confronting the contemporary global economy: the intensifying geoeconomic antagonism between China and the U.S. in what is widely termed a 'trade war' (a far more serious encounter than its name suggests). I subsequently turn to discuss the most vivid example of China's externalisation dynamics: the Belt and Road Initiative (BRI), a potentially transformative attempt to lay the basis for China's regional (some would argue global) hegemony in Southeast and Central Asia (and beyond) through a sweeping round of infrastructural investments. Finally, I consider whether the accumulation of economic problems in China might be evaded by the further expansion of the most dynamic sector of its economy today: the internet and digital services economies. I conclude with a summary of the core theoretical and empirical contributions of this book, and suggest that the emergent social, political and economic crises to which the Covid-19 pandemic has given rise are likely to deepen the trends towards autocentrism, the national territorialisation of capitalist economies, and inter-imperialist rivalry described here.

8.2 The Geopolitical Economy of US Containment: From Geoeconomics to Geopolitics

Chapters 6 and 7 located the genesis of the state capitalist SOA in global economic dynamics from 2008. The global economic crisis punctured the exportist SOA, a mixed economy growth model underpinned by export-led development, and led to a deepening of state intervention in the economy. While economic dynamics initiated this transformation, a sharp rupture in the US' China policy (which became evident early during the Obama administration) exerted further pressure on China's leadership to hedge against reliance upon the exportist SOA. Export-led development was underpinned by a long-run US policy of engaging China and encouraging its integration with the liberal economic order. Obama's Pivot to Asia, by contrast, (published as Defence Strategic Guidance in January 2012 as 'Sustaining US Leadership: Priorities for the twenty-first Century Defence') represented a fundamental reorientation of US grand strategy towards exerting systematic geopolitical, diplomatic and economic pressure balancing against China's rise. This strategic reorientation dovetailed with the global economic downturn to further drive the emergence of an increasingly autocentric state capitalist SOA in China.

Many of the Pivot's core planks were put into place during the second Bush Jr. term—including forward troop positions in Hawaii, Guam and Alaska facilitating rapid access to Asia Pacific, the development of the AirSea battle doctrine (later the Joint Concept for Access and Maneuver in the Global Commons) aimed at upholding US dominance in the Pacific Ocean through enhanced naval and air defence capabilities, and a redeployment of 60% of the US naval fleet to the Pacific by 2009 (Silove 2016). US Strategic Defence Reviews reveal that such decisions were largely based upon military calculations regarding China's increasingly impressive naval capabilities and (Johnson 2018), as its military spending grew commensurately with its economy (maintaining defence spending at a steady rate of just below 2% of GDP through the two decades to 2020). But from the tail end of the second Bush administration into Obama's first term, the US foreign policy establishment came increasingly to view China's economic growth as the major threat to US regional hegemony in its own right, as predictions began to abound that the US role as the predominant economy might be under threat. In this context, Obama's implementation of the Pivot is consonant with the long-held US grand strategy of 'forward defence' which identifies and mitigates against possible rival powers before they emerge, by balancing (where possible) or, more rarely, containment (where not). The diplomatic orientation of Obama's Pivot aimed at replacing bilateral 'hub-and-spokes' relations with a 'networked security architecture', based upon military and diplomatic regional multilateralism (Kolmaš and Kolmašová 2019). But its *realpolitik* arm also included further major military redeployments to the US ring of East Asian and Pacific military bases, bringing the total civilian and military personnel of the Pacific Command stationed in Asia Pacific to around 377,000 (where forces were previously being wound down), increasingly regularised Freedom of Navigation Operations (FONOPs) (naval patrols targeting new Chinese territorial claims in the South China

Sea) and support for Japanese naval activities in the East China Sea (cf. Wilson 2016) from US Seventh Fleet (a permanent presence in the Pacific since 1943), and the rollout of a Terminal High Altitude Area Defense (THAAD) missile system in South Korea (deployed in 2017), which poses a potential threat to the utility of China's nuclear missile capabilities.

The East and South China Sea disputes in particular highlight how serious a security dilemma China confronts in the context of the US pivot to Asia. Critical is the threat of increased US forward presence in the 'first island chain', the string of US military bases surrounding China's seaboards (from Okinawa in the north east, through Taiwan, the Philippines, to the Malay peninsula). As in the 1960s Third Front period (see Chapter 4), the growing presence of US naval vessels in the vicinity of China's critical industrial and financial hubs of the Pearl and Yellow River Deltas, alongside the absence of any Chinese security input over the US$4tn worth of critical raw materials and manufactured goods which flow through the South China Sea and the Malacca straits by cargo ship each year, has sparked profound concern among Chinese elites about potential security vulnerabilities (Zhang 2019). China has consequently embarked upon an impressive expansion of its military capacities and its preparedness to expand its naval reach throughout the South China Sea (justified through the mobilisation of the '9-dash line' as an oceanic sovereignty claim), while challenging Japanese claims to the Diaoyu/Senkaku islands and attempts to establish air defence identification zone in the East China Sea (Rolf and Agnew 2016). A series of Chinese Defence White Papers has committed China to naval expansion in defence of its near seas (which remains its overwhelming commitment) through 'open seas protection' and 'offshore water defence', while also raising the intention to build 'far seas forces': a blue-water navy of its own (Wu 2019; CSIS 2019). On this latter front, the 2016 establishment of a military base in Djibouti has acted as something of an experiment, although it remains principally service-oriented (cf. Styan 2020). This has not stopped lurid fears of a Chinese set of naval bases (a 'string of pearls') in the Indian Ocean Region circulating in US and Indian security circles (see Tariq 2016 for a critique). The bypassing of much of the governmental apparatus by Xi's use of 'small leading groups' further suggests a more coordinated military strategy than some might allow, while a sustained focus on improving China's naval means has been evident since around 2004 (Fravel 2018). But despite the improved A2/AD capabilities and geographical reach of the People's Liberation Navy, its capacities pale in comparison with the military spending and reach of the US—with which a threefold spending gap still exists (and which are spelled out in China's 2019 Defence White Paper). Moreover, even the defensive strategy encompassing securitisation of the China's near seas in the medium term is no modest goal, given that it is perceived with extreme hostility by US regional allies as well as the US itself.

The legacy of China's status as a former victim of colonialism represents a further potent point of geopolitical leverage for the US and its allies. On the one hand, it renders China highly sensitive to charges of imperialist practice in its increasing economic and diplomatic relations with states of the global south (see 8.4). On the other, and despite China's sovereign claims to both, the dense economic and geopolitical interconnections which exist between the ex-colonial 'Greater China' territories of Taiwan and Hong Kong SAR and the US (alongside the rest of the global economy) render any full and formal legal integration of either with the Chinese mainland quite unlikely during the next decade—despite Bejing's best efforts in the Hong Kong case to use national security legislation to pre-empt the expiry of Basic Law (which *de jure* upholds Hong Kong's legal autonomy until 2047). China's territorial vulnerability strikes at a core legitimacy claim of the CCP: its professed capacity to uphold China's territorial integrity and sovereignty and atone for the 'century of humiliation' until 1949 experienced at the hands of colonial powers. For this reason, whatever the motivations of burgeoning independence movements in those states, the increasingly serious social destabilisation in Hong Kong and the strengthening of the nationalist Democratic People's Party in Taiwan will almost inevitably also function as points of US geopolitical leverage over China in the years to come (Wang 2017). Concerns regarding separatist politics in its western and northern frontiers (Yunnan, Tibet, Xinjiang and Inner Mongolia) are further pressure points in this regard.

The sharp rise in military hostility between China and the US outlined here drove China towards a view of economic interdependency with the US as a serious risk, empowering voices within the Xi administration who have long argued for a systematic reduction of China's external reliance on export markets and foreign technology imports through ramping up domestic innovation capacity (goals which Xi has espoused throughout his period of leadership) (Gewirtz 2020). As such, the geopolitical dynamics at play in China's great power relationship with the US also function as critical inputs into the form its ongoing economic transformation is coming to take, just as geopolitical dynamics shaped previous East Asian instances of late development (although in very different ways) (cf. Stubbs 2017; Cumings 2009).

8.3 Trade War: From Geopolitics to Geoeconomics

The Pivot also aimed to orchestrate an economic balancing against China. This was to be achieved through a mixture of deepening US economic ties with allies in the Asia Pacific, strengthening ASEAN and attendant regional multilateral institutions, and reducing China's relative share in regional trade. The roots of this geoeconomic tilt to the US grand strategy again lay in the second term of the Bush administration with the crucial decision to join and shape the Transpacific Partnership (TPP) in February 2008, a multilateral trade agreement encompassing deep reductions in barriers to trade between the US and its Asian regional allies. The agreement represented a naked attempt to dismantle China's growing industrial policy apparatus by excluding it from regional trade deepening until it agreed to far-reaching economic liberalisations of its state and state-embedded sectors (though it was ultimately derailed as Donald Trump took office; see Bhala 2017). As the TPP was taking shape, a welter of disputes were filed at the WTO by the US—23 cases between 2002 and 2018 (the majority of which were brought under the Obama administration, and settled before adjudication or found in the US' favour; see Schott and Jung 2019). Finally, Obama's administration took a hard line against alleged Chinese industrial espionage (see *Executive Office of the President of the United States* 2013), making several high-profile arrests of Chinese citizens and ultimately striking a 'US-China Cybersecurity Agreement' with Xi in 2015 (which temporarily reduced incidences of intellectual property theft but did not survive the following year's US presidential transition). While the principle grand strategic objection of the Bush and Obama administrations was to challenge China's increasing near-sea defence capabilities, the transformed logic of US economic statecraft—away from simply integrating China into the global economic system towards aggressive attempts to transform its economic model—tilted the entire US-China relationship towards a more serious all-encompassing confrontation, intertwining the hitherto separate geopolitical and economic disputes (Löfflmann 2016).

The steady build-up of economic diplomacy pressures under Obama, despite operating through multilateral mechanisms, can consequently be understood as a precursor to (rather than in contrast with) the shock and awe bilateral approach of the Trump administration's 'trade war' on the Chinese government (Office of the US Trade Representative 2015). Trump's determination to confront what he (and US policymakers more generally) had come to view as China's drastically unfair competitive practices manifested in an obsession with reducing the bilateral trade deficit, decisively tackling both IP theft by firms and state actors, and redressing China's alleged currency manipulation. The pre-existing geopolitical anxieties regarding Chinese military expansion became fused with these growing geoeconomic concerns, as the US government explicitly identified interdependencies between military and economic power and labelled the Chinese state a 'revisionist power' and a 'strategic competitor' (a term Bush Jr. had toyed with but not used during his presidency) in Trump's first National Security Strategy published in December 2017 (*The White House* 2017), which explicitly linked Chinese naval activities with its increasing economic prowess. From early in 2018, Section 201 tariffs were imposed on solar panels and washing machines, and a tit for tat between the US and China followed with a rapid escalation over the same year—with Section 301 tariffs of 25% placed on US$50bn worth of Chinese goods, and of 10% on an even broader range of $200bn of Chinese imports (increasing to 25% in 2019). This was followed by two further major tariff increases through 2019 (see Drezner 2019 for a full account). By the end of 2019, tariffs were levied on two-thirds of the US$550bn worth of Chinese imports at an average rate of 19.3%, up from just 3.1% at the beginning of 2018, while China had reciprocated by placing tariffs on almost all its US imports. A 'Phase One' trade deal between the US and China struck in January of 2020 did little to diminish the newly established trade barriers, and threatened to collapse shortly after in the face of the Covid-19 pandemic. The trade war led to a small overall decline in Chinese exports through 2019 (around 1%, though 7% of its US exports). But it nevertheless exposed the fragility of the state capitalist SOA, as it prompted Chinese stimulus of a 1.5 trillion RMB tax cut in 2018 and a 2tn cut in 2019, accompanied by a relaxation of rules to further encourage local governments' debt-based bond financing for construction projects (worth between 1-2tn RMB).

Trade policy formed only one element in an arsenal of economic weapons the Trump administration was prepared to use to achieve its ends. Xi Jinping had long acknowledged the role of 'technological dominance' in the West's 'sway over the world in modern times', while Beijing would need an 'asymmetrical strategy' in order to overturn its subordination (Gewirtz 2019). Targeted attacks on emergent national champions in the state-embedded private sector like ZTE and Huawei in 2019 and 2020 through the use of the US Bureau of Industry and Security's 'entity list'—which forbids (without license) component sales from US companies—caused profound anxiety in Beijing, as this threatened to cut off China's leading electronics firms from their supply of integrated circuits and other critical US-procured components. In a review conducted in 2018 by the Ministry of Industry and Information Technology, 95% of CPU-related chips for their computers and servers of China's biggest technology firms were found to be dependent on US technologies (He 2018), while over US$75bn of semiconductors were sold by the US to China in 2018 (36% of total US output). Moreover, the two major planks of China's technology acquisition programme (abroad and at home) became subject to a barrage of attacks by the US. Trump empowered the US Committee on Foreign Investment in the US (CFIUS) to cut off Chinese acquisitions aimed at technological transfers not achievable through inward FDI, even blocking deals that would only indirectly benefit Chinese firms (such as Singaporean firm Broadcom's attempted acquisition of Qualcomm, which threatened to pull the US chipmaker out of 5G infrastructure provision—leaving the field open to Huawei) (Grimes and Du 2020).[2] Meanwhile, anti-IP theft activities were ramped up, and the FBI reported it was investigating over 1000 cases of Chinese industrial espionage at the beginning of 2020 (*The Guardian* 2020). At the same time, the January 2020 Phase One Trade Deal committed Chinese firms not to include 'forced' technology transfers in joint ventures between US and Chinese firms operating in China, a long bugbear of US multinationals with Chinese manufacturing operations.

The dramatic evolution of the US-China trade war in the context of pre-existing geopolitical tensions is indicative of a broader shift in the contemporary global political economy, whereby the (albeit porous) boundary between geoeconomics and geopolitics established by US

[2] Again, this mechanism was notably used Obama administration in 2016 with an order to block the acquisition of US-held Aixtron assets by the Fujian Grand Chip Investment Fund.

predominance after the Cold War is increasingly fragmenting as alternate centres of economic and geopolitical power emerge (Beeson 2018). Rather than acting to mollify tensions, in this context the economic interdependencies built up under the period of neoliberal globalisation are increasing becoming viewed as potential (and highly effective) weapons in a deteriorating international system (Farrell and Newman 2019). Further elements in this emergent conflict include the growing risk of a 'financial war', where both the dollar's predominance in international payments systems and reliance of Chinese firms upon US capital markets are mobilised as extraterritorial leverage for the US—risking, in turn, further escalation (Dizard 2020). This might manifest through Chinese sales of its US treasury holdings (that this move would do significant damage to Chinese interests does not rule it out. See Plender 2019). It could also take the form of a squeeze on the sizeable US corporate assets held and profits generated in China. In 2018, the total stockpile of such assets was estimate at over US$600bn, with annual profits of $31bn. Meanwhile, many US corporate giants with no critical input function for Chinese firms (i.e., semiconductors) generated large proportions of their global sales revenues in China—like Apple (19.6%), Starbucks (20.2%), Corning (22%), and Nike (12.4%) (Ma 2018). This gives China some leverage in any conflagration. The ongoing fusion of geoeconomics and geopolitics threatens an escalation in any one arena to spill over into another. As Bello (2019, 72) writes, to the present US administration (and by extension that in China), 'there is no "Chinese Wall" between a trade war and a shooting war'.

8.4 Belt and Road Initiative: A Sino-Led World or Managed Competition?

Nowhere is this fusion between geopolitics and geoeconomics more evident that in China's emergent Belt and Road Initiative (BRI)—and the response it has drawn from the US and its allies. China became a net exporter of capital in 2014, and the second largest exporter of FDI in 2016 (when its annual outbound FDI peaked at US$170bn, before falling back to $110bn in 2019; MOFCOM, n.d.), with much (though not all) of this investment representing SOE investments in infrastructural projects. While such a transformation continues and builds upon a legacy of external investment flows since the early 2000s, since late in 2013, China's growing network of overseas investment projects have become subsumed under the overarching 'Belt and Road Initiative' (BRI). The BRI combines a land-based 'Silk Road Economic Belt' (SREB) stretching across Central Asia into Central and Eastern Europe with a 'Maritime Silk Road' (MSR) running through the Asia Pacific, Indian Ocean and the Middle East and North Africa (MENA) region. These two geographically distinct but functionally intertwined projects encompass both a series of discrete infrastructural investments in roads, rail, energy and port infrastructure, part-funded and financed by Chinese capital aimed at boosting land and sea transport connectivity, alongside the increasingly established economic diplomacy relations which accompany these projects' financing and implementation. I briefly outline here three predominant perspectives on the BRI: as an economic outlet for surplus capital; a geoeconomic strategy which uses the capital-outlet function to cohere Eurasia and the Indo-Asia Pacific into a Chinese-centric series of production networks; and a geopolitical grand strategy which aims to displace the US hegemony through expanding Chinese land power across Eurasia (complementing China's naval activities in the Asia-Pacific). I argue that while economic motivations forged the BRI, a changing 'balance of (economic) dependency', the security needs of China's ballooning offshore capital investments, and the threat (perceived or real) which the US and its allies see in China's growing external activities contain an ineluctable drive towards geopolitical competition with the United States.

The surplus-recycling mechanism is best elaborated by Chohan (2018). In this perspective, as trade gains from the exportist SOA have dwindled, China's state capitalist SOA has aimed to stabilise its current account balance by exporting surplus capital and industrial overcapacity to its regional neighbours. Financing exists in the form of aid, preferential loans, development finance, commercial loans and special funding (Liu et al. 2020). BRI capital aims to plug part of an estimated $26tn 'infrastructure gap' identified to exist in the region (over the next two decades) by the Asia Development Bank (ADB 2017), while granting participant states access to China's highly competitive infrastructural know-how and skilled engineering base. A nested institutional structure is overseen by the NDRC, which coordinates industrial restructuring and BRI market activities of provincial level SOEs operating in the following heavy industrial sectors: steel, non-ferrous metals, construction materials, railways, electricity, chemicals, textiles, automotive, information and communications technology, engineering machinery and aerospace and marine engineering

(Kenderdine and Ling 2017). The ramping up of investments such SOEs experienced in the wake of 2008 can, in this way, be relieved without suffering extreme producer price deflation within China while avoiding dumping exports on global markets. Instead, surplus capacity can be productively consumed in the provision of necessary regional infrastructure, while capital on loans extended can be recovered plus interest. Yu et al. (2020) confirm an 8% increase in China's total exports to BRI states from 2010–2015 above its exports elsewhere, while Görg and Mao (2020) find virtually all this increase concentrated in centrally owned SOEs (indicating a much larger benefit for those firms). These surplus-relief programmes grouped under the BRI initiative build upon pre-existing efforts to geographically rebalance the economy by levelling up its relatively underdeveloped Central and Western regions, while up to half of BRI investments were already announced before the emergence of the initiative (Ye 2019).

Despite its economic taproot, a project on such a vast scale could not fail to raise profound diplomatic and security questions given the pre-existing international context described above. Total BRI spending is estimated to exceed US$1.1tn by 2027, and to involve projects in states containing 60% of the global population and 30% of world GDP (Morgan Stanley 2018). Substantial inward capital flows provide individual states—especially those poorest and least well trade-connected economies in the global south—with a mechanism, for the first time since the end of the Cold War, to access capital while bypassing the funding conditions (tacit or explicit) of existing multilateral institutions like the World Bank and the IMF. But participation (depending on the nature of the project) still typically requires substantial indebtedness on the part of the recipient state. Estimates put the total outstanding BRI loan book at US$350bn in 2018, dwarfing the total stock of FDI ($173bn). Projects such as the Asian Infrastructural Investment Bank (AIIB)—a professionalised vehicle for BRI financing which works closely with the existing multilateral institutions—have aimed to assuage Western concerns about Chinese lending practices and to strengthen China's credibility as a responsible stakeholder within the existing multilateral development finance system. But such initiatives are dwarfed by the interests of China's policy banks, with the EXIM Bank, the China Development Bank and Chinese (state-owned) commercial banks collectively accounting for 94.% of BRI loans (versus the AIIB's 2.3%). This mass of lending functions to draw BRI participant states into relations of dependence on China, both for financial capital and subsequently as an end-market which firms utilising the newly constructed infrastructure might serve (Diesen 2017).

Despite risks for China and lending recipients alike, the upshot of enhanced connectivity in BRI countries is the restructuring of regional economies into Sino-centric regional (rather than global) production networks and facilitates the upgrading of domestic Chinese firms as outsourcing opportunities proliferate (Flint and Zhu 2019). Building on legacy of economic diplomacy established during the commodities super-cycle in 2000s (Jepson 2020), this serves to carve out larger spheres of economic territory dependent on Chinese infrastructure, lead firms and markets, underpinned by Chinese standards. As Hillman (2018) consequently argues, 'Chinese technical standards, for everything from high-speed railway systems to wireless networks, would become more widely adopted, as would Chinese preferences for environmental and social safe-guards. Collectively, these changes would push the United States away from its current position in the global economy and move China towards the center'. Geoeconomic readings of the BRI are politically ambiguous, however, as to whether they form a subset of a geopolitical grand strategy (see below) or are principally a side-effect of the surplus-recycling mechanism. Consequently, many have emphasised the positives associated with China's extension of much needed infrastructural financing and development aid to states of the global south—particularly in comparison with dubious Western aid practices and their colonial legacies (e.g., Dunford 2020). Overhyped charges of intentional 'debt-trap diplomacy' are increasingly revealed to be misleading (Brautigam 2020), but it does seem clear that a geoeconomic rationale is nonetheless at play in many instances: As Carmody (2020) observes, many major BRI investments such as Hambantota port evince no obvious commercial logic, but do possess clear geostrategic potentials.

For such reasons, the BRI is also seen by some as primarily geopolitical manoeuvre into which pecuniary concerns play a secondary role to strategic operations. Zhou and Esteban (2018) view the BRI as a means of 'outmanoeuvring' the US's attempt at naval containment and division in its near seas, combining a financial peace-offering to regional littoral states with a turn to focusing on land-based security relations with Central Asian states. The China–Pakistan Economic Corridor (CPEC), for instance, links China to Pakistan both by a sea route through Chinese Overseas Port Holdings' ownership of Gwadar port and by land, over the yet to be completed Karakoram highway which travails the Himalayas.

Both projects raise serious viability concerns, but are interpreted by some as a means to construct a regional anti-Indian coalition (manifest in recent joint China–Pakistan naval drills in the Indian Ocean; see Collin 2019). Drawing upon such examples, Holslag (2017) and Clarke (2020) view the BRI as a (semi-)coherent grand strategy, echoing Kaplan's (2019) prediction of the emergence of Eurasia as a unified supercontinent under the sway of cooperative multinational empires (China, Russia and Iran) working to disintegrate the Westphalian system, the critical mechanism upholding the US-led global order. There are strong reasons to be sceptical of such sensational predictions, not least the self-evident weaknesses to Mackinder's 'Eurasian heartland' thesis upon which they elaborate. Half-empty Chinese freight trains changing gauge three times as they trundle across central Asia, the abrupt conclusion of the proposed Karakoram Highway (and thus the China Pakistan Economic Corridor) in hostile India—facts which do more to expose the fantastical imaginations of US realists than evolving realities of contemporary geopolitics (Babones 2019). Indeed, Gonzalez-Vicente (2019) points out how the BRI has bolstered the Westphalian system through its focus on bilateral national state-to-state agreements which bypass existing multilateral architectures (while disempowering civil society institutions in the process).

More sober analyses don't share the fear of a united Eurasia or a Chinese blue-water naval force dominating Chinese-owned ports in the Asia Pacific and beyond, but do read the BRI in part as another form of grand strategy: a means of promoting a Chinese soft power, or a 'geocultural' project of rewriting China's regional image as a benevolent and transactional economic superpower (Callahan 2016; Winter 2020). This has prompted the US to establish an international Development Finance Corporation (DFC), with the aim of competitively financing infrastructure across the global south (Schindler and Kanai 2018). Interpreted in such a way, the outcomes of the BRI are at best ambiguous. Gong (2019) records significant pushback and hard negotiation over project terms states across South East Asia, while debt and other project failures increasingly serve to alienate participant states. Both Jones and Zeng (2019) and Ye (2019) point out the proliferation of interests which prevent it from operating effectively as a centralised policy. Critically a division between the Ministry of Foreign Affairs (MFA) which favours long-term soft loans to firm up allies, and MOFCOM, which possesses a commercial mandate to oversee and uphold the quality of foreign aid and loans provisioned under the BRI. Meanwhile, provincial and municipal governments tussle for finance and recognition associated with BRI status (Yu 2018). As Narins and Agnew (2019) point out, the absence of a defined and published plan for the BRI is likely testament more to its 'intentional fuzziness' than an unintentional oversight, permitting it to take shape as it unfolds and for the state to attempt to manage the proliferation of sectoral interests being advanced under the framework.

Disaggregating, rather than subsuming all Chinese actors under a monolith national bloc, is important in ascertaining the principle drivers of various BRI-linked projects. But there are three important reasons why it would be an error to conflate this proliferation of often contradictory and sectional interests with an absence of any geopolitical logic to the BRI. First, arguments which emphasise the similarities between China's outbound FDI spree and those of Taiwan, Korea and Japan before it with the implication that it does not represent a threat to the US-led global order (e.g., Babones et al. 2020) forget that China remains outside the US security umbrella. As such, even a 'regular' transformation from net recipient to contributor of FDI means particular investments are often perceived by other states as a potential act of hostility (Meijer 2019). The BRI was enshrined in the Party's constitution in 2017, has become a flagship policy of Xi's administration, and control was assumed by the CCP's Central Foreign Affairs Commission (the successor to the Foreign Affairs Small Leading Group) personally chaired by Xi Jinping in 2018 to overcome bureaucratic wrangling between the MFA and MOFCOM and to manage fallout from negative foreign responses (Cabestan 2019). Whether accurate or not (and there are legitimate reasons for scepticism here), such reshuffling entrenches the views of those who view the BRI as directly and tightly orchestrated by the central government and directly links myriad lower-tier actors to the central government. And, finally, an ad hoc and grassroots-driven BRI will inevitably encounter major indebtedness and security challenges. If there is a near-inevitability that projects *will* go wrong (Carmody 2020), it seems just as inevitable that the increasingly defined 'national interests' of China will have to be defended by both debt reclamation and overseas security initiatives. A precursor is already visible in the highly controversial takeover of Hambantota port in Sri Lanka and in the formation of PLA forces to secure infrastructural assets under construction in Central Asian states (Dave and Kobayashi 2018).

Consequently, BRI is best understood as at once an economic, geoeconomic and geopolitical project, where these discrete logics sometimes coalesce and sometimes conflict with one another (Flint and Zhu 2019). Most politically dangerous in the short run is the emerging conflict between heavily indebted BRI-project states across the global south and China's attempt to recoup capital while retaining its image as a benevolent financier (Kynge and Yu 2020). But, as argued in Chapter 2, economic processes are simultaneously territorial (insofar as they fix capital in specific places) and political (insofar as they interact with and transform or bolster existing institutional arrangements), and the BRI is no exception. In the longer run, the risk is that its overall dynamic adds to the intensifying geopolitical economy rivalry between China and the United States.

8.5 Big Data to the Rescue?

If the BRI is unlikely to provide a panacea for China's mounting economic difficulties, and China's manufacturing firms in the new 'core sectors' of the state-embedded private sector face serious risk of exclusion from US-dominated production networks, what are the prospects for the evolution of Chinese capitalism? A defining question for the future viability of the state capitalist SOA is China's emergent digital economy. Though difficult to measure, a recent OECD (2019) review calculates China's digital economy to represent a remarkable 28% of value-added GDP in 2017 (after stripping out the ICT 'hardware' sector, which accounts for about 5% of value-added in GDP).

China's new digital giants can be assigned to four major categories: **E-commerce platforms** (Taobao, JD, Alibaba), **communication platforms** (WeChat; Weibo; Baidu) **financial intermediaries & fintech/p2p providers** (AliPay, Ant Financial, Yuebao); and **labour management platforms** (Didi, Meituan, Huochebang). Along with Baidu, all of the above firms are either controlled or owned (majority or by substantial minority stake) by Tencent or Alibaba. Together, the 'BATs' have quickly come to dominate China's digital economy using complex cross shareholding business groups analogous to other northeast Asian business groups (Japanese *keiretsu*, Korean *chaebols*). All have high-margin and commercially dominant core business functions: TenCent in mobile messaging (where it possesses almost total market share through WeChat), payments, and gaming; Alibaba in its widely adopted mobile payments systems (AliPay) and e-commerce (where Alibaba has almost 60% of the market); and Baidu (which accounts for 70% of search engine traffic) in web advertising and AI. These core revenue streams are used to cross-subsidise entry into frontier industries, through both acquisitions of startups and R&D.

Some view this emergent digital economy as a bubble waiting to burst. Though they possessed relatively modest assets (US$134bn and US$105.4bn) and generated unremarkable net profits ($10bn and $12bn), Alibaba Group and Tencent were by far and way the highest valued Chinese firms by market capitalisation at the close of 2019 ($481bn and $472bn, respectively), putting them in the top 10 of all global corporations on that metric (*Forbes*, n.d.). Much of this wave of capital market financing spills downwards into the startups which they acquire at rapid pace. In 2016, 43% of all venture capital funding in China emanated from the BATs (*McKinsey* 2017). While the US had 203 'unicorns' (private startup firms valued at over US$1bn) at the end of 2019, China had 206. Of these, around half had received investment from BAT firms, while between 2015–2018 it is estimated that US$1.3tn in investment was pumped into Chinese unicorns. Xia (2018) views the sector as chronically overcapitalised: the average share price-to-earnings-ratio is 66 in China's digital economy, while the global industry average is just 12.5. And significant questions exist as to how much actual economic value is generated within such industries, given their revenue streams are effectively reliant upon advertising which redistributes surpluses generated elsewhere (Lucas 2020). However, the sheer scale and capitalisation levels of these firms means that huge R&D spending (US$22bn by the top 100 firms in 2018) is spawning globally competitive innovation in firms like ByteDance, creator of TikTok (a highly successful video app in Western economies). Further, China's vast manufacturing base permits basic research innovations to be quickly commercialised and applied as general purpose technologies as they proliferate from the design stage through an 'army of tinkerers' (Lee 2018), a distinct strong point of the innovation ecosystem not evident in Silicon Valley. This unique advantage seems to offer at least some protection to leading firms against any major equity price crash.

Virtually all Chinese digital economy firms have, however, benefitted from the erection of the 'Great Firewall' during the 2000s, which has functioned (in part unintentionally) as a form of industrial policy by excluding or severely limiting foreign entry. Facebook, Google, Twitter and WhatsApp are effectively banned, while Uber, Airbnb and eBay confronted various licencing issues leading to their downfall (see Kirby 2016). Digital economy firms can thus benefit from access to China's 1.4bn citizens unimpeded by foreign competition—a user base large enough to generate high quality big data. Some are explicitly backed by the state: Huang and Tian (2019) estimate that over US$520bn has been raised by state-guided venture capital funds since 2000, a good deal of which has flooded into the digital economy since 2012. Public-private partnerships and government procurement contracts proliferate (such as the Ministry of Public Security's substantial contracts with Tencent in areas like cloud computing and data analytics). Many firms can also exploit the interstices of the state economy. Alibaba subsidiary Yuebao, for instance, capitalises on high interbank lending rates to offer consumers wealth management products by parking their underused savings overnight in state banks. The lack of a well-established legal system greater desire for algorithmic contract regulation also increases the attractiveness of blockchain technologies.

Insofar as it is embedded in China's institutional environment, the digital economy also possesses a distinctively territorial logic (cf. Leamer and Storper 2014). The 'great firewall' has already basically enforced a separation of software and hardware infrastructures ('stacks'; Bratton 2016), with China's permeated by state monitoring and control. This gives China's internet economy a distinctive political and geopolitical orientation, tying together national security concerns with the commercial logics of digital platforms into an overlapping set of national interests between state managers and large capitalists (Moisio 2018; Plantings and de Seta 2019). The international race for supremacy in the digital economy is leading to concerns that China is supplanting U.S. firms in aspects of AI capacity (Johnson 2019). Concern is also voiced by US policymakers about the unfair nature competition of 'dual-use technology' development which link civilian and military industries together and draw on Chinese military research budgets, while threatening the US military's technological leadership (see U.S.-China Economic and Security Review Commission 2019). If this is the case, China is likely inspired by Washington's own experience of 'hiding' a developmental state in its military-industrial complex, where substantial R&D expenditures and breakthroughs in basic research undertaken by state-funded military research laboratories were appropriated by private corporate sector and spun into highly successful consumer-facing applications

(Block 2008). Further, the exponential growth of China's technology giants has rendered them ready to internationalise their activities, with overseas adoption of many such applications taking off in South East Asia and the 'Digital Silk Road' an increasingly significant component of the evolving BRI. Debates are now evident over the extraterritorial reach of Chinese censorship of platforms such as TikTok and WeChat. As such, China's digital economy both displays some potential to drive China's economic growth into the future, but risks both exacerbating the risks associated with a more general asset price bubble encompassing other equities and real estate, as well as deepening interstate antagonisms and geopolitical economic rivalry with the United States.

8.6 Summary

This text has developed and operationalised the theory of uneven and combined development in order to untangle the enigma of the Chinese economic 'miracle'. I have advanced a version of Marxist political economy which incorporates geopolitics and territoriality into a spatio-temporal theory of global capitalism, and views the military and economic competition between states (alongside competition between firms) as an upholder and enforcer of the law of value. As such, the capitalist world economy, as a unitary system, is understood to exist according to a 'general condition' of uneven and combined development: in which persistent shifts in the geography of global economic development inevitably generate geopolitical tensions by empowering some states economically and militarily at the expense of others. As this process generates geopolitical tensions and conflicts, these in turn serve to empower and disempower particular class fractions and state institutions and transform states' developmental trajectories. Capitalist competition thus exists on a spectrum, from economic competition between firms, through diplomatic wrangling, and full-blown imperial conflagrations over territory. As such, this uneven and combined developmental dynamic operates both through the international states system while at the same time serving to reproduce it.

I subsequently specified a second, more particular condition of uneven and combined development—as a period of rapid catch-up growth, in which a developing economy is driven by geopolitical threats to mobilise its state apparatus in the service of acquiring techno-economic materials from advanced economies. This permits it to leapfrog stages of development and pursue rapid economic growth on a compressed timescale. This form of UCD, though rare, is a phenomenon which has been repeated throughout the history of the capitalist world economy. Gerschenkron, Lewis, Rostow and many other development economists have understood catch-up development as an enabler of compressed industrialisation and urbanisation. But Trotsky's contribution was to examine in great detail how these achievements typically come at the cost of immense social and geographical dislocations set in motion by the wholesale transformation of the economic base of a society. The class dynamics which emerge from economic turbulence are highly path-dependent, and in turn shape both the form of capitalism which emerges from the period of UCD and the social formation's future relationship with the global political economy. For this reason, 'leapfrogging' is rarely a smooth process of appropriating technologies and arriving at the technological frontier. Instead, it typically results in 'debased adaptation', whereby advanced productive forms bolster regressive socio-economic and political relations and sets off unpredictable political economic trajectories of development.

Building on these insights, I developed, drawing critically upon mainstream and heterodox comparative capitalisms approaches, the notion of a national 'system of accumulation' predicated upon the institutionally mediated transfers of surpluses from 'core economic sectors'. This set of intermediary concepts enabled the operationalisation of uneven and combined development, beyond a mere set of 'background conditions', as an analytical method for capturing the political economic dynamics at work in China. This allowed me to identify the emergence of an 'exportist system of accumulation' operative at its height between 2001 and 2008 (in which private sector export surpluses sustained and revived an ailing state sector) which allowed China's economy to begin a 'leap' towards those of advanced economies, though in a highly uneven way. This gave way to a still emergent 'state capitalist system of accumulation' in the aftermath of the 2008 economic crisis (where widespread state intervention shows promise in developing infant industries at the technological frontier, but presents enormous risks in overproducing heavy goods and over-inflating a real estate asset bubble). As such, these intermediary concepts avoid the problems of stasis and path-dependency afflicting orthodox comparative capitalisms writings, since they remain sensitive to the overall UCD dynamic in which they are embedded.

Trotsky further emphasised how the predominant structural dynamics at work in the global political economy also inevitably shape the form this catch-up development takes. China, engaging in UCD during the emergence of global neoliberalism and a long downturn in the advanced economies, could not escape these strictures. The dynamics of the global production networks through which China engaged the global economy ultimately served to 'trap' its core sectors at a relatively low level of the value chain during the period of the exportist SOA, a structural factor which shaped the response to the crisis of 2008. Simultaneously, a steady but marked deterioration in Sino-US geopolitical relations ultimately drove it to pursue infant industry protections policy in its state-embedded private sector firms. Internally, the pressures of compressed industrialisation and urbanisation associated with catch-up combined development generate idiosyncratic sociological forms in the shape of unusual class formations and relations. In this case, China's engagement with global economic liberalism did not decisively empower a transnationally oriented capitalist class, but instead bolstered the strength of the central state. As the export manufacturing sector fragmented, state activity to sustain growth and development ramped up overaccumulation in staple goods industries, and fed a highly dangerous overinflation of equity values in the real estate sector. As such, the state capitalist SOA possesses potential strengths beside potentially fateful weaknesses.

As this book was going to press, the Covid-19 pandemic threatened to intensify the trade war and empower those on both sides of the US-China dispute pushing for a more profound economic decoupling. As such, it accentuated all the tendencies towards autocentrism, the national territorialisation of economic growth, and inter-imperialist rivalry described here. A great deal now hinges on the outcome of China's infant industry policy and the capacity in particular of its new digital economy to continue produce global leaders in technological innovation. A lot also rides on the BRI. Rather than dump surplus capacity onto world markets, China has attempted a vast expansion of its regional power and influence by offering them on relatively favourable terms in the form of infrastructural financing and development. The coming decade will reveal not only how far China's own experience of uneven and combined development has served to resituate it within the hierarchically organised, US-dominated global political economy; but, further, how the highly distinct channels China's outward flows of capital and technology take begin to generate and shape future forms of uneven and combined development in states which follow in its wake (cf. Jepson 2020). The penetration of Africa and Latin America by its thriving technology firms, the flood of infrastructural investment across Eurasia and Southeast Asia, and the intensifying rivalry with the US and its allies in the South and East China Seas are all examples of ripples emanating from China's own experience of UCD which will shape the evolution of the global political economy in the years to come.

References

ADB. 2017. *Meeting Asia's Infrastructure Needs*. Available online at: www.adb.org/sites/default/files/publication/227496/special-report-infrastructure.pdf. Accessed 27 February 2019.

Allison, Graham. 2017. *Destined for War: Can America and China Escape Thucydides's Trap?* Boston: Houghton Mifflin.

Babones, Salvatore. 2019. The Chinese Delusion of a Greater Eurasia. *Quadrant* 63 (3): 10.

Babones, Salvatore, John H.S. Åberg, and Obert Hodzi. 2020. China's Role in Global Development Finance: China Challenge or Business as Usual? *Global Policy* 11 (3): 326–335.

Bello, Walden. 2019. China: An Imperial Power in the Image of the West. *Focus on the Global South.*

Beeson, Mark. 2018. Geoeconomics with Chinese Characteristics: The BRI and China's Evolving Grand Strategy. *Economic and Political Studies* 6 (3): 240–256.

Bhala, Raj. 2017. TPP, American National Security and Chinese SOEs. *World Trade Review* 16 (4): 655–671.

Block, Fred. 2008. Swimming Against the Current: The Rise of a Hidden Developmental State in the United States. *Politics & Society* 36 (2): 169–206.

Bratton, Benjamin H. 2016. *The Stack: On Software and Sovereignty*. Boston: MIT Press.

Brautigam, Deborah. 2020. A Critical Look at Chinese 'Debt-Trap Diplomacy': The Rise of a Meme. *Area Development and Policy* 5 (1): 1–14.

Cabestan, Jean-Pierre. 2019. Political Changes in China Since the 19th CCP Congress: Xi Jinping Is Not Weaker But More Contested. *East Asia* 36 (1): 1–21.

Callahan, William A. 2016. China's "Asia Dream" the Belt Road Initiative and the New Regional Order. *Asian Journal of Comparative Politics* 1 (3): 226–243.

Carmody, Pádraig. 2020. Dependence Not Debt-Trap Diplomacy. *Area Development and Policy* 5 (1): 23–31.

China.org.cn. 2017. Full Text: Xi Jinping's Keynote Speech at the World Economic Forum. Available online at: http://www.china.org.cn/node_7247529/content_40569136.htm. Accessed 18 December 2019.

Chohan, Usman W. 2018. What Is One Belt One Road? A Surplus Recycling Mechanism Approach. In *The Belt and Road Initiative*, ed. Julien Chaisse and Jędrzej Górski, 205–219. Leiden: Brill.

Chung, Jae Ho. 2019. How America and China See Each Other: Charting National Views and Official Perceptions. *The Pacific Review* 32 (2): 188–209.

Clarke, Michael. 2020. Beijing's Pivot West: The Convergence of *Innenpolitik* and *Aussenpolitik* on China's 'Belt and Road'? *Journal of Contemporary China* 29 (123): 336–353.

Clover, Charles, and Lucy Hornby. 2015. China's Great Game: Road to a New Empire. *Financial Times*, October 12. https://www.ft.com/content/6e098274-587a-11e5-a28b-50226830d644.

Collin, Koh Swee Lean. 2019. China-India Rivalry at Sea: Capability, Trends and Challenges. *Asian Security* 15 (1): 5–24.

Cordesman, Anthony. 2019. China's New 2019 Defense White Paper: An Open Strategic Challenge to the United States, But One Which Does Not Have to Lead to Conflict, Center for Strategic and International Studies (CSIS), 24.

Cumings, Bruce. 2009. *Dominion from Sea to Sea: Pacific Ascendancy and American Power*. New Haven: Yale University Press.

Dave, Bhavna, and Yuka Kobayashi. 2018. China's Silk Road Economic Belt Initiative in Central Asia: Economic and Security Implications. *Asia Europe Journal* 16 (3): 267–281.

de Graaff, Naná, and Bastiaan Van Apeldoorn. 2018. US–China Relations and the Liberal World Order: Contending Elites, Colliding Visions? *International Affairs* 94 (1): 113–131.

Diesen, Glen. 2017. Russia, China and 'Balance of Dependence' in Greater Eurasia. Available online at: http://valdaiclub.com/files/13795/. Accessed 13 September 2019.

Dizard, John. 2020. US-China Financial War Is Just Beginning to Take Shape. *Financial Times*, January 3.

Drezner, Daniel. 2019. Economic Statecraft in the Age of Trump. *The Washington Quarterly* 42 (3): 7–24.

Dunford, Michael. 2020. Chinese and Development Assistance Committee (DAC) Development Cooperation and Development Finance: Implications for the BRI and International Governance. *Eurasian Geography and Economics* 61 (2): 125–136.

Economist. 2020. Private Companies Have Put Down Strong Roots in China. April 30.

Executive Office of the President of the United States. 2013. Administration Strategy on Mitigating the Theft of U.S. Trade Secrets. Available online at: https://www.justice.gov/criminal-ccips/file/938321/download. Accessed 11 August 2018.

Farrell, Henry, and Abraham L. Newman. 2019. Weaponized Interdependence: How Global Economic Networks Shape State Coercion. *International Security* 44 (1): 42–79.

Farrell, Henry, and Abraham Newman. 2020. Chained to Globalization: Why It's Too Late to Decouple. *Foreign Affairs*, January/February.

Flint, Colin, and Cuiping Zhu. 2019. The Geopolitics of Connectivity, Cooperation, and Hegemonic Competition: The Belt and Road Initiative. *Geoforum* 99: 95–101.

Forbes. n.d. *Global 2000*. Available online at: https://www.forbes.com/global2000/#7b47de6335d8. Accessed 12 January 2020.

Fravel, M. Taylor. 2018. Shifts in Warfare and Party Unity: Explaining China's Changes in Military Strategy. *International Security* 42 (3): 37–83.

Gewirtz, Julian. 2019. China's Long March to Technological Supremacy. *Foreign Affairs*. Available online at: https://www.foreignaffairs.com/articles/china/2019-08-27/chinas-long-march-technological-supremacy. Accessed 19 December 2019.

Gewirtz, Julian. 2020. The Chinese Reassessment of Interdependence. *China Leadership Monitor* 64. Available online at: https://www.prcleader.org/gewirtz. Accessed 30 May 2020.

Gong, Xue. 2019. The Belt & Road Initiative and China's Influence in Southeast Asia. *The Pacific Review* 32 (4): 635–665.

Gonzalez-Vicente, Ruben. 2019. Make Development Great Again? Accumulation Regimes, Spaces of Sovereign Exception and the Elite Development Paradigm of China's Belt and Road Initiative. *Business and Politics* 21 (4): 487–513.

Görg, Holger, and Haiou Mao. 2020. Does the Belt and Road Initiative Stimulate Chinese Exports? The Role of State-owned Enterprises. KCG Working Paper no. 21. Available online at: https://www.econstor.eu/bitstream/10419/213420/1/1688460241.pdf. Accessed 14 May 2020.

Gourevitch, Peter. 1978. The Second Image Reversed: The International Sources of Domestic Politics. *International Organization* 32 (4): 881–912.

Grimes, Seamus, and Debin Du. 2020. China's Emerging Role in the Global Semiconductor Value Chain. *Telecommunications Policy* (Published online before print). Available at: https://doi.org/10.1016/j.telpol.2020.101959. Accessed 21 April 2020.

He, Huifeng. 2018. Beijing Did a Tech Reality Check on Its Industrial Champions. The Results Were Not Amazing. *SCMP*, July 18.

Hillman, Jonathan. 2018. 'China's Belt and Road Initiative: Five Years Later', Statement Before the U.S.-China Economic and Security Review Commission. Available online at: https://www.uscc.gov/sites/default/files/Hillman_USCC%20Testimony_25Jan2018_FINAL.pdf. Accessed 11 February 2019.

Holslag, Jonathan. 2017. How China's New Silk Road Threatens European Trade. *The International Spectator* 52 (1): 46–60.
Huang, Zhaojun, and Xuan Tian. 2019. China's Venture Capital Market. SSRN. Available online at: https://ssrn.com/abstract=3423553. Accessed 11 September 2019.
Ikenberry, G. John. 2018. The End of Liberal International Order? *International Affairs* 94 (1): 7–23.
Jepson, Nicholas. 2020. *In China's Wake: How the Commodity Boom Transformed Development Strategies in the Global South*. New York: Columbia University Press.
Johnson, James. 2018. *The US-China Military and Defense Relationship During the Obama Presidency*. Basingstoke: Palgrave Macmillan.
Johnson, James. 2019. The End of Military-Techno Pax Americana? Washington's Strategic Responses to Chinese AI-enabled Military Technology. *The Pacific Review* (Published Online Before Print). Available at: https://doi.org/10.1080/09512748.2019.1676299. Accessed 11 December 2019.
Jones, Lee, and Jinghan Zeng. 2019. Understanding China's 'Belt and Road Initiative': Beyond 'Grand Strategy' to a State Transformation Analysis. *Third World Quarterly* (published online before print). Available at: https://doi.org/10.1080/01436597.2018.1559046. Accessed 12 December 2019.
Kaplan, Robert D. 2019. *The Return of Marco Polo's World: War, Strategy, and American Interests in the Twenty-first Century*. New York: Random House.
Kenderdine, Tristan, and Han Ling. 2017. International Capacity Cooperation—Financing China's Export of Industrial Overcapacity. *Global Policy* 9 (1): 41–52.
Kirby, William. 2016. The Real Reason Uber Is Giving Up in China. *Harvard Business Review*, August 2.
Kolmaš, Michal, and Šárka Kolmašová. 2019. A 'Pivot' That Never Existed: America's Asian Strategy Under Obama and Trump. *Cambridge Review of International Affairs* 32 (1): 61–79.
Kynge, James, and Sun Yu. 2020. China Faces Wave of Calls for Debt Relief on 'Belt and Road' Projects. *Financial Times*, April 30.
Leamer, Edward E., and Michael Storper. 2014. The Economic Geography of the Internet Age. In *Location of International Business Activities*, ed. John Cantwell, 63–93. London: Palgrave Macmillan.
Lee, Kai-Fu. 2018. *AI Superpowers: China, Silicon Valley and the New World Order*. Boston: Houghton Mifflin.
Liu, Weidong, Yajing Zhang, and Wei Xiong. 2020. Financing the Belt and Road Initiative. *Eurasian Geography and Economics* 61 (2): 137–145.
Löfflmann, Georg. 2016. The Pivot Between Containment, Engagement, and Restraint: President Obama's Conflicted Grand Strategy in Asia. *Asian Security* 12 (2): 92–110.

Lu, Peng. 2019. Chinese IR Sino-Centrism Tradition and Its Influence on the Chinese School Movement. *The Pacific Review* 32 (2): 150–167.
Lucas, Rob. 2020. The Surveillance Business. *New Left Review* 2 (121): 132–141.
Ma, Joy Datong. 2018. China's Trade War Tools and Their Effects on the US Economy. Available online at: https://macropolo.org/chinas-trade-war-tools/. Accessed 11 March 2019.
McKinsey. 2017. *China's Digital Economy: A Leading Global Force*. New York: McKinsey Global Institute.
Mearsheimer, John J. 2014. Can China Rise Peacefully? *The National Interest* 25 (1): 1–40.
Meijer, Sebastian. 2019. The American Response to China's Rise to Power: An Analysis of Think Tanks' Foreign Policy Proposals Towards the Belt and Road Initiative. MS thesis, Leiden University. Available online at: https://openaccess.leidenuniv.nl/handle/1887/77140. Accessed 2 March 2020.
MOFCOM. n.d. Statistics. Available at: http://english.mofcom.gov.cn/statistic/charts.shtml. Accessed 11 April 2020.
Moisio, Sami. 2018. *Geopolitics of the Knowledge-Based Economy*. London: Taylor & Francis.
Morgan Stanley. 2018. *Inside China's Plan to Create a Modern Silk Road*. Available online at: https://www.morganstanley.com/ideas/china-belt-and-road. Accessed 11 March 2019.
Narins, Thomas P., and John Agnew. 2020. Missing from the Map: Chinese Exceptionalism, Sovereignty Regimes and the Belt Road Initiative. *Geopolitics* 25 (4): 809–837.
Nye Jr, Joseph. 2020. Power and Interdependence with China. *The Washington Quarterly* 43 (1): 7–21.
OECD. 2019. *OECD Economic Surveys: China 2019*. Paris: OECD Publishing.
Office of the US Trade Representative. 2015. FACT SHEET: The Obama Administration's Unprecedented Trade Enforcement Record. Available online at: https://ustr.gov/about-us/policy-offices/press-office/fact-sheets/2015/january/fact-sheet-obama-administration's. Accessed 11 April 2020.
Plantin, Jean-Christophe, and Gabriele de Seta. 2019. WeChat as Infrastructure: The Techno-nationalist Shaping of Chinese Digital Platforms. *Chinese Journal of Communication* 12 (3): 257–273.
Plender, John. 2019. The Threat of a US-China Currency War. *Financial Times*, August 6.
Rolf, Steve, and John Agnew. 2016. Sovereignty Regimes in the South China Sea: Assessing Contemporary Sino-US Relation. *Eurasian Geography and Economics* 57 (2): 249–273.
Schindler, Seth, and Juan Miguel Kanai. 2018. US Sparks New Development Race with China—But Can It Win? *The Conversation*. Available online

at: https://theconversation.com/us-sparks-new-devel-opment-race-with-china-but-can-it-win-105203?fbclid=IwAR3g3UnQ9N1ZuWioZ5vScT-jGwPgXh9blpjnbyPgTYWagH87ytYowRv7VrY8. Accessed 24 February 2020.

Schneider-Petsinger, Marianne, Jue Wang, Yu Jie, and James Crabtre. 2019. US–China Strategic Competition: The Quest for Global Technological Leadership. Chatham House Research Paper. Available online at: https://www.chathamhouse.org/sites/default/files/publications/research/CHHJ7480-US-China-Competition-RP-WEB.pdf. Accessed 11 April 2020.

Schott, Jeffrey, and Euijin Jung. 2019. In US-China Trade Disputes the WTO Usually Sides with the United States. *Peterson Institute for International Economics* blog. Available online at: https://www.piie.com/blogs/trade-and-investment-policy-watch/us-china-trade-disputes-wto-usually-sides-united-states. Accessed 6 September 2019.

Shih, Victor. 2018. Cracks in China's Statist Consensus? *China Leadership Monitor*. Available online at: https://www.prcleader.org/cracks-in-statist-consensus. Accessed 12 December 2019.

Silove, Nina. 2016. The Pivot Before the Pivot. *International Security* 40 (4): 45–88.

Stubbs, Richard. 2017. *Rethinking Asia's Economic Miracle: The Political Economy of War, Prosperity and Crisis*. Basingstoke: Palgrave.

Styan, David. 2020. China's Maritime Silk Road and Small States: Lessons from the Case of Djibouti. *Journal of Contemporary China* 29 (122): 191–206.

Tariq, Sidra. 2016. Sino-Indian Security Dilemma in the Indian Ocean: Revisiting the 'String of Pearls' Strategy. *Regional Studies* 34 (3): 3–28.

The Guardian. 2020. China Theft of Technology Is Biggest Law Enforcement Threat to US, FBI Says. February 6.

U.S.-China Economic and Security Review Commission (USESRC). 2019. *2019 Annual Report to Congress*. Available online at: https://www.uscc.gov/annual-report/2019-annual-report. Accessed 14 January 2020.

Wang, Hung-Jen. 2017. Traditional Empire–Modern State Hybridity: Chinese tianxia and Westphalian Anarchy. *Global Constitutionalism* 6 (2): 298–326.

Wilson, Kimberly L. 2016. Reconciling History and International Law: Territorial and Maritime Claims in the South China Sea and East China Sea. PhD dissertation, University of Maryland.

Winter, Tim. 2020. Geocultural Power: China's Belt and Road Initiative. *Geopolitics*. Available online at: https://doi.org/10.1080/14650045.2020.1718656. Accessed 11 May 2020.

Wu, Chengqiu. 2020. Ideational Differences, Perception Gaps, and the Emerging Sino–US Rivalry. *The Chinese Journal of International Politics* 13 (1): 27–68.

Wu, Zhengyu. 2019. Towards Naval Normalcy: 'Open Seas Protection' and Sino-US Maritime Relations. *The Pacific Review* 32 (4): 666–693.

Xia, Bingqing. 2018. Capital Accumulation and Work in China's Internet Content Industry: Struggling in the Bubble. *The Economic and Labour Relations Review* 29 (4): 501–520.

Xinhua. 2017. Secure a Decisive Victory in Building a Moderately Prosperous Society in All Respects and Strive for the Great Success of Socialism with Chinese Characteristics for a New Era. Available online at: http://www.xinhuanet.com/english/download/Xi_Jinping's_report_at_19th_CPC_National_Congress.pdf.

Xu, Jiajun. 2017. *Beyond US Hegemony in International Development: The Contest for Influence at the World Bank*. Cambridge: Cambridge University Press.

Ye, Min. 2019. Fragmentation and Mobilization: Domestic Politics of the Belt and Road in China. *Journal of Contemporary China* 28 (119): 696–711.

Yu, Jie. 2018. The Belt and Road Initiative: Domestic Interests, Bureaucratic Politics and the EU-China Relation. *Asia Europe Journal* 16 (3): 223–236.

Yu, Linhui, Dan Zhao, Haixia Niu, and Futao Lu. 2020. Does the Belt and Road Initiative Expand China's Export Potential to Countries Along the Belt and Road? *China Economic Review*. Available online at: https://doi.org/10.1016/j.chieco.2020.101419. Accessed 30 May 2020.

Zeng, Jinghan, Yuefan Xiao, and Shaun Breslin. 2015. Securing China's Core Interests: The State of the Debate in China. *International Affairs* 91 (2): 245–266.

Zhang, Feng. 2019. China's Long March at Sea: Explaining Beijing's South China Sea Strategy, 2009–2016. *The Pacific Review* (published online before print). Available at: https://doi.org/10.1080/09512748.2019.1587497. Accessed 13 January 2020.

Zhou, Weifeng, and Mario Esteban. 2018. Beyond Balancing: China's Approach Towards the Belt and Road Initiative. *Journal of Contemporary China* 27 (112): 487–501.

Index

S. Rolf, *China's Uneven and Combined Development*, Studies in the Political Economy of Public Policy, https://doi.org/10.1007/978-3-030-55559-7

The manufacturer's authorised representative in the EU is Springer Nature Customer Service Centre GmbH, Europaplatz 3, 69115 Heidelberg, Germany. If you have any concerns regarding our products, please contact ProductSafety@springernature.com

Printed and bound by CPI Group (UK) Ltd, Croydon, CR0 4YY
01/10/2026
02226249-0005